WATFOR
WATFIV
FORTRAN Programming

FREDRIC STUART

QA
76.5
S82

WITHDRAWN

JOHN WILEY and SONS, INC.
New York, London, Sydney, Toronto

OHIO UNIVERSITY
LIBRARY

Copyright © 1971, by John Wiley & Sons, Inc.

All rights reserved. Published simultaneously in Canada.

No part of this book may be reproduced by any means, nor transmitted, nor translated into a machine language without the written permission of the publisher.

Library of Congress Catalogue Card Number: 78-162424

ISBN 0-471-83471-8

Printed in the United States of America

10 9 8 7 6 5 4 3 2 1

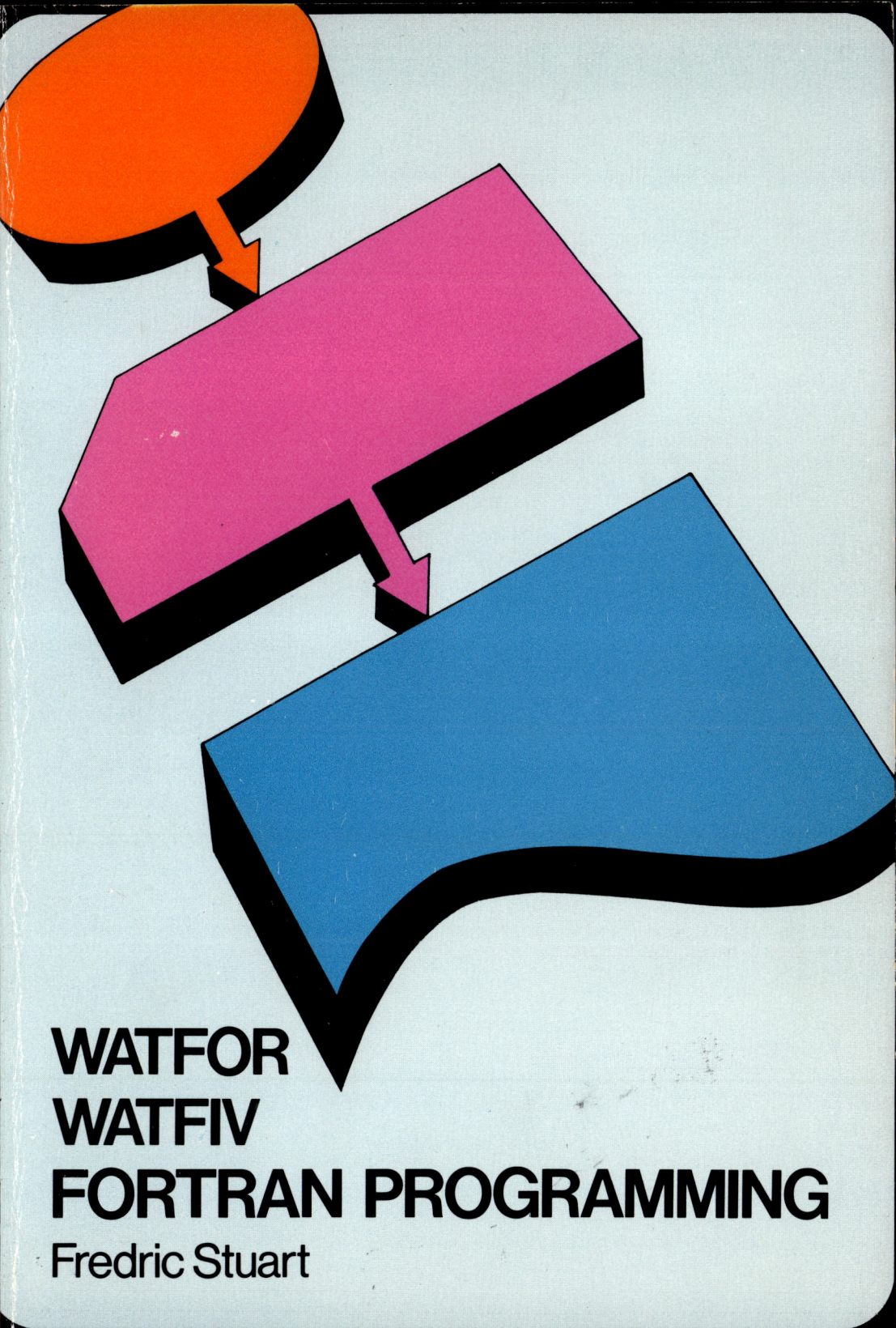

WATFOR
WATFIV
FORTRAN Programming

To Jennifer and Peter

PREFACE

The WATFOR (Waterloo FORTRAN) compiler was designed at the University of Waterloo (Ontario, Canada) with the explicit purpose of solving the problems connected with teaching FORTRAN to large numbers of students under batch-processing conditions. Student exercises produce a large volume of short programs. The programs usually have a high proportion of errors and, therefore, must be compiled several times each, but they have a short, one-time execution stage. And the programmers need more diagnostic help than is offered by most FORTRAN compiler programs.

The WATFOR compiler (and WATFIV, a slightly modified successor) provides an excellent environment for these special learning conditions from the viewpoints of both the student and the University Computer Center.

For the *student:*
1. A formatfree input/output option provides a great advantage for beginning programmers. Nevertheless, the compiler embodies the full FORTRAN IV language, so that students may progress to FORMAT statement usage when they are ready for it.
2. The diagnostic message system is much more extensive than in standard FORTRAN compilers. Additional aids to the debugging process include running in (optional) *debug* mode, in which attempts to use undefined variables are diagnosed at execution time, and *free-run* mode, in which execution may begin despite language errors diagnosed during compilation.
3. Control card requirements are minimal (usually, one JOB card preceding the source program, and one ENTRY card following it). Thus the student is not distracted by having to learn operating system control languages.

For the *Computer Center:*
1. Hundreds of student programs per minute may be compiled and executed. Compile time is at least fifteen times as fast as standard FORTRAN. Furthermore, there is no link-edit of each job; the compiler is an in-core processor that generates object code and executes it immediately when the compilation is completed.

2. Once the compiler is invoked, no intervention from the operating system is required until the batch of WATFOR programs is completed. The compiler program is "load-and-go"; compiler program, object program(s), and all run-time routines are kept in core storage during the whole batch. The compiler provides control options such as limitation of execution time per program, number of pages printed per program, and number of lines per page.

3. The compiler, though designed to be ideal for beginning FORTRAN students, is also useful for experienced programmers' work, particularly when the latter are compiling for error checks, and/or writing programs with low execution/compilation time ratios. As mentioned earlier, the full FORTRAN IV language is implemented, including *complex* and *logical* modes, mixed arithmetic expressions, full subprogram capabilities,[1] FORMAT data arrays, Hollerith constants, etc. In fact, there are several enhancements to standard FORTRAN, such as expressions in output lists and the extended assignment statement.

This textbook is designed to take full advantage of the WATFOR/WATFIV compilers for introducing students to FORTRAN programming. A full FORMAT discussion is deferred until Chapter 9, so that its complexities will not interfere with basic programming concepts and techniques. Thus the order of presentation is, in brief, basic computation (including arithmetic statements and formatfree output), program loops, formatfree input, use of compiler-supplied functions, conditional branching, subscripted variables, subprograms, complex and logical variable modes, FORMAT, and finally an assortment of FORTRAN statements useful for advanced programming. A full treatment of FORTRAN IV language is ultimately provided, but the order of subjects is specifically arranged for beginning students and for the WATFOR/WATFIV environment.

Experience with beginning students points to two indispensable aids to learning programming: *reading* programs, and *writing* programs. Therefore, the text contains more than 100 *sample* programs, and 81 *exercise* problems, each calling for a complete program.

The *sample* programs appear at frequent intervals throughout the text (7 chapters each contain 13 or more samples), to show particular statement forms and techniques. Although they are complete programs, they are short, since each attempts to illustrate only one point at a time. Furthermore, they are frequently redundant as to subject matter—that is, a single problem may be repeated with suitable alterations in successive sample programs. This should facilitate concentration on the techniques being illustrated. For this purpose also, sample program subject matter is kept simple—such topics as

---

[1] Programmer-supplied subprograms must be included as source programs for compilation with the main program.

conversion from Centigrade to Fahrenheit temperatures, computation of examination grades, arithmetic means, profit ratios, and the like are used. Complicated mathematical and engineering problems are avoided in the interest of concentrating student attention on *programming*. Instructors using the text are usually better qualified than textbook authors to select technical examples when appropriate for particular students.

The *exercise* programs are also fairly short and general in subject matter, so that they will be useful practice for students in varying academic disciplines. Where technical matters are mentioned in exercises (e.g., a *standard deviation* is to be computed), necessary formulas and explanations are provided. Thus, all students should be able to complete any of the exercise programs. Appendix B contains sample *output* for each exercise problem, so that the student may fully test his program without descending to hand computation for checking purposes. Furthermore, a standard data set (12 cards, each containing 6 data values), which appears at the beginning of Appendix B, may be used to test all programs that read data. Appendix B shows output resulting from use of this standard data set as input for all such exercises.

As a further aid in the debugging process, Appendix A contains a full listing of WATFOR and WATFIV error codes and diagnostic messages.

My thanks to Dr. Robert Mathis (Ohio State University) for his careful reading of the manuscript and many helpful suggestions.

Fredric Stuart

January 1971

CONTENTS

CHAPTER 1   INTRODUCTION: THE COMPUTER AND THE PROGRAMMING PROCESS   1

    Digital Computers   1
    Component Parts of a Computer System   3
    Computer Storage   5
    Programming Languages   6
    Transmission to the Computer   7
    The Compilation Process   11
    Error Messages   12
    Extension and Warning Messages   12
    Execution: The Debugging Process Continued   13
    Coding Forms   14

CHAPTER 2   INTRODUCTION TO WATFOR PROGRAMMING   17

    Comment Statements   18
    Variables and Constants   18
    Arithmetic Statements; Arithmetic Expressions   19
    Storage Locations   20
    Arithmetic Operators   22
    The STOP Statement; The END Statement   22
    Output Statements   23
    Exponential Notation   23
    Integer Variables and Constants   25
    Explicit Type Specification   27
    Program Loops   28
    Branch Statements and Statement Numbers   29
    A Conditional Branch Statement   30
    Summation and Initialization   30

Exponentiation	31
Hierarchy of Arithmetic Operators; Use of Parentheses in Arithmetic Expressions	33

CHAPTER 3   DO LOOPS AND INPUT   39

The DO Statement	39
General Form	40
Use of the DO Index	41
The Increment Position	41
Algorithms	42
The CONTINUE Statement	43
The READ Statement	44
Placement of Data	46
The Parameter Card	47
Postloop Statements	48
Nested DO Loops	49
Nests Ending at the Same Statement	50

CHAPTER 4   FORTRAN-SUPPLIED FUNCTIONS   57

Function Names and Arguments	57
Square Root	57
Logarithms and Antilogarithms	59
Absolute Value	61
Trigonometric Functions	62
Some Functions Using More than One Argument	63
Some Other Functions	66

CHAPTER 5   CONDITIONAL BRANCHING   71

Two Types of IF Statement	71
The Arithmetic IF Statement	71
Basic Usage	72
Use for Comparison	74
The Logical IF Statement; Relational Operators	75
Logical Operators	77
The Sentinel Card	79
Flowcharting	80
The Computed GO TO Statement	85

CHAPTER 6   SUBSCRIPTED VARIABLES   91

General Purpose and Method	91
The DIMENSION Statement	92
Permissible Subscript Forms	94
Use of the DO Index as Subscript	95
Array Position Versus Array Element Value	96
Indexed Input and Output Lists	97
Operations on Arrays in Storage	98
Interchange of Values in Storage	99
The Sorting Problem	100
Double Dimension	101
The DATA Statement	103
Operations on Two-Dimensional Matrices	104
Triple Dimension	106

CHAPTER 7   SUBPROGRAM ARRANGEMENTS   109

Statement Functions	109
Function Subprograms	112
Main Programs; Calling Programs	114
Conversion of Main Programs to Subprograms	114
Subscripted Variables in Subprograms	115
Subroutine Subprograms	117
The CALL Statement	118
Alteration of Argument Values	119
The COMMON Statement	120

CHAPTER 8   OTHER VARIABLE TYPES   125

Explicit Type Specification	125
Double Precision Variables	125
Double Precision Constants	126
Double Precision Functions	127
Complex Variables	130
Complex Constants	130
Complex Functions	131
Logical Variables and Constants	133
Logical-Valued Expressions	133
Input/Output of Logical Variables	135
The Logical IF Statement Again	135

CHAPTER 9   INPUT/OUTPUT WITH FORMAT; NUMERIC FIELDS   141

I/O Statement Form	141
Equipment Unit Numbers	142
The FORMAT Statement	143
Fields, Records, and Files	143
FORMAT Notation for Numeric Fields	144
F Notation in Output	145
Right-Justification	146
Truncation of Digits; Rounding	146
Size of "w" and "d"	147
I Notation in Output	149
Consistency Between List and Specification Modes	149
E Notation in Output	150
Length of List Versus Number of Specifications	151
D Notation in Output	153
G Notation in FORMAT	153
P Notation: The Scale Factor	155
Input for Numeric Fields	156
Data Condensation	157
F Notation in Input	158
I Notation in Input	159
E and D Notation in Input	160
Complex Variables	162

CHAPTER 10   ALPHAMERIC AND POSITIONAL FORMAT   165

FORMAT Notation for Alphameric Fields	165
Hollerith (H) Strings and Literals (' '), Output	165
Hollerith Strings and Literals in Input	168
"A" Notation for Alphameric Fields	169
The CHARACTER Statement (WATFIV)	173
Logical Fields	174
Positional Notation in FORMAT	174
X Notation in FORMAT	175
T Notation in FORMAT	176
/ Notation in FORMAT	177
Printer Carriage Control	179

| CHAPTER 11 | SOME ADDITIONAL STATEMENTS | 185 |

"Unnecessary" Statements? 185
The EQUIVALENCE Statement 186
The IMPLICIT Statement 187
Storage Length Alteration and Initialization in Explicit
   Type Statements 188
The EXTERNAL Statement 189
Order of Specification Statements 189
The ENTRY Statement 190
Labeled COMMON 191
The BLOCK DATA Subprogram 192
END and ERR Options in the READ Statement 193
I/O Unit Control Statements 194
FORMAT Statements Treated as Data Arrays 195
The Assigned GO TO Statement 197

| APPENDIX A. | WATFOR AND WATFIV DIAGNOSTIC MESSAGES | 199 |

WATFOR 200
WATFIV 212

| APPENDIX B. | TEST OUTPUT FOR EXERCISE PROGRAMS | 225 |

INDEX 235

CHAPTER **1**

INTRODUCTION: THE COMPUTER AND THE PROGRAMMING PROCESS

DIGITAL COMPUTERS

Your purpose in using this book is to learn, as quickly as possible, how to *use*—that is, write *programs* for—the modern electronic computer. Therefore, we shall not indulge in technical descriptions of equipment, beyond a minimum orientation necessary for actual use.

We shall be dealing with *digital*, as opposed to *analog*, computers. The latter type represents numerical quantities as continuous amounts of some measurable entity (e.g., voltage), whereas *digital* computers (the more common type) record such quantities as actual sets of digits. You have used *digital* computation equipment when employing adding machines or desk calculators, and *analog* computation when using a slide rule. Subway turnstile counters are *digital* devices, while thermometers use the *analog* principle.

Some of the advantages of computers are fairly obvious: phenomenal speed and great accuracy usually head the list. Electronic computers perform thousands, in some instances millions, of arithmetic operations per second. Speeds for individual additions, multiplications, divisions, and the like are measured in microseconds (millionths of a second), or even in nanoseconds (billionths of a second). This great speed not only reduces man-days of work to minutes, but also permits freedom to experiment with alternative approaches to time-consuming research problems.

As to accuracy, actual machine errors are very rare; most mechanical and electronic malfunctions are detected by the computer itself, so that wrong answers are almost always traceable to programmer error rather than to the machinery.

The permanent nature of written *programs* makes the electronic computer different from computation devices preceding it (e.g., electric calculators). A *program* is a set of instructions that the computer is to follow during the course of a problem; once written and tested, it may be used over and over again. For example, a program that reads employee payroll records and prepares pay lists and checks need be written (and "debugged") only once, and may then be used every payday; the records themselves change, but the computation procedures do not.

As a corollary advantage over the calculator, the computer user is left with a complete set of machine-readable documents representing the input data (e.g., punched cards or magnetic tape), as well as complete documentation of the operations performed, in the form of the written program itself. The discovery of errors or required alterations to procedures leads to only minutes of rewriting and rerunning, rather than to hours or days of repetition of the work.

The versatility of output arrangements has also been increased by the com-

FIG. 1 A central processing unit (I.B.M. 360).

puter. Printed output may be obtained with elegant labeling, organization into tables, in multiple copies, and on special documents (e.g., paychecks). Furthermore, output may be produced on media that are themselves machine readable (cards, tape, etc.), so that results are directly usable as input for further analysis. Output devices may also include such equipment as plotters (for charting data and/or results), video screens, and remote transmission equipment.

FIG. 2 A card reader (R.C.A. Spectra).

COMPONENT PARTS OF A COMPUTER SYSTEM

A *central processing unit* ("CPU"; see Fig. 1) usually houses the computer "memory," operator controls, internal control circuitry, and any visible registers and light displays. From the programmer's viewpoint, the significant portion of the system housed here is the *primary storage area*, referred to above as the "memory." In this area, provision has been made for electronic recording of information. This information includes, during operation, a set

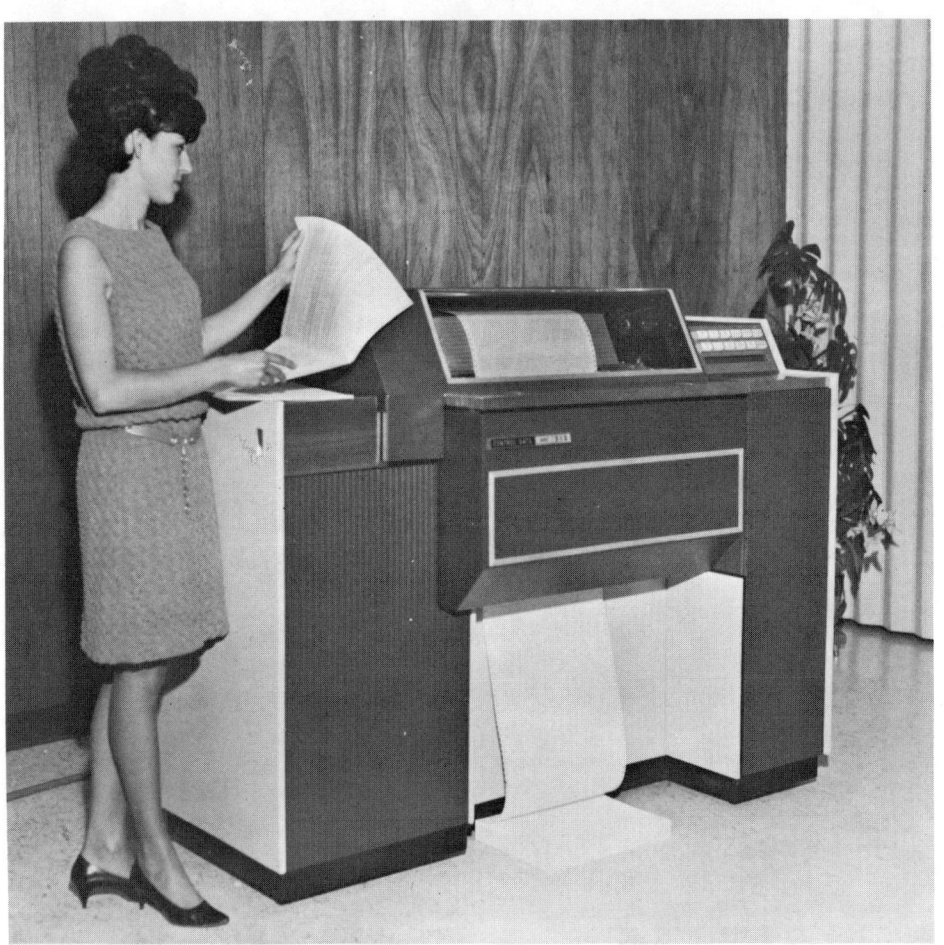

FIG. 3 A high-speed printer (Control Data Corp.).

of instructions (one or more *programs*) that direct the entire system activity, data stored for use during that activity, and intermediate results of the activity.

Other essential components of any computer *system* are *input* (Fig. 2) and *output* (Fig. 3) units. In the most common configurations, punched cards and/or magnetic tape are used for input, and high-speed printers for output.

In addition to the *primary* storage area housed in the CPU, most computer systems now also employ extensive *secondary* storage devices, such as magnetic disks (Fig. 4). Such devices usually can hold much larger quantities of stored information (magnetically recorded) than the *primary* storage area, and are *on-line*—that is, they are accessible to the programmer, via the *primary* storage. Specifically, information may be moved (at the programmer's request) between *primary* and *secondary* storage, in either direction, during operation.

FIG. 4 A magnetic disk storage unit (I.B.M. Corp.).

COMPUTER STORAGE

In both the *primary* and *secondary* storage areas, the actual method of storing information is adapted to the two-state nature of the electronic media that do the recording. That is, each tiny "bit" (plate or cell) may be regarded at any moment as "on" or "off" (e.g., magnetized or unmagnetized). A consecutive string of such "bits" is used to represent a numerical quantity. The storage method usually makes use of the *binary* (base "2") number system. For example,

Computer Storage Representation ("x" represents "on")						Meaning	Binary Notation
(32)	(16)	(8)	(4)	(2)	(1)		
		x		x	x	Number 11	1011
x		x	x			Number 44	101100
				x		Number 2	10
						Number 0	0

Six "bits"

In this example, powers of the base "2" increase from right to left (beginning with 2^0); the sums of these powers are the values stored. In the length shown (not realistic), all integers from 0 through 63 could be represented. The binary number system is thus employed partially as a space-saving device, since the various powers of the base "2" can be summed to code a large (and internally complete) range of integer numbers.

In addition to this *binary* code, the *hexadecimal* (base "16") number system is also used, for coding noninteger values. It should be stressed, however, that the programmer does *not* have to communicate in this fashion; the computer manufacturer provides for translation *by the computer* to these number systems, and translation back again to the common *decimal* notation (base "10" numbers) for output. Alphabetic and special characters — commas, dollar signs, etc. — are represented in storage by fixed combinations of numeric codes.

PROGRAMMING LANGUAGES

Computers do not "think"; they cannot "solve" problems. The computer is in fact capable only of carrying out the instructions of the programmer, who must know perfectly well how to "solve" the problem at hand. The instructions that he writes (the *"program"*) must be complete in that each operation to be performed is fully specified in proper sequence. We shall see, however, that the programmer may call for large amounts of computer work by writing fairly short programs; for he can in effect say, "perform the next instruction 100 times," in lieu of writing it out 100 times. And, even better, he can say, "perform the following set of instructions repeatedly, until . . . ." The condition he names may be the reaching of a certain value in a cumulating storage area, appearance of a specific input value, exhaustion of the input data, etc.

Early electronic computers (post-World War II) could be "programmed" (i.e., supplied with a fresh set of instructions) only by rewiring parts of circuits. *Written* programs appeared shortly thereafter, which could be transmitted to the computer in the same manner as numerical data (using punched cards, paper tape, magnetic tape). These first languages, however, were *machine languages* that conformed to the computer's ability to store only numeric information. They are still provided for each computer model, but are difficult for programmers; they use simple digital operational codes (e.g., "23" may represent "multiply"), and require the programmer to keep track of numerical storage addresses and refer to them in instructions. *Assembler languages* are also provided, which substitute some mnemonic labels for the digital codes (e.g., "M" for "multiply"), and allow alphabetic labels for storage reference. Both types of language have the disadvantage that they are usable only on the computer for which they are designed.

In the late 1950's the idea of intermediate ("problem-oriented, machine-independent") languages reached full development with FORTRAN, still the most widely used *compiler language*. Others include ALGOL, BASIC, COBOL, PL-I, etc. The FORTRAN language is written by the programmer in short phrases ("*statements*"), that combine ordinary English and standard arithmetic notation. For example,

COST = UNITS * PRICE

This instruction may be paraphrased, "look up the values currently stored in the "UNITS" and "PRICE" locations (in primary computer storage) — multiply them, and store the result in the "COST" storage location."

Statements written in this language (or any other *compiler language*) must, however, be translated to the computer's basic *machine language* before execution of the program. Each computer manufacturer provides a FORTRAN *compiler program* (itself a computer program in machine language), which instructs the computer in translating FORTRAN into machine language. Thus the computer, acting under the direction of the FORTRAN *compiler program*, translates the programmer's FORTRAN *source program* into an *object program*, which is in the basic language executable directly by the computer.

In addition to being easy to learn and to remember, the compiler languages have the great advantage that they are not computer-bound. FORTRAN compiler programs for hundreds of computer models provide for identical FORTRAN language (with minor variations) from the programmer's viewpoint, though they translate to completely different machine languages. Thus a FORTRAN source program written for IBM equipment may be run on computers produced by RCA, Honeywell, XDS, CDC, NCR, UNIVAC, etc.

The WATFOR and WATFIV compiler programs specifically referred to in this book represent the sort of "minor variations" mentioned above. FORTRAN stands for "FORmula TRANslation"; the name WATFOR is derived from "WATerloo FORtran." The prefix represents the University of Waterloo, Canada, where the modified compilers were developed. The differences between these and other FORTRAN compiler programs are small (they are pointed out where they occur in the text), so that you will be learning FORTRAN that is easily transferable to any of the hundreds of computers using the general FORTRAN language. But the variations incorporated at Waterloo happen to make life easier for the beginning programming student, and for the computer center serving him.

TRANSMISSION TO THE COMPUTER

Figure 5 shows some commonly used alphabets for card and tape input; each is capable of representing digits 0 through 9, letters A through Z, and selected special characters (plus sign, decimal point, etc.). Careful study of these arrangements is *not* necessary, since the translation from written sym-

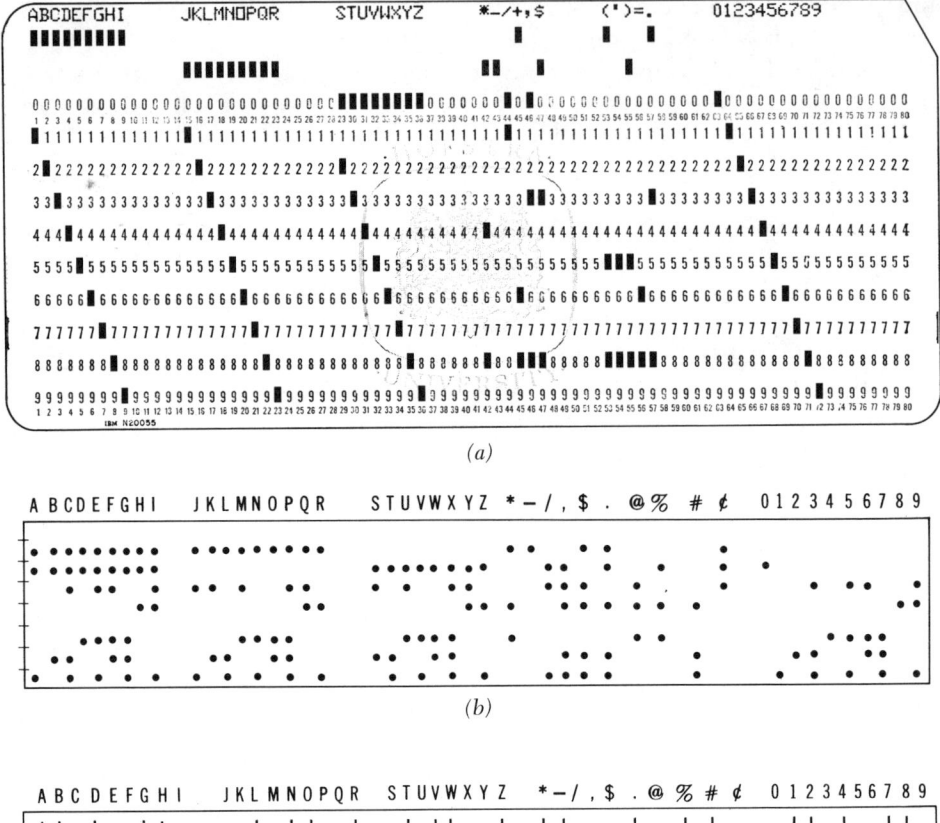

FIG. 5 (a) A punched card alphabet. (b) A paper tape alphabet. (c) A magnetic tape alphabet.

bols is not the programmer's responsibility; it is accomplished by a typewriterlike device such as the *keypunch* machine shown in Fig. 6. The keyboard contains all characters that may be represented; the machine pictured punches the appropriate combination of holes automatically, when any key is depressed by the operator. Note that each character occupies a single column of the 80-column card, requiring from one to three rows of the card for representation. Some such machines produce paper tape, but magnetic

8   INTRODUCTION: THE COMPUTER AND THE PROGRAMMING PROCESS

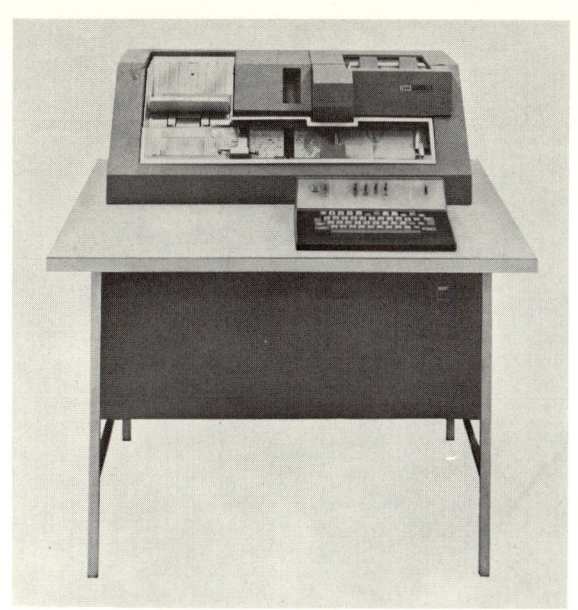

FIG. 6 (a) A keypunch machine (IBM 029). (b) A close view of a keypunch keyboard.

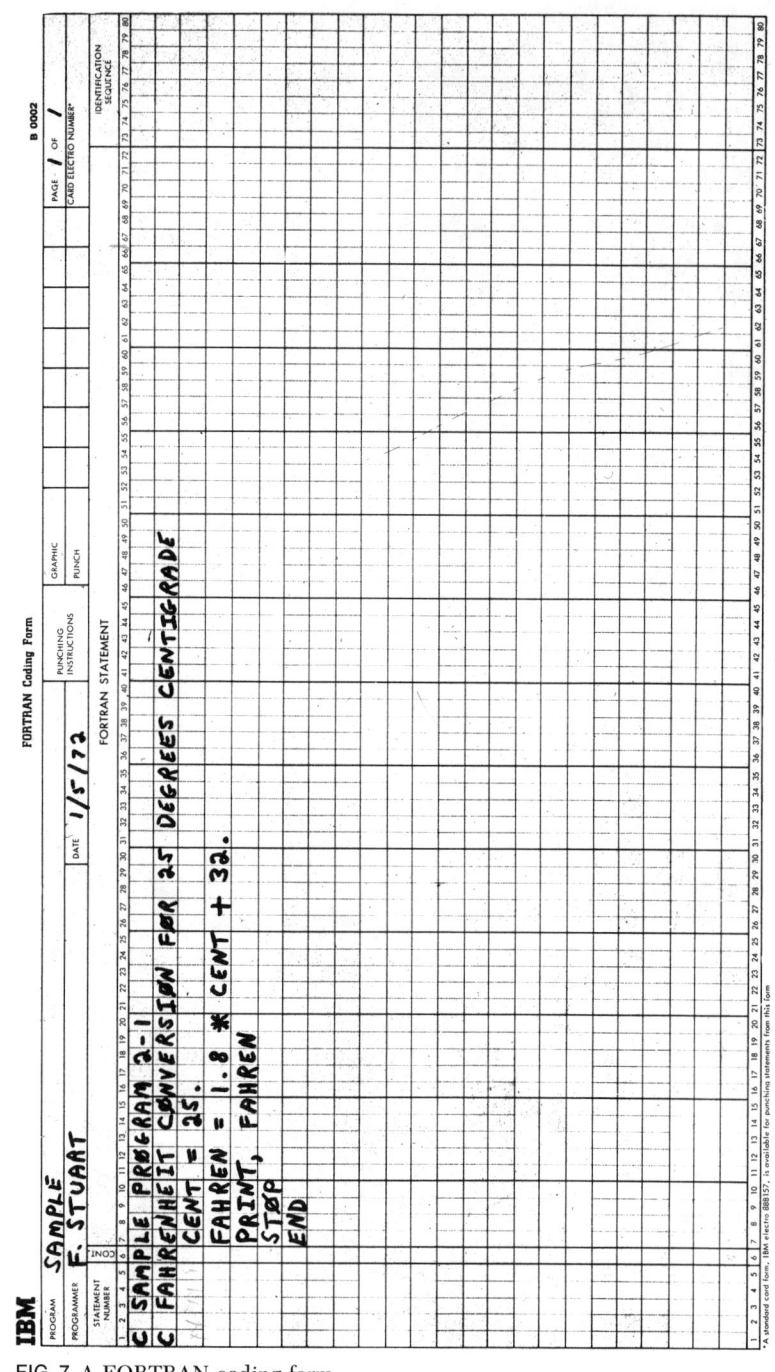

FIG. 7 A FORTRAN coding form.

tape is frequently generated by computers or other machines that transfer directly from punched cards.

The physical programming process actually begins with coding paper (Fig. 7), usually organized in 80 columns to match the standard card. Each line of the coding paper is taken to represent one punch card. Some additional details of organization for FORTRAN programs will be discussed later in this chapter.

When the programmer's work has been transferred to cards via the keypunching process, the deck of cards representing the *source program* (preceded by some *"control"* cards, and possibly followed by cards containing numerical *data*) are read by a *card reader* (see Fig. 2). A typical arrangement consists of 80 wire brushes, which complete electrical contact with a metal plate when a card passing between brushes and plate contains a punched hole. The combination of brush number and timing of the contact defines the character that is to be passed into storage. All 80 columns of the card are read simultaneously, usually at speeds of several hundred cards per minute.

THE COMPILATION PROCESS

One of the important complete programs usually stored on a *secondary* ("on-line") storage medium is the *FORTRAN compiler program*. This program contains thousands of instructions to accomplish translation of FORTRAN statements; it must reside in the *primary* storage area before any FORTRAN *source program is* read. Once in storage, it reads statements of the *source program* and translates them to equivalent sequences of the computer's machine language, producing an *object program*. This process is called *compilation*; while it is taking place, there is no attempt to *carry out* any of the programmer's instructions. If the translation proceeds without difficulty (specifically, if the programmer is not found to have violated any FORTRAN language rules), the *execution* stage follows the successful *compilation*.

When standard FORTRAN compiler programs are used, the *execution* phase requires *replacement* of the FORTRAN compiler program by the *object program*, in primary storage. Therefore, the compiler program must be called back into primary storage prior to entry of *each* FORTRAN source program. However, the WATFOR and WATFIV compiler programs are "core-resident"; that is, they remain in primary storage while execution of the object instructions is taking place. Therefore, a whole "batch" of FORTRAN programs may be compiled (translated) and executed, having called the compiler program into primary storage just once.

Each of the FORTRAN source programs in a WATFOR or WATFIV "batch" therefore requires only two *control cards*: a JOB card ($JOB) at the beginning indicates the commencement of a new job, and an ENTRY card ($ENTRY) at the end serves as a request to execute the object program. (Your local computer installation may require additional keypunching on the $JOB card to supply programmer identification.)

ERROR MESSAGES

At the compilation stage, programmer errors (generally, violations of FORTRAN language rules) may prevent translation of parts of the source program to machine language. The compiler program will produce diagnostic messages designed to help the programmer "debug"—that is, make the necessary corrections before trying again. For example,

$$\text{COST} = \text{UNITS} * + \text{PRICE}$$

would cause the WATFOR compiler to produce the message

$$\star\star\star\text{ERROR}\star\star\star \quad \text{SX-C}$$

which would appear within the reprinted source program, following the erroneous line (statement). The SX-C portion of the error message is part of an error classification system (the SX portion stands for *syntax*), which appears in full in Appendix A. One of the advantages of the WATFOR and WATFIV compilers, as compared with other FORTRAN versions, is the much larger number of such diagnostic messages available.

In this instance, Appendix A says[1]

SX-C   ILLEGAL SEQUENCE OF OPERATORS IN EXPRESSION

The objection is to the appearance of both the asterisk (an *arithmetic operator* calling for multiplication) and the plus sign (calling for addition) side by side. The programmer must make all indicated corrections (usually by repunching some individual statement cards), and reenter the entire corrected source program for compilation.

EXTENSION AND WARNING MESSAGES

The language error we have used as an example makes correction and recompilation mandatory, since the object program is not completely produced. There are, however, two types of diagnostic message that may be received during compilation that do *not* prevent execution of the object program. One of these, the *Extension* message, merely notes that the programmer has used one of the special features of WATFOR or WATFIV that will not be

---

[1] In WATFIV, this message *text* may be included in the output (along with the error *code*), at the installation's option.

acceptable to most FORTRAN compilers. This information is provided to remind the programmer to make appropriate changes if the program is to be run elsewhere. We have already indicated that these differences are few, and will be emphasized in the text as they arise.

A *Warning* message signifies some ambiguity that the compiler program is able to resolve by making some assumption about the programmer's intention. The program will be executed (if no outright language errors are present); but the programmer should make certain that the compiler's assumptions are consistent with his intent. As an example,

$$COST = PRICE * INVENTORY$$

would elicit the WATFOR diagnostic message,

$$**WARNING** \quad VA-2$$

Appendix A indicates the meaning,

VARIABLE NAME LONGER THAN SIX CHARACTERS. TRUNCATED TO SIX

Since the compiler uses a maximum of *six* characters in any *name*, the programmer is warned that the name has been recorded as

$$INVENT$$

He should do something about the warning if, for example, he has used another questionable name such as

$$INVENTION$$

That is, INVENTORY and INVENTION turn out to produce the same name in WATFOR or WATFIV language.

EXECUTION: THE DEBUGGING PROCESS CONTINUED

It has been said that the first axiom of computer programming is: "There is at least one error in every program." It is important to realize that a *compilation* that has proceeded without error messages does not provide proof that the program will execute properly to accomplish the programmer's purpose. Error messages refer only to *language* rule violations; many mistakes in *logic* cannot be detected by the compiler program. If, for example, the programmer has written a sequence of instructions, each meaningful and correctly written, but has placed them in illogical order, the execution may produce some wrong answers, or occasionally no answers at all.

To facilitate complete program testing, Appendix B contains sample output that should be produced by each exercise problem. Exercises requiring *data* have all been tested on a standard data set, which is listed at the beginning of Appenxix B. Since there are usually dozens, occasionally thousands, of alternative methods of writing a computer program to solve a given problem, Appendix B represents the only sort of "answer" key you should need. Any program that produces correct output is a correct program.

Two options provided by the WATFOR and WATFIV compilers aid in the debugging process. One of these allows running in *debug mode* during execution. In this mode, checks are made for *undefined variables*. That is, error messages are produced when any attempt is made to *use* a named value in computations before a value has been assigned to the name. For example,

$$COST = PRICE * UNITS$$

is legal language, but will produce something rational during execution only if PRICE and UNITS have acquired numerical values, earlier in the program. Running in the *debug mode* is slower than normal execution, but often helpful in tracing troubles.

A *free run mode* is also available, in which a program that has produced (language) error messages during compilation may nevertheless be executed; execution terminates when statements containing errors are reached. In this manner, the programmer may get to see partial output, even though the object program is incomplete.

CODING FORMS

The programmer should use a standard FORTRAN coding form (Fig. 7), to facilitate the keypunching process. Note that the form shown provides 80 columns, which correspond to the standard 80-column punched card. Each

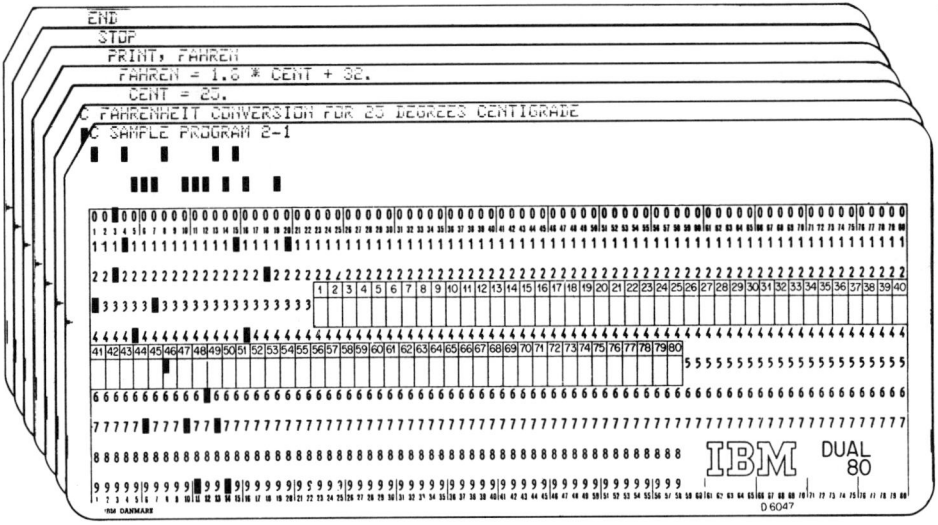

FIG. 8 The Fig. 7 program transferred to punched cards.

FORTRAN statement occupies a separate line; the statement begins in column 7, while statement *numbers* (if used) appear in the first five columns. A statement cannot extend beyond column 72. The last eight columns may be used, however, for nonstatement purposes (e.g., sequence numbers or other identification codes), since they are ignored by the compiler program.

Each line will be keypunched as a separate card (Fig. 8), for the computer analyzes each card as an individual FORTRAN statement. An exception to this rule, in *all* FORTRAN compilers, permits the programmer to *continue* long statements on successive cards, indicating the continuation by placement of a nonzero digit in column 6 of each continuation card, a column otherwise left blank. Cards with blank or zero in column 6 will be interpreted as new statements, while cards containing any other character in column 6 are interpreted as *continuation lines*.

A special exception to the one-card/one-statement rule is provided by the WATFIV compiler, which permits the programmer to include multiple statements on a single line (card), separating them with semicolons. This will be illustrated more fully in Chapter 2.

Columns left blank are usually ignored, and may be used to improve legibility. That is, statements may be "stretched" horizontally by separation of words and symbols. Thus

```
                COST = PRICE * UNITS
```

and

```
            COST    =    PRICE    *    UNITS
```

produce the same effect.

For Review

analog, digital
central processing unit
primary storage, secondary storage
decimal numbers, binary numbers, hexadecimal numbers
machine language, assembler language, compiler language
compiler program, source program, object program
FORTRAN, WATFOR, WATFIV
keypunch
control cards
compilation, execution
error message, extension message, warning message
debugging
debug mode, free run mode
coding form

CHAPTER **2**

INTRODUCTION TO WATFOR PROGRAMMING

Let us examine a complete WATFOR program for a rather trivial problem. We shall have the computer convert a Centigrade temperature (25 degrees) to the Fahrenheit equivalent. We make use of the conversion formula,

$$f = 1.8c + 32$$

```
C SAMPLE PROGRAM 2-1
C FAHRENHEIT CONVERSION FOR 25 DEGREES CENTIGRADE
    CENT = 25.
    FAHREN = 1.8 * CENT + 32.
    PRINT, FAHREN
    STOP
    END
```

The ordinary English words and standard arithmetic notation used in FORTRAN probably make the program fairly easy to follow, even before we discuss the individual statements composing it. Prior to that discussion, we note that only one of the statements,

PRINT, FAHREN

would be unacceptable to most FORTRAN compiler programs. The simplicity of output (and input) instructions in WATFOR and WATFIV are important advantages of these languages for beginners. This will be explained further in this chapter; alternatives common to all FORTRAN compilers appear in Chapter 9.

COMMENT STATEMENTS

The compiler program *ignores* any statement that begins (column 1 of the punched card) with the letter C, which stands for *Comment*. Thus a Comment statement is not *executable;* and in fact is not used during compilation either, since no attempt at translation is made. Consequently, you can write (punch) anything you please in such a statement, without regard to WATFOR language rules.

The Comment statement is designed for the convenience of the programmer and the readers of his program. The inclusion of such a statement at the head of a source program ensures that all such card decks (and all listings made from them) will be readily identifiable. Since any number of Comment statements may appear anywhere in the source program, two other uses are also recommended practice. First, early Comment statements may provide explanatory information—author's name, purpose of the program, required form of input data, and so on. Second, in lengthy programs Comment statements should appear frequently as section headings, so that the programmer (or reader) may locate particular sections easily, and follow the general outline of the program's logic.

VARIABLES AND CONSTANTS

Sample program 2-1 contains two *names* originated by the programmer: CENT and FAHREN. Such names are invented, as needed, to designate *variables*. The actual purpose is to specify *uniquely identified storage locations* for values to be developed during execution of the program. The algebraic meaning of the word *variable* is here copied, since the values *stored* in the named locations may change during the course of execution.

A *constant*, on the other hand, is any value written into the source program as an actual number. There are three constants used in sample program 2-1: 25., 1.8, and 32.

The rules for naming *variables* are as follows:

1. The variable name must *begin* with an alphabetic character. (Note that $ is considered alphabetic.)

2. Following characters may be alphabetic or numeric; but special characters (e.g., plus sign, decimal point, etc.) are not permitted.

3. A maximum of six characters will be used in the name. While the use of more than six produces an error message requiring correction in most FORTRAN compilers, WATFOR and WATFIV produce the sort of *warning* message described in Chapter 1, and the program may be executed without corrections.

4. When any one of the letters I, J, K, L, M, or N (referred to as the "IN-letters") is used as the *first* character of the name, a special type of storage location is reserved, which cannot hold postdecimal content. Such *integer* variables will be discussed later in this chapter.

The following examples illustrate these rules:

Valid Names	Invalid Names
DOG	B1.23 (contains special character)
X	3DIMEN (begins with numeric character)
CASH	A+B (contains special character)
SUM	
SUM2	
A145	
MAX *(integer)*	
KING *(integer)*	
ACCOUNT (but will be recorded as ACCOUN)	

You should adopt the practice of inventing names meaningful to you within the context of the program. This facilitates keeping track of the variables as you write the program, and also makes later reading much easier (especially for the purpose of locating errors). Thus

$$\text{COST} = \text{NUMBER} \star \text{PRICE}$$

is preferable to an alternative,

$$\text{C} = \text{N} \star \text{P}$$

although both are legal.

ARITHMETIC STATEMENTS; ARITHMETIC EXPRESSIONS

There are two *arithmetic statements* in sample program 2–1:

$$\text{CENT} = 25.$$
$$\text{FAHREN} = 1.8 \star \text{CENT} + 32.$$

They are identifiable by the presence of the *equal sign;* the general form for arithmetic statements is

variable name = arithmetic expression

To the left of the equal sign there must appear one (and only one) variable name; but the arithmetic expression may contain combinations of *variables*, *constants*, and *arithmetic operators* (+, −, /, *, **). *Function names* may also appear. They are discussed in Chapter 3.

Arithmetic statements are *executable*—and in fact are the statements that actually call on the computer to perform its fundamental job: computation. The general meaning of any arithmetic statement is: "Perform all computations indicated to the right of the equal sign, and store the result in the location named to its left." Variable names appearing in the arithmetic expression are "looked up" in the referenced location, and the values contained therein at that point in execution are used in the computation. Two important points arise in this connection:

1. Any variable name mentioned in an *expression* (i.e., to the *right* of the equal sign) should already have acquired a numerical value earlier in the execution. Suppose the positions of the two arithmetic statements in sample program 2-1 were *reversed* (vertically). The programmer would then have committed the error of referring to an *undefined variable*. The result would be a wrong answer delivered during execution. (If, however, the program were executed in the *debug mode* available in WATFOR and WATFIV, an undefined variable error message would be delivered as well.)

2. Values in storage locations mentioned in *expressions* are not changed by such usage; but any value already stored in the location mentioned to the *left* of the equal sign *will* be replaced, by execution of the statement. Thus:

	Contents of Storage Locations	
Program Statement	X	Y
X = 2.4	2.4	Undefined
Y = X + 5.0	2.4	7.4
X = Y	7.4	7.4

The X and Y storage locations *both* contain 7.4, after the sequence is executed.

An important corollary of this *replacement* principle is that the following type of statement, which would look like nonsense in algebra, is both valid and highly useful, in programming:

$$X = X + 1.0$$

This produces *incrementation* of the value in the X storage location. (If it appeared at the end of the sequence above, it would produce 8.4 in the X location.)

STORAGE LOCATIONS

We have said that each *variable name* used by the programmer actually represents a separate *storage location*. During compilation, each *new* name mentioned initiates the reservation of a location, which will be filled with digital values during execution. This location, which in machine language has a numerical "address," will be catalogued by the compiler program, so that the proper numerical address will be referenced whenever this variable name is mentioned.

Thus during compilation of sample program 2-1 the first mention of CENT causes a location to be reserved for any numerical values of CENT that may develop during execution. Subsequent mentions (e.g., in the statement assigning a value to FAHREN) do not have this effect, but generate machine language instructions containing the correct address for CENT, determined earlier.

Note that the CENT location is not actually *filled* during compilation with the constant 25. Instructions for filling it are translated to machine language as part of the object program, but have not yet been executed, when compilation is completed.

The decision to provide a storage location for certain values (by assigning a variable name) is usually made when more than one different value is to occupy the location, during execution. In sample program 2-1, we have actually used the CENT storage unnecessarily (with no real harm, of course). The second axiom of computer programming is reputedly, "Every program can be shortened." Sample program 2-2 illustrates the principle:

```
C SAMPLE PROGRAM 2-2
C A SHORTER VERSION OF PROGRAM 2-1
    FAHREN = 1.8 * 25.0 + 32.0
    PRINT, FAHREN
    STOP
    END
```

A further shortening is possible in WATFOR or WATFIV, for these compilers permit the *use of arithmetic expressions in output lists*. This is an extension of ordinary FORTRAN, in which the rule is that *output lists* may contain only the names of variables (i.e., only the names of those storage locations from which values are to be copied for output). Thus:

```
C SAMPLE PROGRAM 2-3
C A WATFOR SHORTENING OF PROGRAM 2-2
    PRINT, 1.8 * 25.0 + 32.0
    STOP
    END
```

This program will elicit the diagnostic message,

EXTENSION   IO-C

Appendix A shows the code translation,

INVALID ELEMENT IN AN OUTPUT LIST

As indicated in Chapter 1, such messages are provided as a reminder to the programmer, but do not indicate illegal WATFOR (or WATFIV) usage; and sample program 2-3 will not be prevented from executing.

(Incidentally, note that the constant "25." appearing in sample program 2-1 is the same as the "25.0" written above; but we shall see shortly that "25," with no decimal point keypunched, would change the meaning slightly.)

A language extension present only in WATFIV permits further *physical* shortening, by including more than one FORTRAN statement per punched card (and/or coding-form line). Semicolons are used to indicate statement endings:

```
C SAMPLE PROGRAM 2-4 (WATFIV ONLY)
PRINT, 1.8 * 25. + 32.; STOP; END
```

ARITHMETIC OPERATORS

We have mentioned that variables and constants are separated, in arithmetic expressions, by *arithmetic operators*. The four operations of simple arithmetic are called for as follows:

+ add
− subtract
/ divide
* multiply

(Another arithmetic operator, ** for exponentiation, will be discussed at the end of this chapter.)

Any number of arithmetic operators may appear in an arithmetic expression. However, arithmetic operators may not appear in succession in expressions. Thus

$$X = A * - B$$

will be rejected during compilation. However,

$$X = A * (-B)$$

is valid. The use of parentheses in arithmetic expressions will be treated systematically shortly.

THE STOP STATEMENT; THE END STATEMENT

STOP is an *executable* statement that terminates execution of the *object* program. END, however, is not executable but merely serves as information to the compiler program that the end of the *source* program has been reached. The word END *must* appear at the end of every source program. Later, we shall examine instances in which more than one STOP statement appears in a program; however, END may appear only once.

OUTPUT STATEMENTS

The simplicity of output statements in WATFOR and WATFIV is based on the use of the optional words, PRINT and PUNCH, to designate the on-line printer and the card punch, respectively. In Chapter 9 we shall examine the more complicated option, WRITE; when the latter is used, the programmer must further specify both the output device to be used, and the *format* in which the output is to appear. The use of PRINT and/or PUNCH in output statements invokes a *fixed format* — that is, the programmer does not choose the horizontal or vertical position for output, the number of decimal places to be printed, etc.[1]

The simplified output statement consists of the word PRINT or the word PUNCH, followed by a comma, and then by the *output list*. The *output list* may contain variables, constants, and arithmetic expressions (in the last case, only the *result* is output), with each element in the list separated from others by commas. For example,

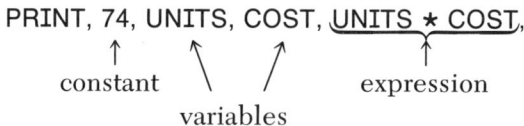

(Remember, however, that *each* of these list elements is itself an *arithmetic expression*, when it appears to the right of an equal sign):

$$K = 74$$
$$X = \text{UNITS}$$
$$\text{TOTAL} = \text{UNITS} * \text{COST}$$

EXPONENTIAL NOTATION

The correct answer to the problem contained in the first four sample programs is exactly 77 degrees Fahrenheit. The computer output appears as follows:

$$0.7700000E\ 02$$

The formatless output statements provided by WATFOR and WATFIV use this *exponential notation*, for noninteger ("*real*") quantities. Following the "E" are two digits indicating the number of places the decimal point is to be moved (from its printed position) to give the actual size of the number, in this case 77.00000.

---

[1] Although this output arrangement (and the READ arrangement described in Chapter 3) represents an *extension* feature of WATFOR/WATFIV — that is, it is not permitted in standard FORTRAN — no EXTENSION message is produced.

You may be familiar with the mathematical notation

$$3(10)^9$$

to represent

$$3,000,000,000$$

or

$$2(10)^{-5}$$

for

$$.00002$$

This notation is adopted in FORTRAN by using "E" followed by up to two digits, to indicate "times ten raised to the following power." The "E" thus stands for "exponent of ten." The exponential format is useful in that very large and very small values may be made to fit into a uniform space. Note that the WATFOR/WATFIV output representation of the two numbers used as examples above would be

$$0.3000000E\ 10$$

and

$$0.2000000E\text{-}04$$

In Chapter 9, we shall introduce programmer-controlled FORMAT, which frees the programmer to select other output forms for *real* (decimal) values.

Exponential notation actually performs a rather important function in computer operations: it provides the basic method for *storing* decimal ("*real*") values. For example, the statement

$$\text{CENT} = 25.$$

actually places, in the CENT location, a two-part representation, the equivalent of

$$2500000\ 02$$

With the decimal position counted from the left, this method stores numbers as follows:

Value	General Storage Form
8456.78	8456780 04
.25	2500000 00
.00000628	6280000 −05
123,456,789,000	1234567 12

Note that each of the storage examples on the right contains *seven* digits of the number itself, and *two* digits of the exponent. In the fourth example, the

24 INTRODUCTION TO WATFOR PROGRAMMING

number is actually *truncated* to fit the storage area, but the exponent value records the actual size of the number as usual.

The *seven* digits are a limit on *precision* of values stored (e.g., IBM 360 series, RCA Spectra series). A common *range* limit, or maximum size of the *exponent*, is approximately ±75. Thus a 75-digit number may be "stored" — but only seven significant digits are actually represented.

INTEGER VARIABLES AND CONSTANTS

We have just referred to decimal numbers as *"real."* An alternative number form is referred to in FORTRAN as *"integer."* Neither word is being used in the strict mathematical sense; for our purposes, *"integers"* are values that *cannot* acquire postdecimal content, while *"real"* values *may* (or may not) have postdecimal digits. The table below shows how the distinction is actually made by the programmer (and recognized by the compiler program):

	Real Mode	Integer Mode
Variable	First character of name is A-H or O-Z	First character of name is I-N
Constant	Decimal point appears in number	No decimal point appears in number

Examples conforming to these conventions appear below.

Real Variables	Integer Variables	Real Constants	Integer Constants
CASH	MONEY	7.	7
X	KX	8.0	8
DIME	NICKEL	.875	31289
S1972	I1972	3.65E2	365

The early constant examples illustrate that it is the presence or absence of the decimal point that distinguishes *real* from *integer*, rather than the actual presence of postdecimal digits. The last real constant shown is in exponential notation.

The use of *integer mode* for values in the program is most commonly *not* for computation, but for purposes of *counting*. There are in fact three disadvantages of integers, for ordinary computation:

1. The obvious one: no postdecimal content can be developed in answers. (There is no provision for an *exponent*, in integer storage locations.)

2. The *range* of values that may be stored in integer locations is limited. While 75-digit numbers may be represented in real mode (see last section), 9- or 10-digit numbers are frequent limits in integer locations. (For IBM 360 and RCA Spectra, the limit is $2^{31} - 1 = 2{,}147{,}483{,}647$.)

3. A corollary of (1) above produces truncated answers in integer *division*. The result of 7/2 is 3.

Since none of these disadvantages would actually cause problems in sample program 2-1, we may convert to integer mode where possible, to illustrate the conventions:

```
C SAMPLE PROGRAM 2-5
C SAMPLE PROGRAM 2-1 REWRITTEN TO USE INTEGERS, BY IMPLICIT
                                                  TYPE SPECIFICATION
      ICENT = 25
      NFAREN = 1.8 * ICENT + 32
      PRINT, NFAREN
      STOP
      END
```

The output from this program will be

$$77$$

since exponential notation is not used for integer variables in the output list.

Note that the arithmetic statement computing NFAREN contains a *"mixed"* arithmetic expression; that is, an expression in which both integer and real values appear. The actual evaluation of the expression is performed in *real* mode, for the compiler treats such mixtures by giving precedence to real arithmetic.[2] Therefore, the expression result is actually developed as

$$7700000\ 02$$

—but the programmer's request to store the result in an *integer* location results in truncation to integer 77.

The first disadvantage above—failure to retain decimal content of answers—is illustrated in sample program 2-6; for 26 degrees Centigrade, the correct answer *should* be 78.80000 degrees Fahrenheit. Instead, the output is

$$78$$

```
C SAMPLE PROGRAM 2-6
C USE OF INTEGER MODE MAY LEAD TO WRONG ANSWERS
      ICENT = 26
      NFAREN = 1.8 * ICENT + 32
      PRINT, NFAREN
      STOP
      END
```

---

[2] Some compiler programs declare mixed expressions illegal, however; the programmer must convert all values to one mode or the other.

Note also that the wrong answer could not be avoided by changing ICENT back to CENT, and/or 32 back to 32.0. Storage in the NFAREN (integer) location loses the postdecimal content. Remember that the *mixed* expression is being evaluated in *real* mode by the compiler with or without these changes.

Sample program 2-7 applies a common version of the temperature conversion formula,

$$f = 9/5 \, c + 32$$

to illustrate problem (3) mentioned above (truncation of decimals in integer division). Even though *real* storage locations (i.e., real variables) are specified, the integer division *instantly* loses the postdecimal portion of the result (the division *"remainder"*), so that a wrong answer is produced. Specifically, 9/5 is evaluated as integer 1; and the succeeding arithmetic produces

$$1 \star 25. + 32. = 57.$$

```
C SAMPLE PROGRAM 2-7
C FAILS BECAUSE OF TRUNCATION RESULTING FROM INTEGER
                                                  DIVISION
      CENT = 25.
      FAHREN = 9/5 * CENT + 32.
      PRINT, FAHREN
      STOP
      END
```

This error may be corrected, by placing a decimal point on *either* the 9 or the 5 (or, of course, on both):

$$\text{FAHREN} = 9./5 \star \text{CENT} + 32.$$

will produce the correct result, 77.0 degrees. (This works because 9./5 is now treated as a *mixed expression*, and evaluated in *real* mode.)

EXPLICIT TYPE SPECIFICATION

A Comment statement in sample program 2-5 remarks that *implicit type specification* has been used to declare the integer mode for the ICENT and NFAREN storage locations. That is, the compiler program recognizes the first characters (I and N) as dictating integer mode. Sample program 2-8 shows an alternative in which the programmer declares *exceptions* to the implicit typing rules; this must be done at the beginning of the program.

```
C SAMPLE PROGRAM 2-8
C USE OF INTEGERS IN SAMPLE PROGRAM 2-1, BY EXPLICIT TYPE
                                               SPECIFICATION
      INTEGER CENT, FAHREN
      CENT = 25
```

```
FAHREN = 1.8 * CENT + 32
PRINT, FAHREN
STOP
END
```

The output from this version is the same as that for sample program 2-5:

```
77
```

The opposite kind of reversal is arranged by

```
REAL ICENT, NFAREN
```

If this statement were inserted at the top of sample program 2-5, the output would be once again

```
0.7700000E 02
```

In most cases, it is probably better to use *implicit* type specification to arrange appropriate storage—that is, to follow the "IN-letter" rule, even though misspelling is required. For example,

```
KOUNT = 1
```

rather than

```
INTEGER COUNT
COUNT = 1
```

and

```
AMAN = 76.3
```

in preference to

```
REAL MAN
MAN = 76.3
```

Programmers who use *explicit* type specification frequently forget their own usage later in the program.

Integers require less storage space than decimal (real) values, and operations involving integers are executed more quickly than real arithmetic. The integer mode is useful in many counting situations and occasional computation situations; the restrictions on usefulness should be remembered, however.

PROGRAM LOOPS

The programs shown thus far make little use of the computer's important advantages over hand calculation. The computer becomes really useful when a *repetitive* procedure is required. For this reason, almost every computer program contains at least one *loop:* a sequence of statements that is to be repeated during execution.

```
C SAMPLE PROGRAM 2-9
C FAHRENHEIT CONVERSION, FOR CENTIGRADE TEMPERATURES FROM
C    ZERO DEGREES AND UP, USING AN ENDLESS LOOP
        KCENT = 0
7       FAHREN = 1.8 * KCENT + 32
        PRINT, KCENT, FAHREN
        KCENT = KCENT + 1
        GO TO 7
        END
```

Sample program 2-9 applies the temperature conversion formula to Centigrade temperatures 0, 1, 2, 3, ..., etc. Note that integer mode is used for these temperatures, and real mode for the Fahrenheit equivalents, so that output appears

```
        0    0.3200000E 02
        1    0.3380000E 02
        2    0.3560000E 02
        3    0.3740000E 02
            etc.
```

(The bracket drawn on the left in sample program 2-9 shows the *range* of the program *loop*. It has no FORTRAN meaning; we shall use it in sample programs for the reader's convenience.)

BRANCH STATEMENTS AND STATEMENT NUMBERS

A *branch* instruction is one that causes the computer to depart from top-to-bottom execution of statements, branching back *or* forward to the statement whose *statement number* is mentioned. The statement

GO TO

is an *unconditional* branch statement; that is, no alternative routes are specified. Its usage creates an *endless loop* in sample program 2-9. That is, computation of FAHREN, output of KCENT and FAHREN, and *incrementation* of KCENT are repeated endlessly, until execution is halted either by manual interruption at the computer console (by an operator), or by reaching of a per-program time limit automatically imposed by the operating system. Note that insertion of a STOP statement between GO TO 7 and END would be logically incorrect, since it can never be reached in execution. The programmer can control the number of repetitions in a loop, by using some form of *conditional* branch statement (see the following section).

When a statement is to be *numbered* by the programmer, the number must appear within the first five columns of the card (coding paper). Statement numbers are in *integer* mode, and may have values between 1 and 99999. Most statements do not *require* numbering. A statement number is generally used only when the statement being written is to be referred to by another statement.

When statement numbers are used, they need not be in sequence and need not represent actual card position in any way. The only consistency required is that between a statement's number and the number mentioned in the statement designed to refer to it.

A CONDITIONAL BRANCH STATEMENT

In sample program 2–10, sample program 2–9 is rewritten, replacing the GO TO statement with a *conditional branch* statement. The effect is to halt execution when a Centigrade temperature of 101 degrees has been reached.

```
C SAMPLE PROGRAM 2-10
C LIMITATION OF THE LOOP, IN SAMPLE PROGRAM 2-9
      KCENT = 0
7     FAHREN = 1.8 * KCENT + 32
      PRINT, KCENT, FAHREN
      KCENT = KCENT + 1
      IF (KCENT .LE. 100) GO TO 7
      STOP
      END
```

A *conditional branch* statement is one that provides two or more alternative routes. A varied set of such statements will be discussed in Chapter 5. We shall merely observe here, in connection with sample program 2–10, that

.LE.

is a *relational operator* having the meaning *"is less than or equal to."* The periods on either side are necessary parts of the operator. The full meaning of the statement as written in the sample program is, "If KCENT is less than or equal to 100, GO TO 7; otherwise, proceed downward." Control passes to the statement to the right of the parenthetical expression only if the expression is "true."

SUMMATION AND INITIALIZATION

One of the important operations that may be accomplished by a *loop* is *summation*. Sample program 2–11 prints the sum of integers 1 through 50:

```
C SAMPLE PROGRAM 2-11
C SUM OF FIRST FIFTY INTEGERS
```

```
               NUMSUM = 0
               NUMBER = 1
        94    ┌ NUMSUM = NUMSUM + NUMBER
              │ NUMBER = NUMBER + 1
              └ IF (NUMBER .LE. 50) GO TO 94
               PRINT, NUMSUM
               STOP
               END
```

This program produces only one line of output,

$$1275$$

Notice the necessity for assigning a (zero) value to NUMSUM *before* its appearance on the right side of an arithmetic statement. This is referred to as *initialization*; it avoids the "undefined variable" error. Note also that *summation* and *incrementation* statements have the same general form, in that each logically requires the mention of the same variable name on *both* sides of the equal sign:

```
    NUMSUM = NUMSUM + NUMBER    (summation)
    NUMBER = NUMBER + 1         (incrementation)
```

However, *incrementation* adds a *constant* to the named location, while *summation* usually involves addition of a *variable* quantity to the location.

EXPONENTIATION

A fifth *arithmetic operator*, **, denotes *exponentiation;* that is, the expression appearing to its left is raised to the power indicated by the expression on the right. For example, X^{12} is computed in FORTRAN by writing

$$X ** 12$$

Some further examples appear below:

	Algebraic Expression	FORTRAN Expression	
(1)	a^3	A ** 3	
(2)	x^{378}	X ** 378.	
(3)	3^r	3. ** R	or 3 ** NR
(4)	4.3^d	4.3 ** D	
(5)	$b^{5.6}$	B ** 5.6	
(6)	$g + h^2$	G + H ** 2	
(7)	$(r + s)^5$	(R + S) ** 5	
(8)	$w^{1/3}$	W ** (1./3.)	
(9)	a^{n-1}	A ** (N − 1)	

Real expressions may be followed by *integer* exponents (examples 1, 6, 7, 9); or by *real* exponents (examples 2, 4, 5, 8). The exponent *mode* is of some importance, for

$$X ** 4$$

is executed by successive multiplication, as though the programmer had written

$$X * X * X * X$$

whereas

$$X ** 4.$$

is executed by employing logarithms:

$$\text{antilog } (4 \log X)$$

Therefore, *real* exponents are useful when (a) large powers could lead to a time-consuming multiplication process (example 2), (b) the desired exponent is decimal or fractional (examples 5 and 8). Note that the omission of decimal points in example 8 would lead to evaluation of the expression as

$$W^0 = 1$$

because of truncation in integer division. (You should also remember that decimal exponents require logarithmic treatment, with or without computer help).

Example 3 illustrates that *integer* expressions may be followed only by *integer* exponents (this follows from the fact that the *logarithm* approximation requires *real* mode). Note also that *negative*-valued expressions may be followed only by *integer* exponents, since logarithms cannot be developed for negative numbers.

Examples 7, 8, and 9 illustrate the need for parentheses in certain instances. Omission in these three cases would produce improper grouping:

(7)	$(r+s)^5$	written	R + S**5	would be evaluated as $r + s^5$
(8)	$w^{1/3}$	written	W ** 1./3.	would be evaluated as $\dfrac{w^1}{3}$
(9)	a^{n-1}	written	A ** N −1	would be evaluated as $a^n - 1$

The use of parentheses in expressions is more fully explained in the next section.

Sample program 2–12 uses the exponentiation operator to produce the sum of the squares of the first 50 integers:

```
  C SAMPLE PROGRAM 2-12
  C SUM OF SQUARES, USING EXPONENTIATION OPERATOR
    NSUM = 0
    N = 1
  5 ┌ NSUM = NSUM + N ** 2
    │ N = N + 1
    └ IF (N .LE. 50) GO TO 5
    PRINT, NSUM
    STOP
    END
```

HIERARCHY OF ARITHMETIC OPERATORS; USE OF PARENTHESES IN ARITHMETIC EXPRESSIONS

Arithmetic expressions may be lengthy. A basic advantage of FORTRAN is suggested by its title—the programmer is able to translate any "formula" in its entirety in a single FORTRAN statement. Thus

$$a = \frac{b+c}{3b^2}$$

may be evaluated by a single FORTRAN statement. However,

$$A = B + C / 3 * B ** 2$$

will not accomplish the desired result. The five arithmetic operators are executed in an order prescribed by these rules:

    **   has highest precedence
    * and / are next (equal in precedence)
    + and − are lowest (equal in precedence)

In the event of "ties," operators equal in precedence are executed *from left to right*. Thus the statement shown above is executed in the following order:

$$\begin{array}{cccc} & 4 & 2 & 3 & 1 \\ A = B & + & C\;/\;3 & * & B\;**\;2 \end{array}$$

The result of this ordering is

$$a = b + \frac{c}{3} \times b^2$$

However, operations *in parentheses* have highest precedence. Therefore, as in algebra, desired *grouping* of operations may be accomplished by the use of parentheses. Thus

$$A = (B + C) / (3. * B ** 2)$$

accomplishes the desired result in the case above. In general, when an *algebraic* expression would be written with parentheses, they may be copied directly into the FORTRAN statement. Thus

$$(g + h)^8$$

becomes

$$(G + H) ** 8$$

There are, however, two major instances in which parentheses are unnecessary to indicate proper grouping in algebra, but become necessary in FORTRAN:

1. *Fractional expressions* are clearly grouped in algebra by vertical separation of numerator and denominator. As illustrated in our first "formula" example, *numerator and denominator may each require a set of parentheses*, for proper FORTRAN grouping.

2. *Exponent expressions* in algebra are clearly grouped by elevation to the right of the expression being raised to a power. *Exponents consisting of expressions require a set of parentheses*, for proper FORTRAN grouping. Thus

$$X^{a+b}$$

must be written

$$X ** (A + B)$$

When sets of parentheses are *nested* (i.e., appear inside one another), the innermost set is evaluated before outer sets. This problem is illustrated in sample program 2-13, which finds the larger root of a quadratic equation, from the formula

$$r = \frac{-b + \sqrt{b^2 - 4ac}}{2a}$$

```
C SAMPLE PROGRAM 2-13
C QUADRATIC EQUATION SOLUTION FOR LARGER ROOT, IN THE
C    EQUATION 2X**2 + 6X + 4 = 0
     A = 2.
     B = 6.
     C = 4.
     ROOT = (−B + (B**2 − 4.*A*C)**.5) / (2.*A)
     PRINT, A, B, C, ROOT
     END
```

One place where parentheses are *not* permitted is at the *beginning* of an *output list*. Thus

$$PRINT, (A + 6.2) / B$$

is illegal.[3] However,

PRINT, 1./B * (A + 6.2)

accomplishes the same result, and is valid.

For Review

	Examples
comment statement	C PAYROLL PROGRAM
variables	A, B, C, DEVIL, JOKER
constants	1., 1.0, 3.6, 1.2E3, 426
arithmetic statement	A = B + 6.3
arithmetic expression	B + 6.3
incrementation	J = J + 1
output statement	PRINT, A, J, 3.0, A + 9.35
output list	A, J, 3.0, A + 9.35
arithmetic operator	+, −, /, *, **
STOP statement	STOP
END statement	END
exponential notation	0.6E−5, 1.0E+10 0.1234567E+38
precision, range	1234567, E± 38
integer variable	I, J, KING
integer constant	32, 7, 971
real variable	A, B, DOG
real constant	3., 3.5, 3.5E9
truncation	7/2 (result 3)
explicit type specification statement	REAL, INTEGER
unconditional branch statement	GO TO 9
loop, endless loop	
conditional branch statement	IF (M .LE. 3) GO TO 4
relational operator	.LE.
summation	SUM = SUM + X
initialization	SUM = 0.
exponentiation	X**12, X**(1./3.)
operator hierarchy	**, * and /, + and −
grouping	$\dfrac{a}{2b}$ A/(2. * B)
	r^{n-1} R ** (N − 1)

---

[3] The reason is that the output list expression would be mistaken for an *indexed list;* the latter form is discussed in Chapter 6.

Programming Exercises

Notes
1. Do not write "endless" loops; use the form shown in sample programs 2–10, 2–11, and 2–12, rather than the 2–9 technique.
2. Sample correct output for all exercise programs appears in Appendix B. You should always check your program's output, since the absence of error messages does not guarantee against logic errors. In addition, a glance at the Appendix B output *prior* to writing the program may clarify the required form of output.

2–1. If a "consumption function" in economic theory is estimated as

$$\text{consumer expenditures} = 78.3 + 0.83 \text{ (income)}$$

write a program that will produce a table of consumer expenditures for incomes of 100, 110, 120, 130... up to (and including) 350. Print the first column (incomes) in *integer* mode, and the second (expenditures) in *real* mode.

2–2. An object dropped from a height travels the distance

$$d = 1/2 \text{ at}^2$$

where a = 32.16 (the gravitational constant) and t = time (seconds). Write a program that will generate a table of distances for times of 1 second, 3 seconds, 5 seconds, ..., 59 seconds. Print time in *integer* mode, and distance in *real* mode.

2–3. The speed of a chemical reaction *doubles* for every 10-degree (Centigrade) rise in temperature. At 0°C the reaction time is 3414 seconds. Write a program that will output a table showing the reaction time for temperatures of 0°, 10°, 20°, 30°, ..., 100°C. Output should include temperatures (*integer* mode) and times (*real* mode).

2–4. The sum to infinity of

$$1 + 1/2^2 + 1/3^2 + 1/4^2 + \ldots$$

is $\pi^2/6 = 1.644934$. Write a program that will produce the sum of the first 1000 terms. The sum should be the *only* output.

2–5. An item is to be sold for either $6.49 or $7.98 per unit. Write a program that will produce a table showing on each line total revenue at each price, from the sale of 1 dozen, 2 dozen, 3 dozen, 4 dozen, ..., 12 dozen units. Print the *number of dozens* in *integer* mode, and the revenues in *real* mode.

2-6. Write a program that will produce a table of *factorial* numbers
$$n! = 1 \times 2 \times 3 \times 4 \ldots \times n$$
beginning with 1!, 2!, 3!, ... through (and including) 20! (The table should have two columns, showing the integer and its factorial, on each line.) Use real mode for the numbers. (Why?)

2-7. Rewrite program 2-6 (above), so that it outputs only (a) the value of 20!, and (b) the *sum* of the first twenty factorial numbers.

2-8. Write a program to find, for $X = 5(10)^9$, the square root of X, cube root of X, fourth root of X, ... through and including the tenth root of X. Print results as a two-column table, with the root number in *integer* mode.

2-9. Rewrite program 2-8 (above), so that the *only* output is the *sum* of the second through the tenth roots of $5(10)^9$.

2-10. The sum of the squares of the first n natural integers is given by
$$S = \frac{n(n+1)(2n+1)}{6}$$
Write a program that will find S for n = 10, 20, 30, 40, ..., 100. Perform all computations and output in *integer* mode.

CHAPTER **3**

DO LOOPS AND INPUT

THE DO STATEMENT

"*Endless*" loops are easily formed, by using the GO TO statement; but no real problem requires *unlimited* repetition of any procedural sequence. Efficient programming requires the capability for limiting execution of any loop to some specific number of repetitions. The use of a *conditional branch* statement (to replace the unconditional GO TO) was introduced in Chapter 2. However, most compiler languages provide some shorthand method for specifying the number of repetitions desired in a loop. In FORTRAN, the DO statement serves this purpose.

Sample program 3–1 employs a DO statement to arrange 100 temperature conversions and output lines:

```
C SAMPLE PROGRAM 3-1
C TABLE OF FAHRENHEIT CONVERSION, FROM 1 TO 100 CENTIGRADE
                                      DEGREES, USING DO LOOP
      ⎡DO 16 I = 1, 100
      ⎢FAHREN = 1.8 * I + 32.
   16 ⎣PRINT, I, FAHREN
       STOP
       END
```

The effective meaning of the DO statement in sample program 3–1 is, "Do everything between here and statement number 16 (inclusive) 100 times." This effect could be duplicated by the programmer using a larger number of statements:

39

Using the DO Statement	Without the DO Statement

```
      ┌ DO 16 I = 1, 100
      │ ---------------------
      │ ---------------------
  16  └ ---------------------
```

```
            I = 1
      15  ┌ ---------
          │ ---------
          │ ---------
          │ I = I + 1
          └ IF (I .LE. 100) GO TO 15
```

Thus the programmer using the DO statement accomplishes three steps in one: a counter (the DO loop *index*) is initialized, and at the same time arrangement is made for both its incrementation and the conditional branch test for its desired limit. Note that a GO TO statement, or an IF statement, is *not* used at the bottom of the DO loop, to arrange the return to the top.

GENERAL FORM

The general form of the DO statement is

Effect During Execution

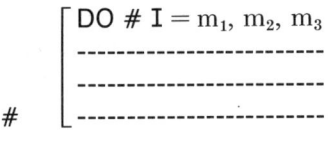
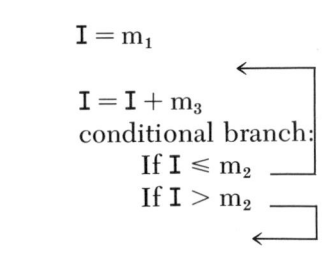

where

　　　　# is a statement number (as usual, an integer constant)
　　　　m_1, m_2, and m_3 may be either integer *constants* or integer *variables*;
　　　　　　if m_3 does not appear, its value is assumed to be equal to 1
　　　　I must be an integer *variable*

When the DO statement is reached during execution, the following sequence has been arranged by the compiler program:

1. I, the *index*, is assigned the value m_1.

2. Immediately following each execution of statement number #, the index will be incremented by m_3.

3. A conditional branch instruction (supplied by the compiler program) is executed. If the incrementation has produced I less than or equal to m_2, the program branches *back* to the first executable statement after DO; when the incrementation has produced I greater than m_2, control transfers to the

next executable statement following statement number #.[1]

USE OF THE DO INDEX

The DO loop *index* may be treated as an ordinary integer variable in arithmetic expressions, output statements, etc., but should not appear within the range of the loop on the *left* of an equal sign. That is, it should not be assigned a new value within the loop.

In sample program 3-1, the *index* is in fact used to represent successive Centigrade temperatures. Sample program 3-2 shows a modification that also uses the *index* as a basis for computing temperatures.

```
C SAMPLE PROGRAM 3-2
C PROGRAM 3-1 MODIFIED TO INCLUDE ZERO DEGREES CENTIGRADE
      ┌ DO 16 I = 1, 101
      │ FAHREN = 1.8 * (I − 1) + 32.
   16 └ PRINT, I − 1, FAHREN
        STOP
        END
```

Remember that the use of *expressions* in output statements (I − 1, in the sample program) is an extension feature of WATFOR and WATFIV. Also note that the DO *index* cannot start at zero. In fact, m_1, m_2, and m_3 must all be *positive integers*.

Finally, note the use of parentheses in the FAREN computation, to "upgrade" the low precedence of the minus sign.

THE INCREMENT POSITION

In sample programs 3-1 and 3-2 the absence of information in the m_3 (increment) position is interpreted by the compiler as though the programmer had written a "1". Sample program 3-3 uses the increment position to compute for Centigrade temperatures 0, 3, 6, 9, ..., 99.

```
C SAMPLE PROGRAM 3-3
C TABLE OF FAHRENHEIT CONVERSION, INCREMENTING BY THREE
                                      DEGREES CENTIGRADE
       ┌ DO 444 NCENT = 1, 100, 3
       │ FAHREN = 1.8 * (NCENT − 1) + 32.
   444 └ PRINT, NCENT − 1, FAHREN
         STOP
         END
```

---

[1] Thus, subsequent to a normal exit from the loop, the storage situation is I>m_2. Note that a DO loop is executed *at least once*, even when m_1 is larger than m_2 in the DO statement.

Statements in the loop are executed for the last time when NCENT = 99; the next index value, 102, is higher than m_2, and therefore causes a branch to the STOP statement.

ALGORITHMS

We digress for a moment to observe that sample programs 3-2 and 3-3 contain simple examples of an important programming technique: the design of *algorithms*. An *algorithm* is a specific computation method that will always produce a desired result. (The American College Dictionary defines *algorithm* as "any peculiar method of computing.") In the programs referred to above, systematic adjustment of the DO index to produce the desired Centigrade temperature illustrates the creation of the *algorithm*.

Suppose the problem in sample program 3-1 were to compute and print the temperature conversions for Centigrade temperatures incrementing by one tenth of a degree: 1.0, 1.1, 1.2, 1.3, ..., 100.0. Sample program 3-4 shows an algorithm based once again on the DO index:

```
C SAMPLE PROGRAM 3-4
C TEMPERATURE CONVERSION BY TENTHS OF CENTIGRADE DEGREES
      DO 16 I = 10, 1000
      FAHREN = 1.8 * I/10. + 32.
   16 PRINT, I/10., FAHREN
      STOP
      END
```

For another example, suppose an examination is to contain 79 questions. The grader needs guidance on the appropriate percentage grade for various possible numbers of *wrong* answers. If the DO index is to be used as the basis for computation, then the numbers 1 through 79, ascending, must be converted to the percentage grade. If these numbers ("K") are treated as the number of *wrong* answers, then logically the number of *correct* answers is

$$79 - K$$

and the ratio of correct answers to the total is

$$\frac{79 - K}{79}$$

Since this is to be treated as a *percentage*,

$$\frac{79 - K}{79} \times 100$$

is the required algorithm. Sample program 3-5 shows the method.

```
C SAMPLE PROGRAM 3-5
C TABLE OF PERCENTAGE GRADES, FOR 79-QUESTION EXAMINATION
```

```
        ┌DO 4 K = 1, 79
        │GRADE = (79 − K)/79.0 * 100.
    4   └PRINT, K, GRADE
         STOP
         END
```

THE CONTINUE STATEMENT

Sample program 3–5 would not be changed, in execution, by this alteration:

```
    C SAMPLE PROGRAM 3-6
    C USE OF THE CONTINUE STATEMENT IN PROGRAM 3-5
        ┌DO 4 K = 1, 79
        │GRADE = (79 − K)/79.0 * 100.
        │PRINT, K, GRADE
    4   └CONTINUE
         STOP
         END
```

The statement CONTINUE is translated to a machine language instruction signifying "no operation." There is only one legitimate use for such a statement, and that is as *the last statement of a DO loop.* When so used, it is there because the programmer wishes to *branch* to the end of the loop in order *to preserve the count by incrementing and testing the DO index.*

Thus, although its use does no damage, CONTINUE is not really needed in sample program 3–6; for the CONTINUE statement is required only when one or more IF statements are used within the loop, and one of the alternative routes desired by the programmer is simply "the bottom of the loop." This usage is illustrated in sample program 3–7, which evaluates the function

$$Y = 1.6X^3 - 7.2X^2 + 2.1X$$

for X values 1, 2, 3, 4, ... etc. to determine the point at which Y becomes positive.

```
    C SAMPLE PROGRAM 3-7
    C DEMONSTRATION OF THE CONTINUE STATEMENT
        ┌DO 1 I = 1, 50
        │Y = 1.6 * I ** 3 − 7.2 * I ** 2 + 2.1 * I
        │IF (Y .LE. 0.) GO TO 1
        │PRINT, I
        │STOP
    1   └CONTINUE
         END
```

In the IF statement written into sample program 3–7, the programmer is in effect saying, "If the computation has produced a result less than or equal to zero, *continue* execution of the DO loop." The branch to statement 1 causes incrementation of the DO index, whereas a branch back to the computation statement ("Y = ...") would have the effect of repeating the prior computation. Note that the arithmetic expression representing the function is written as a *mixed* expression, which we have observed is evaluated in *real* mode — that is, the results of I**3, I**2, and I are each *"floated"* to real form before the multiplications are performed.

(The CONTINUE statement is needed in sample program 3-7 in its present form. It could, of course, be written without any DO statement at all, in which case there would be no use for a CONTINUE statement. And in Chapter 4 other alternatives will appear, which can eliminate the need for CONTINUE, even when the DO loop is used for this sort of problem.)

THE READ STATEMENT

The programs shown thus far have been self-contained in that no data were required during execution; all necessary numerical values were inserted as constants within the source program. In actual practice, such programs are in a small minority, as the phrase "data processing" implies. The computer is particularly useful where a problem of a specific kind must be handled over and over again, for *different* data sets.

In business, monthly inventory or payroll computations are examples. In statistics, such general methods as correlation analysis or variance analysis may be programmed once for operation on varying data sets. In mathematics, the problem of solving systems of simultaneous equations may be programmed for systems of any size, the size and specific coefficients to be entered when a specific problem is to be executed. In every field, there are recurring problems for which the data may change, but the principles of computation, applicable formulas, and required output form do not change.

In sample program 3-5, we computed a table showing percentage grades for various numbers of wrong answers (in a 79-question examination). An *input statement* may be used to alter the purpose, so that the program *reads* values representing the number of wrong answers for each of 300 students, and computes and prints the appropriate grade for each student. This is done in sample program 3-8:

```
C SAMPLE PROGRAM 3-8
C THIS PROGRAM USES AN INPUT STATEMENT, TO PRODUCE GRADES
C    FOR EACH OF 300 STUDENTS, ON A 79-QUESTION EXAMINATION
      DO 4 K = 1, 300
      READ, NWRONG
      GRADE = (79. − NWRONG)/79. * 100.
    4 PRINT, K, GRADE
```

```
STOP
END
```

The simple READ statement, of the form

> READ, input list (variable names separated by commas)

is an extension feature of the WATFOR and WATFIV compiler programs. In Chapter 9 the FORMAT references and statements required by most compilers (and available as options in WATFOR and WATFIV) are introduced. The simpler form we are now using presupposes that the data values appear on punched cards, and are organized with reference to the following rules:

1. The word READ causes selection of a new data card, each time it is encountered during execution. Thus

```
READ, X
READ, Y
```

requires two separate data cards, and

```
      ⎡ DO 1 I = 1, 20
      ⎢ READ, X
   1  ⎣ PRINT, X
```

requires 20 data cards.

2. An *input list* may be longer than one variable name; and a data card may contain more than one value. The statement

> READ, X, Y, Z

may be satisfied by using *one* data card punched with three (or more) separate numerical values, separated by one or more blank column or by commas:

> 7.56   8.2E+12,   74.0

or by using more than one data card; successive cards will be selected until the *input list* has been satisfied, by *nonblank* data items (i.e., blank cards or portions of cards will not be interpreted as zero values). Thus the following data arrangement would also supply the values of X, Y and Z:

> 7.56   (first card)
> 8.2E+12   (second card)
>   74.0   (third card)

3. When *real* variables appear in the *input list*, data values may be in ordinary decimal, exponential, *or* "integer" form. That is,

> READ, A, B, C

could be matched with the data

> 3.45   9.E-8   176

with the C value interpreted as 176.0000. However, *integer* variables in the input list must be matched with integer constants (i.e., no decimal point!) in the data deck. Thus

$$\text{READ, A, B, I}$$

would be legal, for the data shown above: but the data

$$3.45 \qquad 9.\text{E-}8 \qquad 176.$$

would then cause an execution error message (FM-0; INVALID CHARACTER IN INPUT DATA). The decimal point following 176 is the "illegal character" referred to.

4. "Extra" values on data cards are ignored. Thus

$$\text{READ, G, H}$$
$$\text{READ, J}$$

in connection with the data cards

$$7.33 \qquad 8.22 \qquad 956 \qquad \text{(first card)}$$
$$714 \qquad\qquad\qquad\qquad \text{(second card)}$$

produces the value 714 in storage for J.

Unlike PRINT and PUNCH statements, the READ statement may contain *only* the names of variables. Constants and/or expressions are not permitted. Thus

$$\text{READ, X, Y, 35.3}$$

and

$$\text{READ, J} + 6$$

are invalid.

PLACEMENT OF DATA

Actual entry of data cards is accomplished during *execution* of the program; there is no need for data values during *compilation*, and certainly no logical place for data *values* within the source program. The important idea, in fact, is that the source program refers to such values only *by name* (i.e., as *variables*), whereas they appear in the data deck only *as numerical values*. This makes the source program a general statement of method, which is independent of the actual values used in computation. The entry sequence is:

$$\text{\$JOB}$$
$$\text{source program}$$
$$\text{\$ENTRY}$$
$$\text{data cards}$$

Variables mentioned in the *input list* need *not* have been defined earlier in the program; the READ statement serves to define them. Thus the number appearing on the first data card will be stored in the NWRONG location (sample program 3–8) when K (the loop index) is equal to 1; when K = 2 (second pass through the loop), the number on the second data card will *replace* the first value stored.

THE PARAMETER CARD

Sample program 3–8 is written explicitly for *300* student examination records. In light of our earlier statement that recurrent problems may be programmed once for use on different data sets, it would be useful to *generalize* the program further, to allow for a *variable* number of students. This is done in sample program 3–9:

```
C SAMPLE PROGRAM 3-9
C GRADES FOR EACH OF N STUDENTS, ON A 79-QUESTION EXAMINATION
      READ, N
     ┌ DO 4 K = 1, N
     │ READ, NWRONG
     │ GRADE = (79. − NWRONG)/79. * 100.
   4 └ PRINT, K, GRADE
      STOP
      END
```

In this version, N is referred to as a *parameter*[2] entered at execution time. The first data card contains an integer indicating the number of student records to be processed; it must then be followed by N data cards.

A further step suggests itself for complete generalization of the examination-grade program. Since every examination does not contain exactly 79 questions, why not make the number of questions a variable, also? Then *two* parameters must be read in at execution time:

```
C SAMPLE PROGRAM 3-10
C GRADES FOR EACH OF N STUDENTS, ON A J-QUESTION EXAMINATION
      READ, N, J
      FJ = J
     ┌ DO 4 K = 1, N
     │ READ, NWRONG
     │ GRADE = (FJ − NWRONG)/FJ * 100.
   4 └ PRINT, K, GRADE
      STOP
      END
```

---

[2] The terminology comes from statistics. A *parameter* is any characteristic of a population of values. In this instance, the relevant parameter is the population's size, symbolized by N.

Note that a *real* version of J has been used (FJ) in computing GRADE. If you do not see why, consider the result of

$$\text{GRADE} = (J - \text{NWRONG})/J * 100.$$

The truncation resulting from integer division would make all grades *zero*, for less than perfect examinations. Another alternative,

$$\text{GRADE} = (J - \text{NWRONG})/(1. * J) * 100.$$

would consume more execution time.

POSTLOOP STATEMENTS

Most of the programs we have been dealing with have a certain simplicity in common: after exit from the loop, execution is halted (by STOP). A more frequent form for practical programs is:

preloop: initialization, reading of parameters
loop: data reading, summation, multiline output if required
postloop: terminal computations (frequently involving sums), final output

A basic example of this form in statistics appears in sample program 3–11:

```
      C SAMPLE PROGRAM 3-11
      C ARITHMETIC MEAN OF N DATA VALUES
            SUM = 0.
            READ, N
            DO 9 I = 1, N
            READ, X
    9       SUM = SUM + X
            XMEAN = SUM/N
            PRINT, XMEAN
            STOP
            END
```

In this type of program, it is important to remember that statements *in* the loop are repeated, while statements *outside* the loop are not. A common logical error is to *initialize* a sum or counter within the loop (e.g., SUM = 0.). This leads to wrong answers, since the storage location is inadvertently cleared to zero on each pass through the loop.

The inclusion of *terminal formulas* (e.g., XMEAN = SUM/N) within a loop is also a common programmer error, which may ultimately not lead to wrong answers, but consumes significant amounts of unnecessary execution time.

Sample program 3–12 shows the addition of a mean-grade computation to sample program 3–10. Observe the different locations of the two PRINT statements. Does any error result from the use of the variable name GRADE after exit from the loop?

```
C SAMPLE PROGRAM 3-12
C PROGRAM 3-10 MODIFIED TO PRODUCE ARITHMETIC MEAN OF GRADES
      READ, N, J
      FJ = J
      SUM = 0.
      DO 4 K = 1, N
      READ, NWRONG
      GRADE = (FJ − NWRONG)/FJ * 100.
      SUM = SUM + GRADE
4     PRINT, K, GRADE
      GRADE = SUM/N
      PRINT, GRADE
      STOP
      END
```

NESTED DO LOOPS

Consider the following modification to the problem solved by sample program 3-12: there are 10 separate classes taking the same examination. The program should compute and print a grade for each student in each class, and also compute and print 10 separate arithmetic means. In effect, the required modification is simply to make sample program 3-12 run 10 successive times.

```
C SAMPLE PROGRAM 3-13
C TREATMENT OF STUDENTS AS 10 CLASSES OF N STUDENTS EACH
      READ, J
      FJ = J
      DO 8 I = 1, 10
      SUM = 0.
      READ, N
      DO 4 K = 1, N
      READ, NWRONG
      GRADE = (FJ − NWRONG)/FJ * 100.
      SUM = SUM + GRADE
4     PRINT, I, K, GRADE
      GRADE = SUM/N
8     PRINT, I, GRADE
      STOP
      END
```

The adjustment merely required insertion of a new DO statement and addition of an appropriate statement number to the final PRINT statement. Both PRINT statements have also been altered, to supply a class number ("I") for each grade and mean printed.

The program shows the use of a set of *nested DO loops*. In this sort of arrangement, you should see that statements in the *inner* loop are executed more times than statements in the *outer* loop. In this example, if there are an average of 30 students per class, inner-loop statements will each be executed 300 times, while outer-loop statements are executed only 10 times.

NESTS ENDING AT THE SAME STATEMENT

The nest of loops in sample program 3–13 has the general form

$$\begin{bmatrix} \begin{bmatrix} \\ \end{bmatrix} \end{bmatrix}$$

In some programs nest formation may be more complicated:

$$\begin{bmatrix} [\\ [\end{bmatrix} \quad \text{or} \quad \begin{bmatrix} \begin{bmatrix} [\end{bmatrix} \end{bmatrix}$$

A form of DO statement nesting *not* permitted is

$$\begin{bmatrix} \\ \begin{bmatrix} \\ \end{bmatrix} \end{bmatrix}$$

However, two or more DO loops may end on the same statement (i.e., the DO statements refer to the same statement number):

$$\begin{bmatrix} \\ \begin{bmatrix} \\ \end{bmatrix} \end{bmatrix}$$

In such cases, an execution-precedence rule comparable to that for nested parentheses is used: *inner* loops have precedence over *outer* loops. Thus, in sample program 3-14 (below), I remains at 1 while J changes from 1 through 6; then I becomes 2, and J again runs from 1 through 6, and so on.

```
C SAMPLE PROGRAM 3-14
C POSSIBLE RESULTS OF TWO DICE TOSSED — NESTED LOOPS ENDING
                                             AT THE SAME STATEMENT
      ⎡  DO 1 I = 1, 6
      ⎢⎡ DO 1 J = 1, 6
1     ⎣⎣ PRINT, I, J
         STOP
         END
```

Sample program 3-14 produces 36 lines of output, representing the 36 possible *permutations* of the digits 1 through 6. In some problems, it is useful to deal only with *combinations*:

Permutations, Digits 1 to 6		Combinations, Digits 1 to 6	
1	1	1	2
1	2	1	3
1	3	1	4
1	4	1	5
1	5	1	6
1	6		
		2	3
2	1	2	4
2	2	2	5
2	3	2	6
2	4		
2	5	3	4
2	6	3	5
		3	6
3	1		
3	2	4	5
3	3	4	6
3	4		
3	5	5	6
3	6		
4	1		
4	2		
— etc. —			
6	6		

NESTS ENDING AT THE SAME STATEMENT

As the table on page 51 indicates, there are only *15* possible *combinations*. Sample program 3–15 produces the combinations output, by arranging that the inner-loop index has a beginning value ("m_1") one number higher than the outer-loop index value. That is, m_1 in the inner DO statement is a *variable*, whose value is assigned by an *algorithm* ($N = I + 1$) using the outer-loop index.

```
C SAMPLE PROGRAM 3-15
C MODIFICATION OF PROGRAM 3-14 TO PRODUCE COMBINATIONS
                                    INSTEAD OF PERMUTATIONS
      DO 1 I = 1, 5
      N = I + 1
      DO 1 J = N, 6
    1 PRINT, I, J
      STOP
      END
```

Note that the statement

$$\text{DO 1 J} = \text{I+1, 6}$$

would not be legal; that is, arithmetic operators are not permitted within the DO statement.

Another method for achieving the *combinations* result may be written following this plan: let both loop indexes run from 1 through 6, but print only those index combinations for which I is less than J. This is done in sample program 3–16:

```
C SAMPLE PROGRAM 3-16
C ANOTHER METHOD FOR THE COMBINATIONS PROBLEM
      DO 1 I = 1, 6
      DO 1 J = 1, 6
    1 IF (I .LT. J) PRINT, I,J
      STOP
      END
```

This program introduces another *relational operator*,

.LT.   "is less than"

and illustrates also that the statement to the right of the conditional expression need not be a GO TO statement; any *executable* statement is legal, with the exception of *branch* statements and *DO* statements.

When I is *not* less than J, the conditional statement "PRINT, I, J" is not executed; but the position of the IF statement at the end of the DO loops causes the index incrementation/test sequence to be initiated, regardless of whether the conditional statement has been executed. Thus a DO loop may end on this type of ("Logical") IF statement; but the program's execution would not be altered by using CONTINUE instead:

$$\begin{array}{l}\left[\begin{array}{l}\text{DO 1 I} = 1, 6 \\ \left[\begin{array}{l}\text{DO 1 J} = 1, 6 \\ \text{IF (I .LT. J) PRINT, I, J} \\ \text{CONTINUE}\end{array}\right.\end{array}\right. \\ \text{STOP} \\ \text{END}\end{array}$$

1 (label on CONTINUE)

Note, however, that the branch statement in sample program 3–16 is *not* being used to branch back to the top of the loop, for this is done "automatically" by the placement of statement 1 on the statement. And, in fact, a simple "GO TO" statement would be *illegal* at the bottom of a DO loop, since it would be regarded by the compiler as conflicting with the branching instructions generated by the DO statement. That is,

```
1     ┌ DO 2 I = 1, 100
      │ -------------------
2     └ GO TO 1
```

would be illegal.

For Review

DO statement
DO index
increment position
DO loop

algorithm
input statement
input list
input data
parameter entry
parameter card
nested DO loops

combinations, permutations
CONTINUE statement

Examples

DO 4 I = 1, 100, 3
    I
        3
4   ⎡DO 4 I = 1, 100, 3
    ⎣PRINT, I

READ, A, B, KID
    A, B, KID
7.5, 8.2E12, 36
READ, N
    300

```
          ┌ DO 2 J = 1, 10
          │ ┌ DO 1 I = 1, 5
       1  │ └ PRINT, I
       2  └   PRINT, J
```

```
          ┌ DO 1 I = 1, 10
          │ IF (I .LT. 5) PRINT, I
       1  └ CONTINUE
```

Programming Exercises

Notes
1. Use the DO statement to form loops, where necessary.
2. Program exercises requiring data have been tested on a standard data set (12 cards) listed at the beginning of Appendix B. The resulting output appears as usual in that appendix; therefore, to test your programs, always place the entire standard data set behind the $ENTRY card following your source program.

3-1. A certain microbe culture doubles every hour. Write a program to compute how many microbes will inhabit the culture after 50 hours, starting with one microbe. There should be no output until the final result. Also let the program compute and output 2^{50}, using the exponentiation operator, for comparison.

3-2. Write a program that will produce only the following output:

```
    1       20
    2       19
    3       18
    4       17
    — etc. —
    20       1
```

3-3. Adjust program 3-2 (above) so that only the odd-numbered lines (i.e., those lines with odd numbers on the *left*) are produced in output.

3-4. Write a program that reads 12 real data values and prints only the sum of all the values.

3-5. Write a program that reads 12 real data values and reprints only those that are less than or equal to 75.0.

3-6. Write a program that will number 15 lines, as follows:

```
    1
    2
    3
    1
    2
    3
    — etc. —
```

3-7. The *geometric mean* is defined as the nth root of the product of n numbers. For example, for the numbers 2, 4, and 8

$$G = \sqrt[3]{2 \times 4 \times 8} = \sqrt[3]{64} = 4$$

Write a program that reads four sets of three real values each, and computes and outputs four *geometric means*. (Consider values to be keypunched one per data card; use a double DO loop.)

3-8. Rewrite the program in Exercise 3-4, so that it prints the sum of "N" real values, "N" to be read from a parameter card. Test your program by keypunching "8" as the parameter.

3-9. Adjust program 3-7 (above) so that it works for "N" sets of "K" values each, N and K to be entered on a parameter card at execution time. Test with N = 4, K = 3 (you keypunch the parameter card).

CHAPTER **4**

FORTRAN-SUPPLIED FUNCTIONS

FUNCTION NAMES AND ARGUMENTS

In Chapter 2 (sample program 2-13), we obtained a square root by raising an expression to the 0.5 power:

(B**2 − 4. * A * C) ** .5

We could alternatively have written

SQRT(B**2 − 4. * A * C)

All FORTRAN compiler programs, including WATFOR and WATFIV, provide computation routines for many mathematical *functions* that are useful in a wide variety of problems. These may be used in arithmetic expressions (i.e., on the *right* side of arithmetic statements), since they call in a shorthand manner for arithmetic computation. The *function name* (e.g., SQRT) must be followed by parentheses that contain the *argument(s)* — the value (or values) on which the required computations are to be performed.

The *argument* itself is an arithmetic expression, and therefore may be a single variable or constant, or combinations of these separated as usual by arithmetic operators, parentheses, and other function names.

SQUARE ROOT

Neither computer nor compiler contains prepared tables of such functions as square roots, logarithms, cosines, and so on. Each of these functions is approximated by a computation routine, which is generated in machine language when the programmer uses the appropriate FORTRAN word *(function name).* Thus, "SQRT" acts as a convenient substitute for a whole series of FORTRAN statements that might be written by the programmer who remembers how to obtain a square root by some method employing addition, subtraction, multiplication, and division. The parentheses following each function name indicate the extent of the *argument,* and must appear even when the argument is a single variable or constant. Some examples:

Algebraic Expression	FORTRAN Expression
$\sqrt{65.6}$	SQRT(65.6)
$\sqrt{b}$	SQRT(B)
$\sqrt{2a}$	SQRT(2.* A)
$\sqrt{b^3}$	SQRT(B**3)
$4\sqrt{w}$	4. * SQRT(W)
$\sqrt{g+h}$	SQRT(G + H)
$\sqrt{g}+h$	SQRT(G) + H
$\sqrt{\log_e g}$	SQRT(ALOG(G))

The first letter of a function name indicates the mode of the returned value, following the customary implicit system for variable names. Thus the fact that SQRT begins with S signifies *real* mode for the computation result. (This explains why the abbreviation used for *logarithm* is "ALOG", rather than "LOG".) In most (but not all) instances, the *arguments* to be used must be in the same mode as the result. This is true for SQRT; that is, the argument must be in *real* mode (though it may be a *mixed* expression, since such expressions are, in effect, converted to real mode by the computer). In sample program 4–1 (below) the statement

$$\text{SUM} = \text{SUM} + \text{SQRT(I)}$$

would not be legal.

```
      C SAMPLE PROGRAM 4-1
      C SUM OF SQUARE ROOTS, FOR THE FIRST FIFTY INTEGERS
            SUM = 0.
            DO 1 I = 1, 50
            X = I
    1       SUM = SUM + SQRT(X)
            PRINT, SUM
            STOP
            END
```

LOGARITHMS AND ANTILOGARITHMS

In case you have forgotten, a *logarithm* is actually an *exponent*. Having selected a *base* for any logarithm system, the logarithm of any number is that exponent which, when applied to the base, produces the number. Thus, for base 10 ("common") logarithms,

$$\text{since} \quad 10^2 = 100,$$
$$\text{then} \quad \log_{10} 100 = 2$$

and

$$\text{since} \quad 10^3 = 1000,$$
$$\text{then} \quad \log_{10} 1000 = 3$$

If, however, you wanted to find the logarithm (base 10) of the number 500 (i.e., to find what exponent applied to 10 would yield the result 500), you would (without computer help) have to consult a prepared table of logarithms, to find

$$\log_{10} 500 = 2.69897$$

(that is, $10^{2.69897} = 500$).

In FORTRAN, the value 2.69897 will be stored in ANSWER as the result of

$$\text{ANSWER} = \text{ALOG10(500.0)}$$

That is, ALOG10 is a *function name;* the function returns the logarithm (base 10) of the *argument* (which should be in *real* mode).

The process of obtaining the *antilogarithm* (base 10) is not the subject of a prepared function in most compilers, but from the definition may be performed as follows:

$$\text{THIS} = 10. ** 2.69897$$

places the antilogarithm (base 10) of the exponent in the THIS location; that is, 500.0 is the stored result.

Logarithms to the base e ("*natural*" logarithms)[1] are obtained by

$$\text{ALOG(argument)}$$

For this logarithm system, an *antilogarithm* function is also provided:

$$\text{EXP(argument)}$$

That is, EXP(X) calls for e^x.

In Exercise 2-6 you were asked to compute factorial numbers, up to 20! Since n! becomes very large as n is increased, most factorial numbers cannot be stored (in most systems, 33! or 57! reach the computer's *range* limit).

[1] e is the mathematical constant, approximately 2.718281828459045.

The *logarithms* of the factorials may be obtained, instead. Sample program 4-2 (below) computes

$$\log_{10} 100!$$

by computing

$$\log_{10}1 + \log_{10}2 + \log_{10}3 \ldots + \log_{10}100.$$

```
C SAMPLE PROGRAM 4-2
C LOGARITHM OF FACTORIAL 100
      FACTL = 0.
      DO 1 I = 1, 100
      X = I
    1 FACTL = FACTL + ALOG10(X)
      PRINT, FACTL
      STOP
      END
```

Since the computer multiplies and divides very rapidly, you should *not* resort to logarithms merely as a computation alternative. For example, it would be foolish to substitute for

$$A = B*C/D$$

by writing

$$A = EXP(ALOG(B) + ALOG(C) - ALOG(D))$$

Though the result would be the same, the latter would be slower in execution, as well as bulkier to write and keypunch and more likely to produce rounding error in answers. Also note that one type of problem that would force you to use logarithms when computing by hand, finding a specific *root*, may be handled in FORTRAN without mention (by the programmer) of logarithms. For example, the fourth root of X, written algebraically

$$\sqrt[4]{x} \quad \text{or} \quad x^{1/4}$$

may be written in FORTRAN

$$X ** (1./4.) \quad \text{or} \quad X ** .25$$

We observed earlier that the compiler program itself arranges use of logarithms for decimal exponents. Therefore, this is really executed as though the programmer had written

$$EXP(ALOG(X) * (1./4.)) \quad \text{or} \quad EXP(ALOG(X) * .25)$$

Some usage examples for the ALOG, EXP, and ALOG10 functions appear on the next page:

Algebraic Expression	FORTRAN Expression
$\log_e x$	ALOG(X)
$3\log_e d$	3. * ALOG(D)
$\log_{10}(a + b)$	ALOG10(A + B)
$\text{antilog}_e 3.5$	EXP(3.5)
$\text{antilog}_{10} h$	10. ** H
e^x	EXP(X)
$\log_e \sqrt{r}$	ALOG(SQRT(R))

Sample program 4–3 produces a reference table frequently found in mathematics texts. For values of X from 0.1 to 100.0, incremented by tenths, the program computes X^2, $\sqrt{X}$, $\sqrt[3]{X}$, and $\log_{10} X$.

```
C SAMPLE PROGRAM 4-3
C TABLE OF SOME FUNCTIONS OF X
      DO 1 I = 1, 1000
      X = I/10.
      A = X ** 2
      B = SQRT(X)
      C = X ** (1./3.)
      D = ALOG10(X)
    1 PRINT, X, A, B, C, D
      STOP
      END
```

ABSOLUTE VALUE

The function ABS returns the *absolute* value of the real argument. That is, the sign of the result is made positive, regardless of whether the actual result of the argument arithmetic is positive or negative. Thus

Algebraic Expression	FORTRAN Expression
$\|a - b\|$	ABS(A − B)
$\|b^2 - 4ac\|$	ABS(B**2 − 4.*A*C)
$\|i - j\|$	IABS(I − J)

As the last example illustrates, the function name IABS is used for *integer* arguments, and returns an *integer* result.

Sample program 4–4 illustrates the usefulness of the ABS function; for 31 daily temperature observations, the program computes *average deviation* from 70 degrees, disregarding sign (direction) of the deviations. Thus, 65 degrees and 75 degrees are both recorded as deviations of (plus) 5 degrees.

```
C SAMPLE PROGRAM 4-4
C AVERAGE DEVIATION FROM 70-DEGREE TEMPERATURE (ONE MONTH)
      SUM = 0.
     ┌DO 1 I = 1, 31
     │READ, TEMP
1    └SUM = SUM + ABS(TEMP − 70.)
      AVGDEV = SUM/31.
      PRINT, AVGDEV
      STOP
      END
```

TRIGONOMETRIC FUNCTIONS

For angles expressed in *radians*, several trigonometric functions are usually provided:

Trigonometric Function	FORTRAN Function Name
sine	SIN
cosine	COS
tangent	TAN
cotangent	COTAN
hyperbolic sine	SINH
hyperbolic cosine	COSH
hyperbolic tangent	TANH

For the opposite computation (e.g., to find the angle in radians for which the argument is the sine):

Trigonometric Function	FORTRAN Function Name
arc sine	ARSIN
arc cosine	ARCOS
arc tangent	ATAN
arc tangent of a/b	ATAN2(A,B)

Thus

```
ANGLE = 0.6
COSINE = COS(ANGLE)
FINAL = ARCOS(COSINE)
```

This sequence of statements computes the cosine of an angle measured as 0.6 radians, and stores the result in the COSINE location (a *variable* name, not a *function* name); and then stores the original value (0.6) in the FINAL location.

A method for computing the area of a triangle, given two sides (a,b) and their included angle (C) is

$$\frac{ab\ \sin C}{2}$$

Sample program 4–5 reads 20 data cards, each containing the side-angle-side information (in that order), and computes and prints the 20 areas.

```
      C SAMPLE PROGRAM 4-5
      C COMPUTATION OF AREA FOR TWENTY TRIANGLES
            DO 1 I = 1, 20
            READ, A, C, B
            AREA = A * B * SIN(C)/2.
    1       PRINT, A, C, B, AREA
            STOP
            END
```

Again note that the angle is keypunched in radians, not degrees.

SOME FUNCTIONS USING MORE THAN ONE ARGUMENT

The last function name mentioned in the trigonometric list (ATAN2) requires *two* real arguments; these are separated by a comma within the argument parentheses. Several other useful functions are designed to operate on more than one argument.

DIM (for real arguments) and IDIM (for integer arguments) are functions requiring exactly *two* arguments. The second argument is subtracted from the first. If the result is positive (i.e., if the first argument is larger than the second), this result is returned. But for *negative* results, *zero* is returned. That is,

DIM(C, D)   If c > d, returns the value (c-d)
              If c ≤ d, returns the value 0.0

Sample program 4–6 makes use of the DIM function to compute *degree-days*, which are defined as the total number of degrees *below* 65 shown by daily average temperatures.

```
      C SAMPLE PROGRAM 4-6
      C COMPUTATION OF TOTAL DEGREE-DAYS, FOR ONE MONTH
            SUM = 0.
            DO 20 I = 1, 31
            READ, TEMP
   20       SUM = SUM + DIM(65., TEMP)
            PRINT, SUM
            STOP
            END
```

Four separate functions deal with selection of the *largest* of the listed arguments. *Any number* of arguments may appear.

AMAX1(A,B,C,D...)   returns the largest of the values mentioned. Note that the arguments are in *real* mode, and so is the returned value.

AMAX0(I,J,K,L...)   is used to select the largest of a set of *integer* arguments—but the value returned is in *real* mode.

MAX1(A,B,C,D...)   selects the largest of a set of *real* arguments, but returns a value in *integer* mode.

and finally,

MAX0(I,J,K,L...)   selects the largest of a set of *integer* arguments, and returns that value in *integer* mode.

Four functions are also available to do the opposite—that is, to select the *smallest* of the arguments. The meanings parallel those of the "MAX" functions above, substituting "MIN":

AMIN1   real arguments, real value returned
AMIN0   integer arguments, real value returned
MIN1   real arguments, integer value returned
MIN0   integer arguments, integer value returned

In sample program 4–7, AMAX1 and AMIN1 are used to produce one-month means for daily *high* and *low* temperatures by selecting the highs and lows from six readings taken each day.

```
C SAMPLE PROGRAM 4-7
C MEANS OF DAILY HIGH AND DAILY LOW TEMPERATURES
      SHIGH = SLOW = 0.
     ┌DO 11 I = 1, 31
     │READ, T1, T2, T3, T4, T5, T6
     │SHIGH = SHIGH + AMAX1(T1, T2, T3, T4, T5, T6)
   11└SLOW = SLOW + AMIN1(T1, T2, T3, T4, T5, T6)
      PRINT, SHIGH/31., SLOW/31.
      STOP
      END
```

Sample program 4–7 also illustrates the *extended assignment* statement, a feature of WATFOR and WATFIV not found in most FORTRAN compilers.

That is, the first arithmetic statement contains more than one equal sign, and assigns initial values of zero to both the SHIGH and SLOW locations. Thus

$$A = B = C = D = E = 6.5$$

is legal in WATFOR and WATFIV, and places 6.5 in each of the five mentioned locations. A WARNING code (EQ-A) is delivered for this extension feature; "Appendix A indicates the meaning, "MULTIPLE ASSIGNMENT STATEMENTS NOT IN STANDARD FORTRAN."

The SIGN function requires two *real* arguments; ISIGN performs the same function for two *integer* arguments. In each case, the function returns the *value* of the *first* argument, with the *sign* of the *second* argument. Thus

$$A = A + SIGN(.5, A)$$

succeeds in *adding* 0.5 to *positive* values of A, and *subtracting* 0.5 from *negative* A values.

This idea is incorporated within sample program 4–8 (below), which reads revenue and cost information (in dollars and cents), computes profits (revenue minus cost), and then converts the profit result to the *nearest whole dollar* (in integer mode). The conversion provides for appropriate *rounding*, by adding .50 to positive profits, and subtracting .50 from negative profits, just prior to storage in integer mode (which, of course, truncates the postdecimal content). For example,

These cases are rounded "upward"		The rounding arrangement does not change these dollar values	
NPROF =	106.71 + .50	NPROF =	720.45 + .50
=	107.21	=	720.95
=	107	=	720
NPROF =	−106.71 − .50	NPROF =	−720.45 − .50
=	−107.21	=	−720.95
=	−107	=	−720

```
C SAMPLE PROGRAM 4-8
C THE SIGN FUNCTION USED FOR ROUNDING
      DO 1 I = 1, 500
      READ, REV, COST
      PROFIT = REV - COST
      NPROF = PROFIT + SIGN(.50, PROFIT)
    1 PRINT, I, NPROF
      STOP
      END
```

AMOD uses two real arguments, while MOD is the equivalent function for two integer arguments. The function produces the "remainder" resulting from division of the first argument by the second. For example,

$$R = AMOD(19.0, 4.0)$$

produces R = 3.0 (since the division would result in 4¾).

SOME OTHER FUNCTIONS

In sample program 3–10 (and also in 3–12 and 3–13) we read a parameter (J) in *integer* mode and then proceeded to store the same value in *real* mode so that it could be used conveniently in real arithmetic. We accomplished this by

$$FJ = J,$$

a procedure called *"floating"* the integer value. This step could be eliminated, by computing

$$GRADE = (J - NWRONG)/FLOAT(J) * 100.$$

That is, the function name FLOAT returns a *real* version of the *integer* argument (without changing J in storage). Conversely,

$$INT(G)$$

returns an *integer* version of the *real* argument, having truncated (i.e., simply dropped) the postdecimal portion of the argument. (Another function usually provided, IFIX, duplicates this effect.)

Finally, the function AINT accomplishes *truncation* of a real argument, but preserves the real mode of the result. That is, the postdecimal digits of the argument are converted to zeros. Thus

$$X = 5.75$$
$$Y = AINT(X)$$

results in Y stored as 5.00. The difference between AINT and INT is illustrated by the example below:

$$X = 5.75$$
$$A = AINT(X)/2 \quad \text{(result: A is stored as 2.50)}$$
$$B = INT(X)/2 \quad \text{(result: B is stored as 2.00)}$$

The "A" statement results in division of "real" 5 by "integer" 2, and this mixed expression is evaluated in real mode, producing 5.0/2.0 = 2.50. But the "B" statement calls for division of "integer" 5 by "integer" 2, and the truncation resulting from integer division produces the result "integer" 2, which is then stored in B as "real" 2.00.

A summary of the functions we have discussed appears in Table 1.

TABLE 1

One Argument		Two Arguments		Two or More Arguments	
Real Argument	**Integer Argument**	**Real Arguments**	**Integer Arguments**	**Real Arguments**	**Integer Arguments**
SQRT		ATAN2		AMAX1	AMAX0
ALOG		DIM	IDIM	MAX1	MAX0
ALOG10		SIGN	ISIGN	AMIN1	AMIN0
EXP		AMOD	MOD	MIN1	MIN0
ABS	IABS				
SIN					
COS					
TAN					
COTAN					
SINH					
COSH					
TANH					
ARSIN					
ARCOS					
ATAN					
AINT					
INT or IFIX	FLOAT				

Some other functions commonly provided will be discussed in Chapter 8, in connection with DOUBLE PRECISION and COMPLEX variable modes.

For Review

FORTRAN-supplied function	*Examples*
function name	A = SQRT(75.6) + AMAX0(I, J, K)
	SQRT AMAX0
function arguments	75.6 I, J, K
square root	SQRT( )
logarithm (base e)	ALOG( )
logarithm (base 10)	ALOG10( )
antilogarithm (base e)	EXP( )
antilogarithm (base 10)	10.** ( )
absolute value	ABS( ), IABS( )
trigonometric functions	SIN, COS, TAN, COTAN, SINH, COSH,
	TANH, ARSIN, ARCOS, ATAN, ATAN2
truncation	AINT( ), INT( ), IFIX( )
conversion to real	FLOAT( )

SOME OTHER FUNCTIONS

largest argument	AMAX1, AMAX0, MAX1, MAX0
smallest argument	AMIN1, AMIN0, MIN1, MIN0
subtraction; positive or zero result	DIM(,), IDIM(,)
first value, second sign	SIGN(,), ISIGN(,)
division remainder	AMOD(,), MOD(,)

Programming Exercises

4-1. The *quadratic mean* is defined as the square root of the mean square of a set of values. For example, for the numbers 1 and 7,

$$Q = \sqrt{\frac{(1)^2 + (7)^2}{2}} = \sqrt{\frac{50}{2}} = \sqrt{25} = 5$$

Write a program that reads 12 real data values, and computes and outputs their *quadratic mean*.

4-2. Find the sum of the terms

$$(\sqrt{a})^{a-1}$$

for a from 1 to 10. Let the sum be the only output.

4-3. Compare the results of

(1) $b^{1/4}$

(2) $\sqrt{\sqrt{b}}$

(3) $\text{antilog}_e(\log_e b/4)$

(4) $\text{antilog}_{10}(\log_{10} b/4)$

for b = 256. (Do it all in one program.)

4-4. Evaluate the function

$$\frac{X + 4}{5 \log_{10} X}$$

for X from 20 to 40 (i.e., show 21 lines of output).

4-5. The law of cosines says that

$$a^2 = b^2 + c^2 - 2bc(\cos A)$$

where a, b, and c are the lengths of sides of a triangle and A is the angle opposite a. Write a program to find the length a for a triangle with b = 3 feet and c = 4 feet, for angles A = 1.39 radians, 1.41 radians, 1.43 radians,

... 1.67 radians. (Try assigning the A value with an *algorithm* based on a DO loop index.)

4-6. Write a program that will read six data cards, each containing three real values. For each set of three read in, output (*a*) the smallest of the three, (*b*) the smallest *absolute value* (i.e., disregarding sign), (*c*) the *remainder* from the division

$$\frac{a + c}{\log_{10} b}$$

4-7. Rewrite program 4-6 (above) so that the data values are converted to integer mode (after they are read in); and then produce only the (*a*) and (*b*) output, for the integers.

4-8. Write a program that reads 12 real data values, and produces as output each of these values stated as the nearest whole integer (properly rounded).

CHAPTER **5**

CONDITIONAL BRANCHING

TWO TYPES OF IF STATEMENT

We have already seen examples of, but have not fully discussed, the *Logical IF statement*. We shall also examine an alternative form, the *Arithmetic IF statement*. The following two statements have precisely the same result during execution:

Logical IF   Arithmetic IF

IF (X .LT. 0.) GO TO 8   IF (X) 8, 9, 9
9 ----------------------------   9 ----------------

While the set of parentheses on the left contains a *logical-valued expression* and is followed by an *executable statement*, the set on the right contains an *arithmetic expression* and is followed by *three statement numbers*, separated by commas. We shall examine the *arithmetic* form first.

THE ARITHMETIC IF STATEMENT

The general form for Arithmetic IF statements is

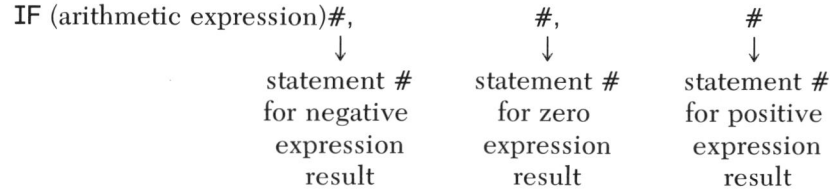

Thus the statement

$$\text{IF (X) 3, 1, 2}$$

may be paraphrased, "If X is negative, GO TO 3; if X is zero, GO TO 1; if X is positive, GO TO 2." In this example, a branch to one of three different statements will take place as soon as the current value of X has been looked up in storage. More work must be performed prior to branching if the arithmetic expression (all of which must be enclosed by parentheses) is longer. For example,

$$\text{IF (B} \ast \ast 2 - 4. \ast \text{A} \ast \text{C) 17, 10, 10}$$

Note that two of the statement numbers are identical in·this instance, so that the branch is to statement 17 for a negative result, and to statement 10 for zero *or* positive results. All three numbers must still be written in such cases.

It would *not* be logical to write *three* identical numbers, since

$$\text{IF (X) 7, 7, 7}$$

has the same effect as saying

$$\text{GO TO 7}$$

Similarly, the arithmetic expression should contain at least one *variable*, since

$$\text{IF (17.2} - \text{38.6) 8, 9, 3}$$

should really be written

$$\text{GO TO 8}$$

BASIC USAGE

Conditional branch statements appear to allow the computer to "make decisions" during execution of the program. It should be evident, however, that all such "decisions" are preplanned by the programmer, who must fully describe all alternative routes and the conditions under which each shall be taken.

A basic use for the Arithmetic IF statement is discrimination between negative, zero, and positive values for single variables, particularly where such values have been read as input data. This usage is illustrated in sample program 5–1:

```
C SAMPLE PROGRAM 5-1
C THIS PROGRAM OBTAINS THE SUM OF POSITIVE DATA VALUES ONLY,
C BY CONVERTING NEGATIVE DATA ITEMS TO ZEROS BEFORE ADDING
```

```
         SUM = 0.
        ┌DO 2 I = 1, 50
        │READ, B
        │IF (B) 1, 2, 2
1       │B = 0
2       └SUM = SUM + B
         PRINT, SUM
         STOP
         END
```

The conditional branch test is executed after each B value is read; for zero and positive data values, the program branches "around" statement 1 to execute the summation (statement 2). Since the latter statement is at the end of the DO loop, execution then proceeds with the next READ or (when I = 51) to the PRINT statement.

The procedure used in sample program 5-1, changing negative values to zero to avoid including them in the sum, is actually a bit awkward. The process should remind you of the DIM function (Chapter 4), which *returns* zero values in place of negative subtraction results. Sample program 5-2 illustrates that the DIM function could, in fact, be used in lieu of the prior conditional arrangement.

```
C SAMPLE PROGRAM 5-2
C AN ALTERNATIVE TO PROGRAM 5-1, USING THE DIM FUNCTION
         SUM = 0.
        ┌DO 2 I = 1, 50
        │READ, B
2       └SUM = SUM + DIM(B, 0.)
         PRINT, SUM
         STOP
         END
```

This digression illustrates that some of the FORTRAN–supplied functions incorporate *conditional branch* instructions in the prepared procedure invoked by the function name. More to the point in our current discussion, the change-negative-to-zero procedure may also be eliminated by using the CONTINUE statement in another version of program 5-1, to branch "around" the summation statement when input values are negative:

C SAMPLE PROGRAM 5-3
C AN ALTERNATIVE TO PROGRAM 5-1, USING THE CONTINUE
                  STATEMENT

```
        SUM = 0.
       ┌DO 2 I = 1, 50
       │READ, B
       │IF (B) 2, 2, 1
   1   │SUM = SUM + B
   2   └CONTINUE
        PRINT, SUM
        STOP
        END
```

In sample programs 5-1 and 5-3, only a single variable name appears in the conditional arithmetic expression. In sample program 5-4 (below), the IF statement is used to isolate negative results for a more complex expression. The problem is to read a data deck containing quadratic equation coefficients and punch a new data deck by eliminating those instances in which

$$\frac{-b \pm \sqrt{b^2 - 4ac}}{2a}$$

would produce *imaginary* roots (because $b^2 - 4ac$ is negative).

```
C SAMPLE PROGRAM 5-4
C THIS PROGRAM READS QUADRATIC EQUATION COEFFICIENTS, AND
C       REPUNCHES ONLY THOSE HAVING REAL ROOTS
       ┌DO 2 I = 1, 100
       │READ, A, B, C
       │IF (B**2 − 4.*A*C) 2, 1, 1
   1   │PUNCH, A, B, C
   2   └CONTINUE
        STOP
        END
```

USE FOR COMPARISON

The statement

$$\text{IF } (A - B) \ 6, 6, 7$$

has the interesting meaning to the programmer, "If A is smaller than or equal to B, GO TO 6; if A is larger than B, GO TO 7." Another example of this *comparison* usage,

$$\text{IF } (M - 100) \ 3, 4, 3$$

may be paraphrased, "If M is exactly equal to 100, GO TO 4; otherwise, GO TO 3." This very common technique is illustrated in sample program 5-5, in which members of integer data pairs are compared.

```
C SAMPLE PROGRAM 5-5
C THIS PROGRAM PRINTS THE SMALLER OF EACH SET OF TWO DATA
                                                       VALUES
      ┌DO 2 I = 1, 70
      │READ, K, L
      │IF (K − L) 2, 2, 1
   1  │K = L
   2  └PRINT, K
       STOP
       END
```

Once again, we could employ a FORTRAN-supplied function to accomplish the same result. In sample program 5-6, the MIN0 function, which itself contains conditional branch instructions, does the job:

```
C SAMPLE PROGRAM 5-6
C AN ALTERNATIVE TO PROGRAM 5-5, USING THE MIN0 FUNCTION
      ┌DO 2 I = 1, 70
      │READ, K, L
   2  └PRINT, MIN0 (K, L)
       STOP
       END
```

THE LOGICAL IF STATEMENT; RELATIONAL OPERATORS

We have encountered two of the six available *relational operators* in earlier programs. The full list is:

Relational Operator	Verbal Meaning	Algebraic Notation
.EQ.	equal to	$=$
.NE.	not equal to	$\neq$
.LT.	less than	$<$
.GT.	greater than	$>$
.LE.	less than or equal to	$\leq$
.G.E.	greater than or equal to	$\geq$

As we have observed earlier, use of these *relational operators* create *logical-valued expressions*. The general form for the Logical IF statement is

IF (logical-valued expression) executable statement
                                      ↓
                                (this statement will be executed only if
                                the logical-valued expression is "true";
                                otherwise, control passes to the statement below "IF")

In sample program 5-3, an Arithmetic IF statement was used to isolate negative values of B. Sample program 5-7 shows the substitution of a Logical IF statement to accomplish the same job.

```
C SAMPLE PROGRAM 5-7
C AN ALTERNATIVE TO PROGRAM 5-3, USING LOGICAL IF
      SUM = 0.
     ┌DO 2 I = 1, 50
     │READ, B
     │IF (B .LE. 0.) GO TO 2
     │SUM = SUM + B
    2└CONTINUE
      PRINT, SUM
      STOP
      END
```

There are, of course, other ways of obtaining the same effect. Sample program 5-8 substitutes the .GT. operator for the .LE. operator:

```
C SAMPLE PROGRAM 5-8
C ANOTHER ALTERNATIVE, STILL USING LOGICAL IF
      SUM = 0.
     ┌DO 2 I = 1, 50
     │READ, B
    2└IF (B .GT. 0.) SUM = SUM + B
      PRINT, SUM
      STOP
      END
```

Sample programs 5-7 and 5-8 illustrate that the *Arithmetic* IF statement generates more frequent need for the CONTINUE statement than the *Logical* IF statement. While a Logical IF statement may be used as the last statement of a DO loop, the Arithmetic IF is prohibited in this position. For example,

```
     ┌DO 2 I = 1, 50
     │-----------------
     │-----------------
    2└IF (B) #, #, #
```

would be illegal. This prohibition is a natural extension of the same restriction placed in the unconditional GO TO statement, in Chapter 3, for the Arithmetic IF statement has the effect of up to three separate GO TO statements.

Some statement sequences accomplishing identical results appear below:

		Arithmetic IF	Logical IF
(1)		IF (X − Y) 1, 1, 2	IF (X .LE. Y) X = X ∗ 20.
	1	X = X ∗ 20.	DO 3 I = 1, 25
	2	DO 3 I = 1, 25	
(2)		IF (B − 50.) 4, 3, 4	IF (B .EQ. 50.) STOP
	3	STOP	INCR = INCR + 1
	4	INCR = INCR + 1	
(3)	8	-----------------	8 --------------------
		IF (ANS) 8, 9, 8	IF (ANS .NE. 0.) GO TO 8
	9	PRINT, ANS	PRINT, ANS
(4)		IF (3∗X − (A+B)) 7, 7, 6	IF (3∗X .GT. A + B) X = X/10.
	6	X = X/10.	PRINT, X
	7	PRINT, X	

It is evident from these examples that Logical IF statements usually require less numbering of statements than Arithmetic IF arrangements. Note also that in example 4 a set of parentheses surrounding the addition has been dropped, in the Logical IF version. This is possible because *relational operators have lower precedence in execution than arithmetic operators*. Therefore, the ".GT." is the *last* operator executed in the example 4 statement.

LOGICAL OPERATORS

Logical-valued expressions may contain *logical operators*, as well as *relational operators*. There are three *logical operators*:

.NOT.
.AND.
.OR.

These have *lower* execution precedence than *relational operators* (and therefore are also lower in the hierarchy than *arithmetic operators*). Therefore

A .GT. B .OR. C .LT. D

is executed as though written

(A .GT. B) .OR. (C .LT. D)

Precedence between the *logical operators* themselves is in the order named above (.NOT. before .AND., and .AND. before .OR.).

Sample program 5-9 requires two *Arithmetic* IF statements, to isolate values between two limits:

```
C SAMPLE PROGRAM 5-9
C THIS PROGRAM REPRINTS DATA VALUES THAT ARE BETWEEN 75.0
                                          AND 85.0 (INCLUSIVE)
      ┌DO 3 I = 1, 300
      │READ, GRADE
      │IF (GRADE − 75.) 3, 2, 1
    1 │IF (GRADE − 85.) 2, 2, 3
    2 │PRINT, I, GRADE
    3 └CONTINUE
       STOP
       END
```

The same job may be accomplished by a *single Logical* IF statement:

```
C SAMPLE PROGRAM 5-10
C ALTERNATIVE TO PROGRAM 5-9, USING RELATIONAL AND LOGICAL
                                                    OPERATORS
      ┌DO 1 I = 1, 300
      │READ, GRADE
      │IF (GRADE .LT. 75. .OR. GRADE .GT. 85.) GO TO 1
      │PRINT, GRADE
    1 └CONTINUE
       STOP
       END
```

There are, as above, usually an assortment of alternative Logical IF statements that will arrive at the same result. For example,

IF (A .GT. B .OR. A .LT. B)

may be written

IF (A .NE. B)

Furthermore, alteration of statement order permits the use of alternative Logical IF statements. This is illustrated in sample program 5-11 (below), which is an alternative to 5-10.

```
C SAMPLE PROGRAM 5-11
C ANOTHER ALTERNATIVE TO PROGRAM 5-10, USING RELATIONAL AND
C                    LOGICAL OPERATORS SOMEWHAT DIFFERENTLY
      ┌DO 1 I = 1, 300
      │READ, GRADE
    1 └IF (GRADE .GE. 75. .AND. GRADE .LE. 85.) PRINT, GRADE
       STOP
       END
```

We have indicated (see sample programs 5–9 and 5–10) that two *Arithmetic IF* statements may frequently be replaced by one *Logical* IF statement. The reverse may be true on occasion, however. The example below requires execution of one of *two* alternative statements, rather than the simpler execute/bypass alternatives at which we have been looking.

	Arithmetic IF		Logical IF
	IF (X − Y) 10, 11, 11		
10	X = 0.		
	GO TO 12		IF (X .LT. Y) X = 0.
11	Y = 0.		IF (X .GE. Y) Y = 0.
12	------------------------	12	-----------------------

Although the second Logical IF statement may at first appear redundant, you should see that it is necessary to prevent execution of *both* arithmetic statements being treated as alternatives. (In this connection, note that it is *not* legal to use more than one executable statement following the logical-valued expression; thus

```
        IF (X .LT. Y) X = 0. GO TO 12
        Y = 0.
12      ----------------------------------
```

would not be valid).

THE SENTINEL CARD

In Chapter 3 we introduced the idea of the *parameter card* as a method of generalizing a program to operate on data sets of variable size. Such a card (as in sample program 3–11) is placed ahead of the actual data cards, and is keypunched with the number of data items to be handled. A statement such as

READ, N

precedes the program's main reading loop. Sample program 5–12 shows another method for generalizing the program, *without* prespecification of the size parameter:

```
C SAMPLE PROGRAM 5-12
C SENTINEL CARD AS ALTERNATIVE TO PARAMETER CARD
C            (SEE PROGRAM 3-11)—ARITHMETIC MEAN OF ANY SET OF
                                          REAL DATA CARDS
```

```
          SUM = COUNT = 0.
    15    ┌READ, X
          │IF (X .EQ. 9999.99) GO TO 86
          │SUM = SUM + X
          │COUNT = COUNT + 1.
          └GO TO 15
    86    XMEAN = SUM/COUNT
          PRINT, XMEAN
          STOP
          END
```

In this method, no *parameter card* precedes the data, but a *"sentinel card"* *follows* the actual data deck. This card contains a number chosen for probable dissimilarity to any actual data value (in the sample program, 9999.99). After each execution of the READ statement a conditional branch statement transfers control either to the summation and counting activities or, when the *sentinel value* is encountered, to the terminal portion of the program. Note that the GO TO 15 statement in sample program 5–12 does not actually create an *endless* loop, since a method of "jumping out" from the middle of the loop has been arranged.

If the *DO statement* is used in conjunction with the *sentinel card* arrangement, the stated index limit (m_2) is selected as a high integer constant representing a *maximum* number of data values that the program can handle. This is illustrated in sample program 5–13:

```
C SAMPLE PROGRAM 5-13
C COMBINATION OF SENTINEL CARD WITH DO LOOP (THIS PROGRAM
C                       WORKS FOR A MAXIMUM OF 10,000 DATA VALUES)
          SUM = 0.
         ┌DO 1 I = 1, 10000
         │READ, X
         │IF (X — 9999.99) 1, 86, 1
    1    └SUM = SUM + X
    86    XMEAN = SUM/(I — 1)
          PRINT, XMEAN
          STOP
          END
```

Note the division by I–1 at statement 86; why is this necessary?

FLOWCHARTING

The use of *conditional branch* statements leads to the creation of separate *branches*—segments of the program that are entered only when certain conditions exist, and may also be exited from conditionally. The complexity that may develop in programs with extensive branching makes the *flow chart* a useful method for both preparing for and documenting the program.

A *flow chart* is a schematic diagram of steps that must be executed to solve a problem. Such a chart need *not* contain actual program statements, nor is it necessary to have a separate cell in the flow chart for every program statement that will be (or has been) written. If this kind of detail is included, the flow chart may fail in its primary purpose as an aid in visualizing the overall program sequence—the general *"flow"* of the program.

Some conventional symbols are in use for flow charts; these are recommended, since a frequent use for the flow chart is *documentation*—it serves as a description of the program for readers other than the programmer. Some common symbols appear below:

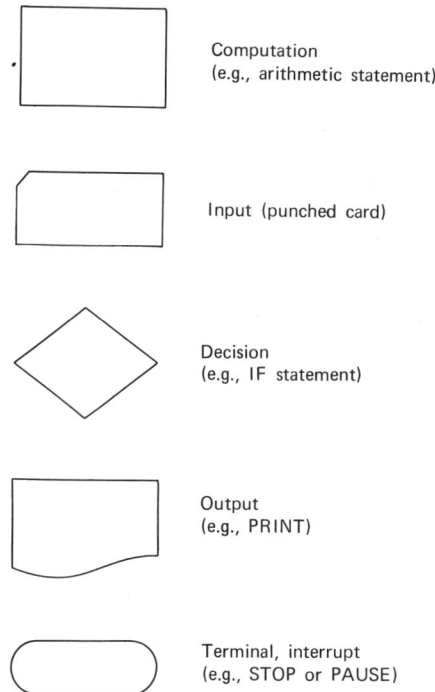

Computation
(e.g., arithmetic statement)

Input (punched card)

Decision
(e.g., IF statement)

Output
(e.g., PRINT)

Terminal, interrupt
(e.g., STOP or PAUSE)

FLOWCHARTING

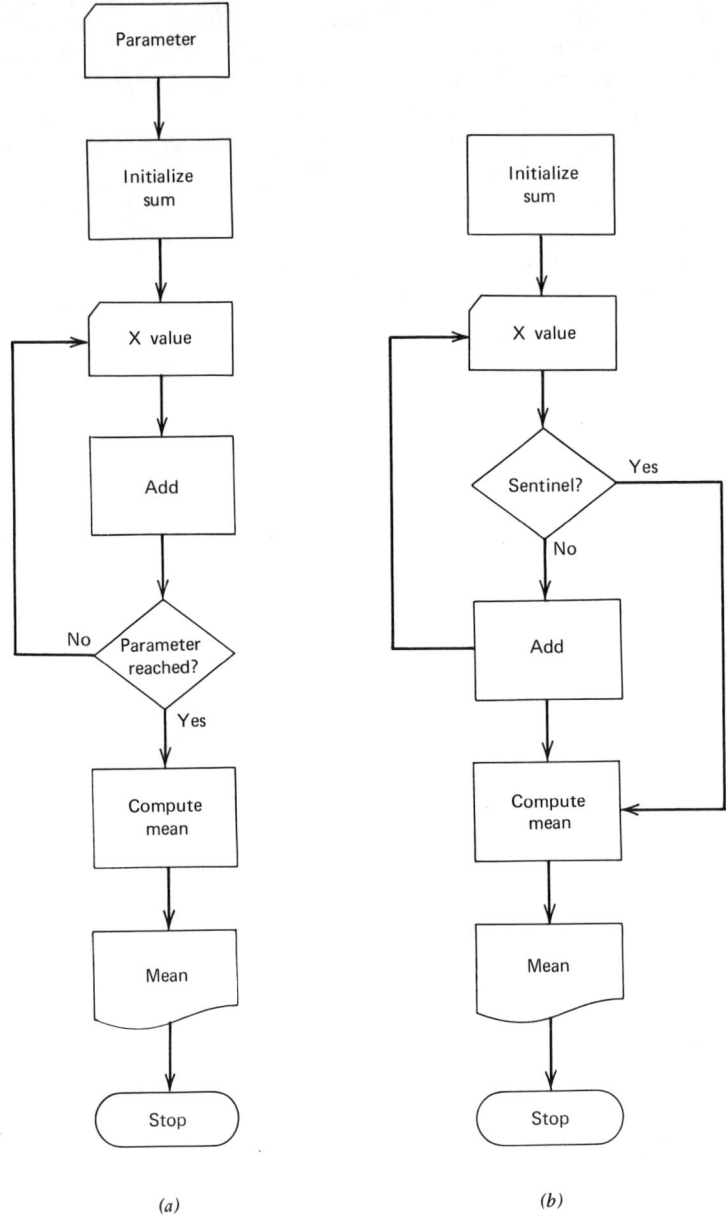

(a)   (b)

FIG. 9 (a) Parameter-card method.   (b) Sentinel-card method.

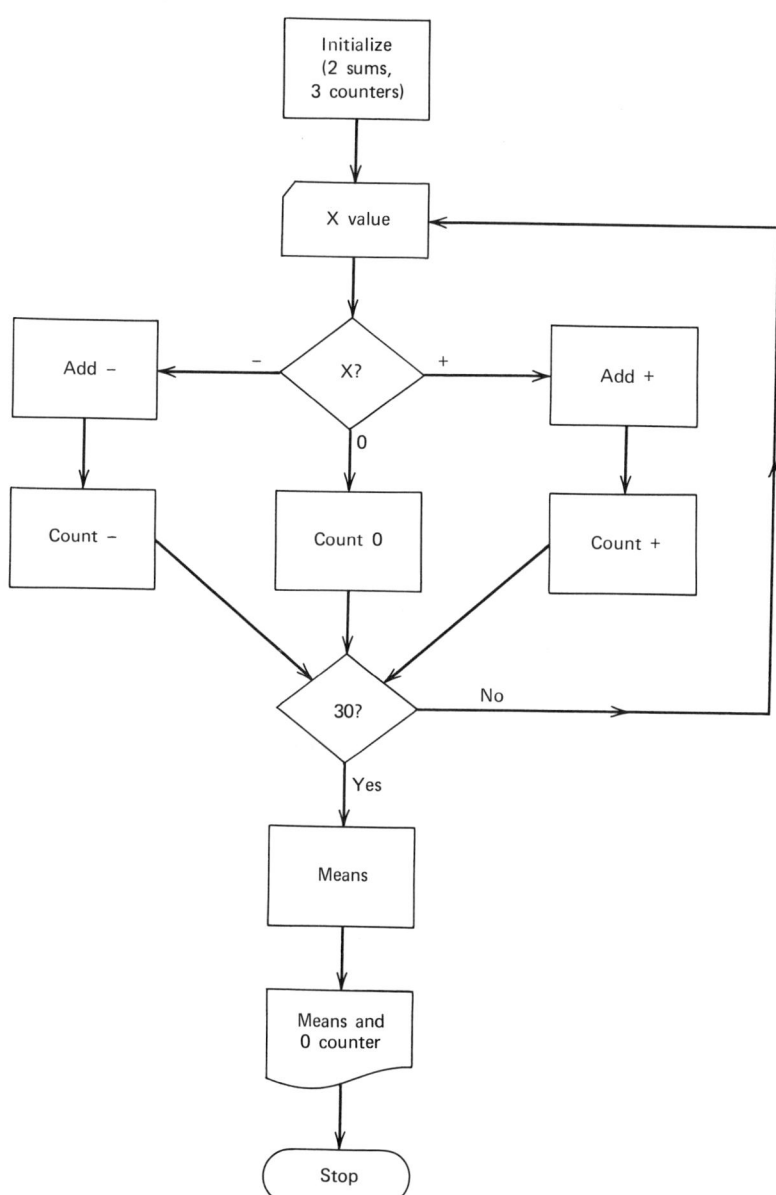

FIG. 10 Program to compute negative and positive means and count zero values.

Figure 9 compares flow charts for the *parameter card* and *sentinel card* methods, as applied to the arithmetic mean problem (see sample programs 3–11 and 5–12).

The more complicated the program, the more useful the flow chart is likely to be. Let us diagram a program that is to read 30 data items, and compute the mean of the *negative* values, the mean of the *positive* values, and the *number* of *zero* values. The flow chart appears in Figure 10. A program written to match the flow chart follows:

```
C SAMPLE PROGRAM 5-14
C THIS PROGRAM COMPUTES SEPARATE MEANS FOR NEGATIVE AND
C POSITIVE DATA VALUES, AND COUNTS THE NUMBER OF ZERO VALUES
        SUMPOS = SUMNEG = NUMPOS = NUMNEG = NUMZIP = 0
1       READ, XITEM
        IF (XITEM) 2, 3, 4
2       SUMNEG = SUMNEG + XITEM
        NUMNEG = NUMNEG + 1
        GO TO 5
3       NUMZIP = NUMZIP + 1
        GO TO 5
4       SUMPOS = SUMPOS + XITEM
        NUMPOS = NUMPOS + 1
5       IF (NUMNEG + NUMZIP + NUMPOS .LT. 30) GO TO 1
        PRINT, SUMNEG/NUMNEG, SUMPOS/NUMPOS, NUMZIP
        STOP
        END
```

In sample program 5–14, note that omission of either "GO TO 5" statement would create a "short circuit" in the flow diagram. But also observe that such a statement is unnecessary, following the positive-count statement (just prior to statement 5).

When the *extended assignment* statement contains both real and integer variables (as above), care should be exercised; any post-decimal content is lost as it "passes through" integer locations. Thus

$$X = A = I = B = 3.15$$

succeeds in placing 3.15 in the B location, but places 3.0 in the A and X locations. Note also that any arithmetic expression (i.e., not just a single constant) may appear to the right of the last equal sign. For example,

$$A = B = C = 8 * SQRT(4. * X)$$

is valid (so long as X has been previously defined, of course).

THE COMPUTED GO TO STATEMENT

The Logical IF statement provides, in effect, for execution of one of *two* alternative statements: the one to the right of the IF parentheses, and the next (executable) statement below. A flow chart of the process might look like that shown below.

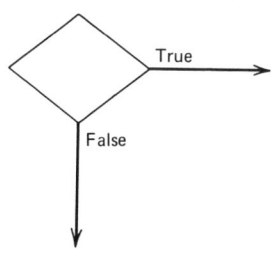

The Arithmetic IF statement provides for execution of one of *two or three* alternative statements (since three different statement numbers may appear after the IF parentheses):

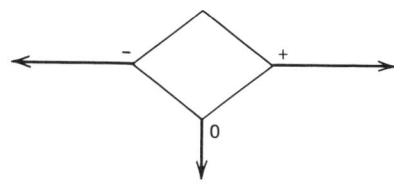

If *more than three* alternative routes are required, a *sequence* of such IF statements might be necessary. For example, the following program segment permits an execution-time option (based on a *parameter card*) involving nine alternatives:

```
        READ, K
        IF (K − 2) 101, 102, 1
    1   IF (K − 4) 103, 104, 2
    2   IF (K − 6) 105, 106, 3
    3   IF (K − 8) 107, 108, 109
```

This is designed to branch to statement 101 if the parameter card contains a "1", to statement 102 if it contains a "2", ..., to statement 109 if it contains a "9". The required sequence is even longer, if written with Logical IF statements.

The *Computed GO TO* statement is capable of producing this multibranch effect in a single statement:

>   READ, K
>   GO TO (101, 102, 103, 104, 105, 106, 107, 108, 109), K

The parentheses contain *statement numbers*, each of which must be matched by a numbered executable statement somewhere in the program (though the statement numbers listed need not all be different). The choice between these routes is conditioned on the current value of the *integer variable* mentioned to the right, which must be within the range 1 through #, where # is the number of statement numbers listed in the parentheses. Thus the general form is

>   GO TO (list of statement numbers, separated by commas; length of the list is #) , integer variable
>   ↓
>   (may have values during execution between 1 and #)

The value of the integer variable is used to count down the line of statement numbers, from left to right. Thus a current value of "5" causes a branch to the fifth statement in the list.

There is no limit to the number of statement numbers that may be included in the parentheses; as mentioned above, some may duplicate others:

>   MVALUE = M − 2 ∗ N
>   GO TO (5, 5, 6, 6, 6), MVALUE

In this example, the branch is to statement 5 if MVALUE is 1 or 2; and to statement 6 if MVALUE is 3, 4, or 5. Note that integer *expressions* are not acceptable in the Computed GO TO statement itself, so that

>   GO TO (5, 5, 6, 6, 6), M − 2∗N

is not valid. However, also note that since only two statement numbers are used in this example, the work could also be accomplished by

>   IF (M − 2 ∗ N − 2) 5, 5, 6

or by

>   IF (M − 2 ∗ N .LE. 2) GO TO 5

86 · CONDITIONAL BRANCHING

Although the Computed GO TO statement is available for multibranch decisions:

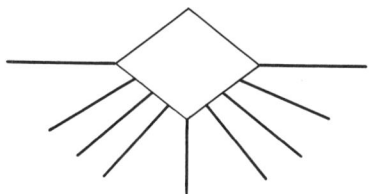

it may be used for as few as two alternative statements. Thus where MARK may have only the values "1" or "2":

IF (MARK − 2) 3, 4, 4

might be replaced by

GO TO (3, 4), MARK

Sample program 5–15 uses the Computed GO TO statement to arrange a parameter-entry selection of one of four types of summation (sum of actual values, sum of base e logarithms, sum of base 10 logarithms, sum of reciprocals):

```
C SAMPLE PROGRAM 5-15
C THIS PROGRAM USES A COMPUTED GO TO STATEMENT, TO BRANCH
C   TO ONE OF FOUR ALTERNATIVES SELECTED BY PARAMETER CARD
      SUM = 0.
      READ, N, KODE
      DO 1 I = 1, N
      READ, X
      GO TO (6, 7, 8, 9), KODE
    6 SUM = SUM + X
      GO TO 1
    7 SUM = SUM + ALOG(X)
      GO TO 1
    8 SUM = SUM + ALOG10(X)
      GO TO 1
    9 SUM = SUM + 1./X
    1 CONTINUE
      PRINT, N, KODE, SUM
      STOP
      END
```

For Review

Arithmetic IF statement
Logical IF statement
logical-valued expression
relational operator
logical operator
operator hierarchy

sentinel card
sentinel card test
flow chart
documentation
Computed GO TO statement

Examples

IF (A − 10.) 3, 3, 4
IF (A .LE. 10.) GO TO 3
  A .LE. 10.
.EQ. .NE. .LT. .GT. .LE. .GE.
.NOT. .AND. .OR.
    **
  * /
  + −
.EQ. .NE. .LT. .GT. .LE. .GE.
  .NOT.
  .AND.
  .OR.
9999.99
IF (X .EQ. 9999.99) GO TO 86

GO TO (7, 8, 9, 10), I

Programming Exercises

5-1. Write a program that reads a *pair* of real values from each of 12 data cards, and reprints only those pairs whose sum exceeds 100.00. (Also print an integer position number (1–12) for each such pair.)

5-2. Adjust program 5-1 (above) so that the number of data cards to be handled is not pre-fixed (maximum 5000); but arrange it so that execution will terminate when the first value of any pair is equal to 8686.86. (Keypunch this *sentinel value*, and place the card behind the *sixth* data card, to test your program.)

5-3. Rewrite program 5-2 (above), substituting Logical IF wherever you used Arithmetic IF, and Arithmetic IF wherever you used Logical IF. Test the program as before.

5-4. Write a program that will read 12 real data values, and compute and print the arithmetic mean of only the *negative* values; but print the *position number* of each *positive* data value encountered (do not print it for zero items).

5-5. Write a program that will read 12 values of A, and reprint only those that satisfy the following condition:

$$15 \leq A < 20 \text{ or } A > 40$$

88 CONDITIONAL BRANCHING

5-6. Write a program that will answer this question: Which factorial number (see Exercise 2-6 for a definition) is the first to exceed the value 100 billion? (Use *exponential notation* for the latter value.)

5-7. Write a program that will read 10 data cards, but will reprint only the first value on the second, fifth, ninth, and tenth cards. (Use a DO loop, and a Computed GO TO statement that refers to its index.)

5-8. The sum to infinity of

$$1 + 1/1! + 1/2! + 1/3! \ldots$$

is equal to e, the base of the natural logarithm system (2.718282). Write a program that answers the question: How many factorial terms are required to obtain a result within 0.00015 of the correct answer?

5-9. Write a program that will read 12 real values, truncate them to integers, and reprint only those that are then *odd* numbers.

5-10. Write a program that *counts* the number of (nonblank) cards in a data deck containing real values. The deck will be followed by a *sentinel card,* bearing the value 999.999.

CHAPTER **6**

SUBSCRIPTED VARIABLES

GENERAL PURPOSE AND METHOD

The statement

READ, X

has the effect, during compilation, of reserving a single storage location for the value "X". Yet we have seen that this statement during execution may actually handle many *different* values of X. Our frequent looping arrangement

1 $\begin{bmatrix} \text{DO 1 I} = 1, \text{N} \\ \text{READ, X} \\ \text{SUM} = \text{SUM} + \text{X} \end{bmatrix}$

repeatedly replaces old values of X with new ones, as the reading proceeds. After exit from the loop, the only value of X *in storage* is the last one read — the nth value.

The purpose of *subscripting* is the simultaneous retention in storage of multiple values of any variable. The method is precisely analogous to mathematical notation:

$$X_1, X_2, X_3, X_4, \ldots, X_n$$

becomes in FORTRAN

$$X(1), X(2), X(3), X(4), \ldots, X(N)$$

The entire set of values thus designated is frequently referred to as an *array*; individual values are *array elements*.

91

As an example of the technique, let us write a program to compute the *average deviation* for up to 1000 data values. This measure is the mean of *absolute* deviations from the arithmetic mean; that is,

$$\text{A.D.} = \frac{\Sigma |X - \overline{X}|}{n}$$

where $\overline{X}$ is the arithmetic mean. *Subscripting* is necessary, since individual values of X must be available for computation of deviations from the mean, *after* the latter has been produced. Sample program 6–1 shows the method.

```
C SAMPLE PROGRAM 6-1
C AVERAGE DEVIATION, FOR N DATA VALUES (MAXIMUM NUMBER 1000)
      DIMENSION X(1000)
      SUM = SUMD = 0.
      READ, N
     ┌DO 1 I = 1, N
     │ READ, X(I)
   1 └SUM = SUM + X(I)
      XMEAN = SUM/N
     ┌DO 2 J = 1, N
   2 └SUMD = SUMD + ABS(X(J) − XMEAN)
      AVGDEV = SUMD/N
      PRINT, XMEAN, AVGDEV
      STOP
      END
```

THE DIMENSION STATEMENT

The programmer's intention to store multiple values of a variable must be expressed at the beginning of the source program by use of a DIMENSION statement.[1] The DIMENSION statement in sample program 6–1 has the effect during compilation of setting aside 1000 *real* locations in storage, and referencing these as $X_1, X_2, X_3, X_4, \ldots, X_{1000}$. Each variable for which subscripts are to be used must be declared in a DIMENSION or explicit type specification statement. Conversely, any variable thus declared to be an *array* must be

---

[1] If, however, a variable that is to be subscripted is also to be "typed" by an *explicit type specification* statement (e.g., REAL or INTEGER), its dimensions should be declared in the type statement, which *precedes* any DIMENSION statements. Dimension information so appearing should not be repated in DIMENSION. For example,
```
            REAL ITEM(10)
            INTEGER PROD(20), CLIMB(20)
            DIMENSION FAULT(20)
```

provided with a subscript each time it is mentioned in the source program, with two general exceptions.

The first of these exceptions appears in *input* and *output* statements, and is illustrated with regard to input in sample program 6–2:[2]

```
C SAMPLE PROGRAM 6-2
C THIS PROGRAM READS AN ARRAY OF EXACTLY FIFTY ELEMENTS,
C                            AND REPRINTS IT IN REVERSE ORDER
      DIMENSION PRICE(50)
      READ, PRICE
      DO 1 I = 1, 50
      J = 51 - I
1     PRINT, PRICE(J)
      STOP
      END
```

The *omission* of any subscript reference in the READ statement, though PRICE has been declared as an array of 50 elements, has the effect of including *all* elements of the array in the input list. That is,

```
      DIMENSION A(7)
      READ, A
      PRINT, A
```

has the same effect as writing,

```
      DIMENSION A(7)
      READ, A(1), A(2), A(3), A(4), A(5), A(6), A(7)
      PRINT, A(1), A(2), A(3), A(4), A(5), A(6), A(7)
```

Since the ommission of the subscript reference causes the compiler program to include the full array (as dimensioned) in the list, this method would *not* work in sample program 6–1. Look back at that program to make sure you see the reason for this.

This sort of omission is *not* valid in arithmetic statements. That is, in the sequence

```
      DIMENSION A(7)
      SUM = 0.
      READ, A
      SUM = SUM + A
```

the READ statement is legal, but the arithmetic statement following is not.

---

[2] The second exception concerns the use of array names in *subprograms* (e.g., programmer-supplied functions) and statements *calling* subprograms. This will be discussed in Chapter 7.

A DO loop is usually the most convenient technique for traveling through the array after it has been stored. Thus

> DIMENSION A(7)
> SUM = 0.
> READ, A
> ⎡DO 1 METHOD = 1, 7
> 1 ⎣SUM = SUM + A(METHOD)

The sequence above accomplishes the required arithmetic correctly.

The parentheses of the DIMENSION statement must contain an integer *constant*. An integer variable is not acceptable, even when previously defined. The reservation of storage locations for all variables is a *compilation* activity; variables are not represented by actual values in storage until *execution* time, when it is too late to make such reservations. Thus

> DIMENSION PRICE(N)

is not valid.[3] This is the reason, in sample program 6–1, for selecting 1000 as a *maximum* size for the array, in a program written to be general as to size of the data set.

The DIMENSION statement may include declarations for more than one variable at a time, in which case commas are used for separation:

> DIMENSION A(20), B(20), C(50), J(75)

This statement reserves a total of 90 *real* locations and 75 *integer* locations.

PERMISSIBLE SUBSCRIPT FORMS

The subscript appears in parentheses immediately following the name of the variable being subscripted, and is treated as a part of that name. In standard FORTRAN, the subscript must be in *integer* mode; but some compiler programs, including WATFOR and WATFIV, permit the use of *any arithmetic expression* as subscript. If, however, the subscript expression is in real mode, its result is truncated to integer for the purpose of locating the array element. Thus

> X(SQRT(12.))

would be interpreted as

> X(3)

In our examples thus far, we have used a single integer constant and a single integer variable as subscripts. The latter usage is probably the most common, in connection with the convenient use of the *DO loop index* as the subscript.

Since the computer locates the array elements in storage by subscript *number* (having "looked up" the current value of any integer variable men-

---

[3] An exception, for subprograms, is mentioned in Chapter 7.

tioned in the subscript), the programmer is not committed to any particular subscript usage. That is, in later parts of the program he need not repeat the integer variable originally used as subscript. This is illustrated in sample program 6-1 (above), where I is used in the first DO loop, and J appears in the second.

In standard FORTRAN, a limited set of integer *expressions* are also usable as subscripts. For most FORTRAN compilers, the full list follows (where v represents any integer variable, and c and d represent any integer constants):

	General Form	Example
(1)	v	X(MAX)
(2)	c	X(36)
(3)	v + c	X(K + 2)
	v − c	X(JOB − 5)
(4)	c ⋆ v	X(2 ⋆ M)
(5)	c ⋆ v + d	X(2 ⋆ M + 1)
	c ⋆ v − d	X(4 ⋆ LUMP − 3)

In types 3, 4, and 5, the *order* of these expressions must be rigidly adhered to. That is, the following examples do *not* contain legal subscripts:

X(3 + K)   (wrong order, #3)
X(K ⋆ 3)   (wrong order, #4)
X(6 + 3 ⋆ K)   (wrong order, #5)

For this reason, the following rearrangement of sample program 6-2

```
        DO 1 I = 1, 50
1       PRINT, PRICE(51 − I)
```

contains a subscript that would be illegal in most FORTRAN versions; but it is acceptable in WATFOR and WATFIV.

USE OF THE DO INDEX AS SUBSCRIPT

There is no *necessary* connection between the DO loop and subscripted variables; it is a matter of *convenience* for the programmer. That is,

```
        DIMENSION ITEM(20)
        SUM = 0.
        READ, ITEM
        K = 1
5       ⎡SUM = SUM + ITEM(K)
        ⎢K = K + 1
        ⎣IF (K .LE. 20) GO TO 5
```

The arrangement above works. But as we observed in Chapter 3, the use of the DO statement shortens the program:

```
       DIMENSION ITEM(20)
       SUM = 0.
       READ, ITEM
       DO 6 K = 1, 20
   6   SUM = SUM + ITEM(K)
```

The DO index is always in the proper (integer) mode, and it "automatically" represents an ascending series of values.

The *increment* (m_3) position in the DO statement is useful for traveling *selectively* through an array in storage. This is illustrated in sample program 6–3, which selects a *systematic* sample:[4]

```
C SAMPLE PROGRAM 6-3
C THIS PROGRAM PRODUCES THE MEAN OF A SYSTEMATIC SAMPLE
                                        (EVERY 5TH ELEMENT,
C STARTING WITH THE FIRST), FROM AN ARRAY OF 1,000 ELEMENTS
       DIMENSION X(1000)
       READ, X
       SUM = 0.
       DO 1 I = 1, 1000, 5
   1   SUM = SUM + X(I)
       PRINT, SUM/200.
       STOP
       END
```

ARRAY POSITION VERSUS ARRAY ELEMENT VALUE

A common source of confusion concerns the distinction between an array element's *position* and its *value*. The former is a number from 1 through the integer mentioned in the DIMENSION statement parentheses; it is represented by an integer subscript in the program. The *value*, however, is in *real* mode or *integer* mode depending on the implicit or explicit typing of the variable *name;* it is stored in the *position* in storage indicated by its subscript. In rare instances, *position* and *value* may be arranged to be identical. Thus, for example:

---

[4] A systematic sample is defined as every jth element of a population of values, where j is selected at random from the digits 1 through k; the value of k depends on the relative sizes of population and required sample size. Specifically,

$$k = \text{population size/sample size}$$

```
            DIMENSION NUMBER(10)
           ┌DO 1 I = 1, 10
      1    └NUMBER(I) = I
```

In sample program 6-4 (below), both array *position* and *value* of some elements are printed in output—that is, both subscript and subscripted name are included in the output list.

```
C SAMPLE PROGRAM 6-4
C THIS PROGRAM PRINTS THE ARRAY POSITION AND VALUE OF ALL
C            DATA ITEMS SMALLER THAN THE ARITHMETIC MEAN ITEM
      DIMENSION GRADE (300)
      READ, GRADE
      SUM = 0.
     ┌DO 1 I = 1, 300
   1 └SUM = SUM + GRADE(I)
      XMEAN = SUM/300.
     ┌DO 2 I = 1, 300
   2 └IF (GRADE(I) .LT. XMEAN) PRINT, I, GRADE(I)
      STOP
      END
```

INDEXED INPUT AND OUTPUT LISTS

The statement

PRINT, (X(I), I = 5, 9)

has the same effect as if the programmer had written

PRINT, X(5), X(6), X(7), X(8), X(9)

The form shown first is called the *indexed list* or, occasionally, the *implied DO loop*. Like *omission* of the subscript reference, discussed earlier, it is valid only in *input* and *output* statements. Thus

SUM = SUM + (X(I), I = 5, 9)

is not valid.

The *indexed list* is a convenient input/output method when a generalized program employs the parameter card arrangement to vary the data set size. As we have seen, (a) such programs utilize a constant in the DIMENSION statement that serves as a *maximum* size for the data set, and (b) the *omission* of the subscript reference in input/output statements would not work, since the *maximum* number of elements would thus be automatically included in the lists. Sample program 6-5 shows a solution using *indexed lists*.

```
C SAMPLE PROGRAM 6-5
C THIS PROGRAM USES INDEXED LISTS TO HANDLE INPUT AND
                                                  OUTPUT
      DIMENSION X(1000)
      READ, N
      READ, (X(I), I = 1, N)
      PRINT, (X(I), I = 10, N, 10)
      STOP
      END
```

For a parameter card keypunched "36", this program would read 36 data values, and reprint only the 10th, 20th, and 30th values.

When more than one subscripted variable is to appear in input and/or output statements, the list order is developed as follows:

(1)   DIMENSION A(3), B(3)
       READ, A, B

the order is A(1), A(2), A(3), B(1), B(2), B(3)

(2)   DIMENSION A(3), B(3)
       READ, (A(I), I = 1, 3), (B(I), I = 1, 3)

the order is A(1), A(2), A(3), B(1), B(2), B(3)

(3)   DIMENSION A(3), B(3)
       READ, (A(I), B(I), I = 1, 3)

the order is A(1), B(1), A(2), B(2), A(3), B(3)

Thus in sample program 6-6 (below), the *input* data is organized in the order X — Y — X — Y — etc.; but the *output* order is changed to print first all the X values, and then all the Y values. The output statement would have the same effect if it were changed to

PRINT, X, Y

```
C SAMPLE PROGRAM 6-6
C INDEXED LIST WITH TWO VARIABLES INTERSPERSED IN DATA
      DIMENSION X(50), Y(50)
      READ, (X(I), Y(I), I = 1, 50)
C THE OUTPUT ORDER IS CHANGED
      PRINT, (X(I), I = 1, 50), (Y(I), I = 1, 50)
      STOP
      END
```

OPERATIONS ON ARRAYS IN STORAGE

We have seen (e.g., sample programs 6-2, 6-3, 6-4) that once an array of values has been stored it is a relatively simple matter to "travel through" the array in various directions and for various purposes, usually employing the DO loop as the means of transportation. Some of the more interesting and useful applications of the technique involve *comparison* of values stored (using, of course, *IF statements* within loops).

Sample program 6–7 shows such an application, comparing elements of an array with one another to find all pairs equal in value. Note that the double-loop *combinations* technique is the one introduced earlier, in sample program 3–15.

```
C SAMPLE PROGRAM 6-7
C THIS PROGRAM PRINTS THE ARRAY POSITIONS OF ALL EQUAL PAIRS
                                                    OF VALUES
      DIMENSION X(50)
      READ, X
      DO 1 I = 1, 49
      K = I + 1
      DO 1 J = K, 50
1     IF (X(I) .EQ. X(J)) PRINT, I, J
      STOP
      END
```

The useful ability to *order* values as to size is also based on repetitive use of IF statements. To begin with a relatively simple problem, let us consider selecting the *largest* value from a stored array. The technique in sample 6–8 (below) is (a) place the first array element in the "BIG" location, (b) compare each of the other array elements in turn with the "BIG" value, *replacing* "BIG"'s contents each time a value larger than the current "leader" in that location is encountered.

```
C SAMPLE PROGRAM 6-8
C THIS PROGRAM FINDS THE LARGEST VALUE, IN A SET OF 300
      DIMENSION GRADE (300)
      READ, GRADE
      BIG = GRADE(1)
      DO 1 I = 2, 300
1     IF (GRADE(I) .GT. BIG) BIG = GRADE(I)
      PRINT, BIG
      STOP
      END
```

INTERCHANGE OF VALUES IN STORAGE

In sample program 6–8, each array element is examined but left undisturbed in storage (since *copying* into the "BIG" location does not alter the location from which the copying is done). In some problems, comparison of values is followed by *interchange* of the values in storage. Given two storage locations whose values are to be switched, how may the switching be accomplished? If the locations are A and B, the sequence

$$A = B$$
$$B = A$$

does *not* work. You should see that it leaves *both* locations filled with the value originally stored in the B location.

Three statements are required to effect the *interchange*:

$$SAVE = A$$
$$A = B$$
$$B = SAVE$$

In this method, the SAVE location serves as a safe resting place for the "A" value, so that it is not permanently lost when the second statement (A = B) is executed.

THE SORTING PROBLEM

The techniques we have been examining—search through an array for small or large values, and interchange of values in storage—may be applied to the problem of *arranging values in storage in ascending (or descending) order*. This is called *sorting*, a job that has proved difficult for both programmers and computers, and has been accomplished by many different approaches.

A basic technique, which is slower than some others in execution but logically simple, involves a sequence of comparisons made in the *"combinations"* order shown in sample programs 3–15 and 6–7. That is, we first compare

X_1 and X_2
X_1 and X_3
X_1 and X_4

X_1 and X_n

Prior to beginning this set of comparisons, a "1" has been placed in an integer location (called "NSMALL" below) designed to hold the *subscript* (array position) of the *smallest* element. When an array element smaller than X(1) is encountered, the subscript of this element is copied into "NSMALL". As the comparisons proceed, each element that proves smaller than the previous "leader" has its subscript copied into the "NSMALL" location.

When this first set of comparisons is finished, NSMALL contains the *subscript* of the *smallest* array element. The element value corresponding to this subscript is *interchanged* in storage, with the X(1) element. Thus the entire set of comparisons, and the following interchange, moves the smallest X value to the X(1) location. The *next* set of comparisons is

$$X_2 \text{ and } X_3$$
$$X_2 \text{ and } X_4$$
$$\text{---}$$
$$X_2 \text{ and } X_n$$

This set is followed by an interchange which moves the second smallest element into the X(2) location. This process must be repeated (N − 1) times, ending with the comparison

$$X_{n-1} \text{ and } X_n$$

Sample program 6-9 shows this method implemented for N values (using a parameter card; maximum of 1000 values).

```
C SAMPLE PROGRAM 6-9
C A BASIC SORTING METHOD
      DIMENSION X(1000)
      READ, N, (X(I), I = 1, N)
      LIMIT = N − 1
      DO 2 INDEX = 1, LIMIT
      NSMALL = INDEX
      ISTART = INDEX + 1
      DO 1 I = ISTART, N
1     IF (X(I) .LT. X(NSMALL)) NSMALL = I
      SAVE = X(NSMALL)
      X(NSMALL) = X(INDEX)
2     X(INDEX) = SAVE
      PRINT, (X(I), I = 1, N)
      STOP
      END
```

DOUBLE DIMENSION

It is possible in FORTRAN to assign *two* subscripts to a dimensioned variable. The statement

$$\text{DIMENSION W}(3,4)$$

reserves storage for *12* values of W. They will be referenced as

$W_{1,1}$ $W_{2,1}$ $W_{3,1}$ $W_{1,2}$ $W_{2,2}$ $W_{3,2}$ $W_{1,3}$ $W_{2,3}$ $W_{3,3}$ $W_{1,4}$ $W_{2,4}$ $W_{3,4}$

Note that the *first* subscript varies *first*, in this reference system.

The usual permissible forms of the subscript are available in double dimension. Thus the following are all valid:

W(MAX, J)	(the v form)
W(3,2)	(the c form)
W(ITEM, K + 6)	(the v and v+c forms)
W(3★K+1, N−6)	(the v★c+d and v−c forms)

The reason for using this method instead of

DIMENSION W(12)

is the programmer's conceptual view of the data as a two-dimensional *matrix*, in which identification of each value by two coordinates or characteristics is convenient. Some examples of problems in various disciplines may illustrate the point:

Economics: data representing m industries in n different years
Mathematics: data representing m simultaneous equations, each containing n variables
Business: data representing m products, each subject to n transactions
Statistics: data representing two categorical variables, one with m categories and the other with n categories
Survey Research: data representing m respondents, each answering n questions
Engineering: data representing m materials, each having n characteristics

For a specific illustration, let us assume 10 classes of 30 students each, for whom examination grades have been keypunched. Sample program 6–10 computes 10 class means.

```
C SAMPLE PROGRAM 6-10
C MEAN GRADES FOR 10 CLASSES OF 30 STUDENTS EACH, USING
                                              DOUBLE DIMENSION
      DIMENSION GRADE(30,10), SUM(10)
      READ, GRADE
    ┌ DO 1 I = 1, 10
1   └ SUM(I) = 0.
    ┌ DO 3 I = 1, 10
    │┌ DO 2 J = 1, 30
2   │└ SUM(I) = SUM(I) + GRADE(J, I)
3   └ PRINT, I, SUM(I)/30.
      STOP
      END
```

Observe that the convenient method for "traveling through" a double-dimensioned array employs a nest of two DO loops. Input, on the other hand, has been handled by making use of the *subscript omission* method shown earlier for single-dimensioned arrays. Since the compiler then organizes the input list on the *first-subscript-changes-first* principle, the DIMENSION statement mentions the class size (30) first; that is, the data are keypunched in class order. If the declaration were made as

$$\text{DIMENSION GRADE(10,30)}$$

then the statement

$$\text{READ, GRADE}$$

would generate a list in an order not matching the data organization.

THE DATA STATEMENT

In sample program 6–10 (above), a DO loop (ending at statement 1) is used to *initialize* 10 values of the subscripted variable SUM, at zero. A less bulky arrangement is available in FORTRAN, which *accomplishes initialization at compilation time:*

$$\text{DIMENSION SUM(10)}$$
$$\text{DATA SUM/10} \star \text{0./}$$

This *DATA initialization* statement arranges for insertion of values in certain storage locations during *compilation* of the source program (i.e., insertion directly into the *object* program). Thus

DATA I,J,K/17, 31, 57/, Z95, Z99/1.96, 2.58/, PI/3.141593/, A,B,C/3 $\star$ 1.98/

substitutes for the following *executable* program statements, which would do the same job at execution time:

$$I = 17$$
$$J = 31$$
$$K = 57$$
$$Z95 = 1.96$$
$$Z99 = 2.58$$
$$PI = 3.141593$$
$$A = B = C = 1.98$$

In the prior example, the omission of subscript reference for SUM in the DATA statement indicates initialization for the entire array. If individual elements are to be initialized, subscript references are necessary:

$$\text{DATA SUM(1), SUM(5)/ 2} \star \text{0./}$$

Note that the asterisk is used, following an integer constant, to *repeat* the following constant; that is, 5 $\star$ 1.6 is translated, "five locations in the list are to be initialized at 1.6."

The *indexed list* is also usable within the DATA statement, in some FORTRAN compiler programs. Thus

DATA (SUM(L), L = 1, 5)/ 5 * 0./

There is no limit to the number of variables that may be mentioned in each group. That is, our second example could also be written as a single group:

DATA I, J, K, Z95, Z99, PI, A, B, C/17, 31, 57, 1.96, 2.58, 3.141593, 3 * 1.98/

Whatever the organization into groups, a slash (/) is used to begin and end each list of constants. Note that matching of *modes* is important; that is, real variables in the list must be matched with constants containing decimal points, and integer variables with constants lacking decimal points.

In addition to saving some programming time, the DATA statement also saves storage space, since the machine language instructions generated by *executable* initialization statements are eliminated from the object program, by using DATA. Initial values provided by the DATA statement may be changed later in the program (by executable statements); for example,

SUM(1) = SUM(1) + X

is valid. However, the DATA statement may not be used to cause *reinitialization*, since it is not executable. That is, there can be no transfer (or "branch") to the DATA statement.

OPERATIONS ON TWO-DIMENSIONAL MATRICES

Sample program 6–11 (below) uses the DATA statement to initialize 40 locations. It also illustrates the proper form of the indexed list (in input and output statements) for double-dimensioned variables:

((A(I,J), I = 1, M), J = 1, N)

The form is a set of nested parentheses, with the *first* subscript (i.e., the one in the *inner* set of parentheses) varying *first*, as usual. As in the case of single dimension, the indexed list form proves useful when the data set being handled is smaller than the dimensions mentioned in the DIMENSION statement.

```
C SAMPLE PROGRAM 6-11
C SUMS OF ROWS AND COLUMNS, FOR AN M BY N MATRIX (MAXIMUM
                                                  20 BY 20)
      DIMENSION A(20,20), R(20), C(20)
      DATA R, C/40 * 0./
      READ, M, N
      READ, ((A(I,J), I = 1, M), J = 1, N)
```

```
       DO 1 I = 1, M
       DO 1 J = 1, N
       C(I) = C(I) + A(I,J)
1      R(J) = R(J) + A(I,J)
       DO 2 J = 1, N
2      PRINT, (A(I,J), I = 1, M), R(J)
       PRINT, (C(I), I = 1, M)
       STOP
       END
```

The program accomplishes summation by "rows" and by "columns"; the technique is worth examining closely, since this sort of operation on a matrix of stored values is required in many problems. The double DO loop ending at statement 1 "travels through" the entire matrix, adding each value to the appropriate column and row sums. Observe that the output list at statement 2, although it is an indexed list referring to a double-dimensioned variable, needs only one set of parentheses. This is because only one of the subscripts is to be varied within the list.

Some matrix operations are much simpler in form. For example, for any *square* matrix the *diagonal* elements are those that have identical first and second subscripts. This is illustrated in sample program 6–12:

```
C SAMPLE PROGRAM 6-12
C SUM OF DIAGONAL ELEMENTS OF A SQUARE INTEGER MATRIX
       DIMENSION MATRIX(50,50)
       DATA ISUM/0/
       READ, MATRIX
       DO 1 I = 1, 50
1      ISUM = ISUM + MATRIX(I,I)
       PRINT, ISUM
       STOP
       END
```

Another common form of operation on matrices is shown in sample program 6–13. Two matrices with the same dimensions are added (by adding individual corresponding elements), to produce a third matrix:

```
C SAMPLE PROGRAM 6-13
C SUM OF TWO MATRICES
       DIMENSION A(4,9), B(4,9), C(4,9)
       READ, A, B
       DO 1 I = 1, 4
       DO 1 J = 1, 9
1      C(I,J) = A(I,J) + B(I,J)
```

```
        ┌ DO 2 J = 1, 9
   2    └ PRINT, (C(I,J), I = 1, 4)
          STOP
          END
```

TRIPLE DIMENSION

Most FORTRAN compilers permit the use of *three* subscripts to identify values of a variable (and some allow up to *seven* subscripts). All the arrangements are extensions of the double-dimension idea; thus

$$\text{DIMENSION M(4,5,6)}$$

reserves storage for 120 values of M. The entire array may be read by

$$\text{READ, M}$$

in which case the order of subscript assignment in the input list is

M(1,1,1), M(2,1,1), M(3,1,1), M(4,1,1), M(1,2,1), M(2,2,1) ... etc.

That is, as usual, *first* subscript changes *first*.
An *indexed list* would be of the form:

READ, (((M(I,J,K), I = 1, 4), J = 1, 5), K = 1, 6)

Finally, the technique of "traveling through" a three-dimensional array in storage involves a triple nest of DO loops:

```
        ┌   DO 1 I = 1, 4
        │┌  DO 1 J = 1, 5
        ││┌ DO 1 K = 1, 6
   1    └└└ MSUM = MSUM + M(I,J,K)
```

Three-dimensional data sets are fairly common in real problems. Sample program 6-14 shows the triple-dimension techniques applied to a major league baseball problem, in which a first subscript identifies a particular player, a second subscript specifies a particular team, and the third subscript is used for identification as to league.

```
C SAMPLE PROGRAM 6-14
C THIS PROGRAM PRODUCES 24 TEAM SALARY MEANS – THERE ARE 2
C             LEAGUES, 12 TEAMS IN EACH LEAGUE, AND 25 PLAYERS ON
                                                          EACH TEAM
      DIMENSION PLAYER(25, 12, 2), SUM(12,2)
      DATA SUM/24 * 0./
      READ, PLAYER
```

```
      ┌  DO 2 K = 1, 2
      │  DO 2 J = 1, 12
      │┌ DO 1 I = 1, 25
1     ││ SUM(J,K) = SUM(J,K) + PLAYER(I,J,K)
2     └└ PRINT, J, K, SUM(J,K)/25.
         STOP
         END
```

For Review

subscripted variable
subscripts
DIMENSION statement
array
array element
subscript omission

indexed list

interchange in storage

sorting
double dimension
DATA statement
indexed list
triple dimension
indexed list

Examples

X(K), X(4), X(K+3), X(3∗K), X(3∗K−2)
  K   4   K+3   3∗K   3∗K−2
DIMENSION X(20), ITEM(10)
            X   ITEM
          X(3) ITEM(8)
READ, X
PRINT, ITEM
READ, (X(I), I = 1, 20)
WRITE, (ITEM(I), I = 1, 10)
SAVE = A
A = B
B = SAVE

DIMENSION CAR(7, 12)
DATA CAR/84 ∗ 0.0/
WRITE, ((CAR(I,J), I = 1, 7), J=1,12)
DIMENSION YARD(3, 4, 10)
READ,(((YARD(I, J, K), I=1,3), J=1,4), K=1,10)

Programming Exercises

6-1. Write a program that reads 72 real data values, and computes and prints the measure

$$\frac{\Sigma(X - \overline{X})^3}{n}$$

where $\overline{X}$ is the arithmetic mean, and n is the number of data values.

6-2. Adjust program 6-1 (above) so that it works for a *maximum* of 500 values, and reads a *parameter card* containing the "n" value. Test with a parameter card using 36.

6-3. Write a program that reads 30 data values, and then computes their *range* — that is, the distance between the lowest and highest values.

6-4. Write a program that reads a *parameter card* containing a value for N, then reads N data values, and then prints the array *positions* (1-n) of all values equal to the *last* value. Test with a parameter of 20.

6-5. Write a program that will read the first nine data items (i.e., using only the first two data cards), and produce as output the arithmetic means of all possible *different* samples of two items each. Output should be in five columns, showing for each of the 36 samples the two array position numbers, the two array values, and their mean.

6-6. Write a program that will read ten values of b and one value of X (reading the first two data cards), and compute and print

$$Y = b_1 X^9 + b_2 X^8 + b_3 X^7 \ldots + b_9 X + b_{10}$$

(This should be done in about eight statements, including STOP and END.)

6-7. Write a program that reads the entire data deck as a 6-column by 12-row matrix, and then prints as output the 6 column sums.

6-8. Write a program that reads the first 28 data items as a 7-column by 4-row matrix, keypunched in "column order", and then reprints the matrix as a 4-column by 7-row matrix.

6-9. Adjust program 6-8 (above) so that it works for an m x n matrix (maximum 20 x 20), with these dimensions to be read from a *parameter* card. Test with parameters 7 and 4.

6-10. A checkerboard looks like this, at the beginning of the game:

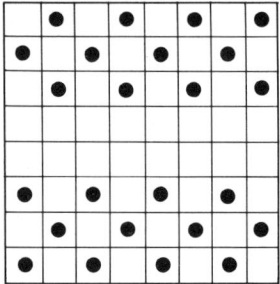

Write a program that will output a "picture" of the board, using the digit 0 for unfilled squares, and the digit 1 for squares occupied by checkers. (The DATA statement should be an easy method for "loading" zeros into a matrix. It may also help to note that checkers may rest only on squares whose two-dimensional subscripts add up to *odd* totals.)

CHAPTER 7

SUBPROGRAM ARRANGEMENTS

STATEMENT FUNCTIONS

In Chapter 4 we examined the use of *functions* supplied by the compiler program. A *function* is one form of the *subprogram:* a set of instructions that may be stored (on a *secondary* storage medium, usually), and called upon *by name* for insertion in the programmer's explicitly written sequence of instructions.

The purpose of *any* subprogram arrangement is avoidance of repetitive programming—a series of computations that is to be repeated may be written once and used many times. The results are savings in programming time, keypunching time, compilation time, and computer storage. In the case of FORTRAN-supplied functions, the writing has been done by the compiler author for certain computation problems that tend to arise repeatedly in a large variety of problems. The square root function is a good example. The statement

$$A = SQRT(X + Y) - B$$

is executed as follows:

1. The values of X and Y are looked up in storage, and the addition performed.
2. The resulting numerical *argument* is operated on by the SQRT subprogram instructions, which produce a new value, the square root of the argument.
3. The computed value is *returned* to take the place of SQRT(X + Y), in the *calling statement.*

4. The rest of the statement is executed (look-up of B, subtraction, and placement of the result in A storage).

Two methods for duplicating this effect—that is, for writing *programmer-originated* functions—are available in FORTRAN: *statement functions* and *function subprograms*. Sample program 7-1 shows a *statement function* of a trivial sort, designed to obtain the *cube root* of any *real argument*.

```
C SAMPLE PROGRAM 7-1
C THIS PROGRAM CONTAINS A STATEMENT FUNCTION, THAT RETURNS
C                      THE CUBE ROOT OF ANY REAL ARGUMENT
      DIMENSION X(20)
      DATA SUM, SUMCR/2 * 0./
      CUBRT(A) = A ** (1./3.)
      READ, X
      DO 1 I = 1, 20
      SUM = SUM + X(I)
1     SUMCR = SUMCR + CUBRT(X(I))
      CRSUM = CUBRT(SUM)
      PRINT, SUMCR, CRSUM
      STOP
      END
```

The program compares, for 20 data values, a sum of cube roots with the cube root of the sum. The statement *defining* the cube root function is

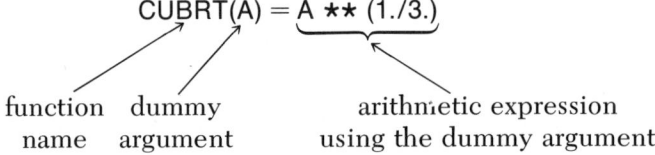

$$\text{CUBRT(A)} = \text{A} ** (1./3.)$$

function name — dummy argument — arithmetic expression using the dummy argument

The rules for defining and using such a *statement function* are:

1. The function definition(s) should appear after nonexecutable *specification* statements (e.g., DIMENSION, REAL, DATA, etc.), but before the first *executable* statement of the program.
2. The *left* side of the definition statement contains:
   (a) an invented *name* for the function. This name follows all the compiler's rules for naming ordinary variables, as to number of characters, permissible characters, and mode implied by first character (unless reversed in an earlier explicit type specification statement).
   (b) parentheses containing at least one *dummy argument* (or several dummy arguments separated by commas). The "A" in our statement function definition (sample program 7-1) simply indicates that a *single real value* must be provided by the "calling" statement

(in which it also will appear in parentheses, following the function name).

3. The *right* side of the definition consists of any legitimate arithmetic expression, which mentions the dummy argument(s) on the left—and shows how they are to be combined to form the required (*"returned"*) value. This expression may contain FORTRAN-supplied or programmer-supplied functions, except that it cannot contain the name of the statement function appearing on the left; that is, your function cannot use itself in computation.

4. Any statement that makes use of the function (a *"calling"* statement) does so according to the usual rules governing FORTRAN-supplied functions. Thus the function name can appear only in *arithmetic expressions* (i.e., only on the *right* side of arithmetic statements, and within parentheses in Arithmetic and Logical IF statements). When it appears, it is followed by parentheses that must contain the required arguments, which may be variables, constants, or more complicated arithmetic expressions. These arguments must match the *dummy* arguments in *number, order,* and *mode,* but *not necessarily in name*. Their values will be substituted (during execution) for the dummy variables representing them in the function definition.

Sample program 7–2 contains *two* statement functions, each operating on *three* arguments.

```
C SAMPLE PROGRAM 7-2
C THIS PROGRAM USES TWO STATEMENT FUNCTIONS, TO OBTAIN
C                            ROOTS OF QUADRATIC EQUATIONS
      ROOT1(A, B, C) = (-B - SQRT(B**2 - 4.*A*C))/(2.*A)
      ROOT2(A, B, C) = (-B + SQRT(B**2 - 4.*A*C))/(2.*A)
      DO 1 I = 1, 12
      READ, X, Y
      A = ROOT1(X, Y, 5.0)
      B = ROOT2(X, Y, 5.0)
      C = ROOT1(2.*X, 3.*Y, 20.0)
      D = ROOT2(2*X, 3.*Y, 20.0)
1     PRINT, X, Y, A, B, C, D
      STOP
      END
```

You should see that the first calling statement

$$A = ROOT1(X, Y, 5.0)$$

results in substitution of the first X value (an input data item) for the dummy argument "A", use of the first Y value for the dummy "B", and use of 5.0 for the dummy "C". Also note that the dummy argument *names* are not "reserved" as storage locations; thus there is no conflict when the names "A", "B", and "C" are used in the executable portion of the program.

FUNCTION SUBPROGRAMS

There are two factors that limit the usefulness of the *statement function:* first, it is available only within the program in which it appears. A statement function must be *written into* any program in which it is to be *called.* By contrast, the SQRT function (and other FORTRAN-supplied functions) are available to all programs, the programmer writing only the function name and the actual arguments.

Second, any statement function is limited to a *single* statement; many problems for which subprogram treatment is convenient require multiple statements for solution.

The *function subprogram* lifts both of these limitations. With regard to the first, let us make the CUBRT function (written as a statement function in sample program 7-1) permanently available:

```
C SAMPLE PROGRAM 7-3
C THIS CONVERTS THE CUBRT FUNCTION TO A FUNCTION SUBPROGRAM
      FUNCTION CUBRT(V)
      CUBRT = V ** (1./3.)
      RETURN
      END
```

The rules for writing *function subprograms* are:

1. The first statement contains only the word FUNCTION, the (invented) *function name,* and the *dummy arguments.* As in the statement function, the latter are variable names representing the values needed for computation, which at execution time will be supplied by the *calling program.* In sample program 7-3,

$$\text{FUNCTION } \underset{\substack{\nearrow \\ \text{function} \\ \text{name}}}{\text{CUBRT}} (\underset{\substack{\nwarrow \\ \text{dummy} \\ \text{argument}}}{\text{V}})$$

the "V" indicates that *one real value* is required for the computation.

2. Somewhere within the function subprogram, the *function name* must be assigned a value. When this is done (as it ordinarily is) in an arithmetic statement,[1] *only* the function name appears to the left of the equal sign. The

---

[1] Another possibility is that the function subprogram may contain a READ statement that treats the function-name value as input; that is, the function name may appear in an *input list.*

dummy argument(s) may appear only on the *right* side of equal signs—that is, in arithmetic expressions. In sample program 7–3,

$$\underset{\text{function name}}{\uparrow}\text{CUBRT} = \text{V} ** \underset{\text{dummy argument}}{\nwarrow}(1./3.)$$

a single statement is sufficient to assign the required value to CUBRT.

3. The word RETURN must appear at least once in the function subprogram. This is a *control statement* (a "branch" statement), which returns control to the *calling statement,* within the *calling program.* The value assigned to the function name by the subprogram is thus made available to the program actually executing.

4. The subprogram must end with an END statement. The *function subprogram* is thus a complete entity, which is *compiled* separately. The resulting object program cannot, however, be *"executed."* (Where would the value of "V" be obtained, if sample program 7–3 were "executed" by itself?) It may be *stored* on a secondary medium (e.g., a magnetic disk), as is the compiler program; and is then available for incorporation into object programs generated from *main* programs that use the function name.

With regard to the second limitation mentioned for statement functions, consider the problem of computing a *factorial number:* By definition,

$$n! = 1 \times 2 \times 3 \times 4 \times \ldots n$$

The following set of statements does the job, for factorial 14:

```
        FACT = 1.0
      ⎡ DO 1 I = 1, 14
   1  ⎣ FACT = FACT * I
```

(Note that real mode is used for FACT, because factorial numbers are very large in size).

To convert this routine to permanent availability as a *function subprogram,* the necessary steps are merely:

    (a) change "14" to "N", to establish a general case;
    (b) write a FUNCTION statement at the top;
    (c) write RETURN and END statements at the bottom.

Sample program 7–4 shows the resulting subprogram, which returns n! for $n \geq 1$:

```
C SAMPLE PROGRAM 7-4
C THIS IS A FUNCTION SUBPROGRAM, RETURNING THE FACTORIAL
C                              NUMBER FOR ANY INTEGER ARGUMENT
      FUNCTION FACT(N)
      FACT = 1.0
      DO 1 I = 1, N
1     FACT = FACT * I
      RETURN
      END
```

MAIN PROGRAMS; CALLING PROGRAMS

All of our sample programs prior to 7-3 were *"main" programs*—that is, they were written to be executed rather than stored awaiting "calls" from other programs. A *calling program* is any program that mentions the name of (and thus "calls") one or more subprograms. Note that a *subprogram* may be a *calling program*—that is, subprograms may themselves mention subprogram names. This will be the case in sample program 7-6. First, however, let us write a *main program*, which *calls* the FACT function subprogram.

The *combinations* formula, useful in probability computations, obtains the number of different combinations of n things taken r at a time, from

$$nCr = \frac{n!}{r!\,(n-r)!}$$

Sample program 7-5 makes use of the formula, to compute the number of different possible (five-card) poker hands that may be dealt:

```
C SAMPLE PROGRAM 7-5
C THIS IS A CALLING PROGRAM, THAT USES THE FACT FUNCTION
      COMB = FACT(52)/(FACT(5) * FACT(47))
      PRINT, COMB
      STOP
      END
```

CONVERSION OF MAIN PROGRAMS TO SUBPROGRAMS

Since the *combinations* evaluation may itself prove useful in other contexts, let us convert from *main program* to *function subprogram* form. Once again, the necessary steps are:

> (a) change "52" and "5" to integer variables;
> (b) write a FUNCTION statement at the top;
> (c) replace "STOP" with "RETURN";
> (d) extract the PRINT statement.

Although output statements are permitted in subprograms, the programmer's intention is usually *not* to output the function result, but to use the returned value in further computations within the calling program.

Sample program 7-6 shows the finished subprogram:

```
C SAMPLE PROGRAM 7-6
C CONVERSION OF A MAIN PROGRAM TO A FUNCTION—THIS MAKES
C          THE COMBINATIONS FORMULA A FUNCTION SUBPROGRAM
      FUNCTION COMB(I, J)
      COMB = FACT(I)/(FACT(J) * FACT(I − J))
      RETURN
      END
```

As mentioned earlier, this is both a *subprogram* and a *calling program*. With this version now available in storage, sample program 7-5 (a *main calling program*) would now be shortened to:

```
C SAMPLE PROGRAM 7-7
C PROGRAM 7-5 MAY NOW BE REWRITTEN THIS WAY
      PRINT, COMB(52,5)
      STOP
      END
```

SUBSCRIPTED VARIABLES IN SUBPROGRAMS

Dummy arguments may be *array names;* in this case, no subscript reference appears in the FUNCTION statement, but a DIMENSION statement must be used to declare the fact that an array is represented by the dummy name. Thus

```
      FUNCTION PROD(A, B, C)
      DIMENSION A(5), B(5), C(5)
```

This beginning indicates that A, B, and C are each *single-dimensioned arrays*. The "5" in each parentheses set does not, however, limit the *size* of the arrays, which are actually determined by a DIMENSION statement in any *calling program*. DIMENSION statements containing dummy arguments do not have the usual effect of reserving storage locations;[2] although the compiler program requires some integer constant in the parentheses, the constant used is immaterial.

---

[2] No subprogram dummy argument, array or not, actually receives an assigned storage location during compilation of the subprogram, since the main program that supplies the actual argument values (in a calling statement) will also have provided their storage locations (passing proper addresses to the subprogram).

The purpose of using *argument arrays* is the convenient transfer of multiple values between main programs and subprograms. We may demonstrate by writing a function subprogram that will compute the *arithmetic mean* of the first N values in a real array:

```
C SAMPLE PROGRAM 7-8
C THIS FUNCTION SUBPROGRAM RETURNS THE ARITHMETIC MEAN OF
C                            ARRAY ELEMENTS 1 THROUGH N
      FUNCTION XMEAN(X, N)
      DIMENSION X(1)
      SUM = 0.
      DO 1 I = 1, N
    1 SUM = SUM + X(I)
      XMEAN = SUM/N
      RETURN
      END
```

The "1" in the DIMENSION statement is merely a placeholder; but the statement indicates that any calling program is to supply a DIMENSION statement declaring the actual size of the argument array.[3] Sample program 7-9 is a calling program written for 300 examination grades:

```
C SAMPLE PROGRAM 7-9
C THIS CALLING PROGRAM USES THE XMEAN AND STDEV FUNCTIONS
      DIMENSION GRADE(300)
      READ, GRADE
      A = XMEAN(GRADE, 300)
      B = STDEV(GRADE, 300)
      PRINT, A, B
      STOP
      END
```

---

[3] However, if a dummy argument array has more than one dimension, the subprogram and main program DIMENSION statements must agree to assure proper referencing during execution. This problem may be handled by writing *maximum* dimensions into the subprogram, which then are used also in calling programs, even though less than the maximum size is to be used. Another solution, *"adjustable dimension"*, is available in some compilers, including WATFOR and WATFIV. Then:

```
          FUNCTION GAME(A, I, J)
          DIMENSION A(I,J)
```

is legal; that is, the exact dimensions of the A array will be passed as arguments in the calling statement.

The first calling statement

$$A = XMEAN(GRADE, 300)$$

supplies the 300 values of GRADE, which fill the place of the dummy X array in the subprogram, and the integer constant 300 to fill the "N" argument position. The STDEV subprogram, shown below, computes the *standard deviation* from

$$S = \sqrt{\frac{\Sigma(X - \overline{X})^2}{n}}$$

That is, this statistical measure is defined as the square root of the mean-squared deviation from the arithmetic mean.

```
C SAMPLE PROGRAM 7-10
C THIS FUNCTION SUBPROGRAM RETURNS THE STANDARD DEVIATION
C                       OF ARRAY ELEMENTS 1 THROUGH N
      FUNCTION STDEV(X, N)
      DIMENSION X(1)
      XM = XMEAN(X,N)
      SUM = 0.
      DO 1 I = 1, N
1     SUM = SUM + (X(I) − XM)**2
      STDEV = SQRT(SUM/N)
      RETURN
      END
```

SUBROUTINE SUBPROGRAMS

Two factors preclude the use of the *function subprogram* form in some instances. First, only one value may be returned to the calling program. Suppose, for example, that we want to design a subprogram that will compute *both* arithmetic mean and standard deviation. Should such a subprogram be named "XMEAN" or "STDEV"? Since we want to return both computed values to the calling program, the answer is "neither—make it a *subroutine subprogram*, and give it some neutral name." By "neutral" we mean that the *name* of a *subroutine subprogram* does not acquire a value during execution of the subprogram. However, XMEAN and STDEV will be included in the *dummy argument list*. This is possible because dummy arguments in *subroutine subprograms*, unlike those in *function subprograms*, may be mentioned on the left side of arithmetic statements—that is, they may be assigned values in the subprogram.

Sample program 7-11 shows the form, as applied to the problem described above.

```
C SAMPLE PROGRAM 7-11
C THIS SUBROUTINE SUBPROGRAM RETURNS BOTH MEAN AND
C    STANDARD DEVIATION, FOR ARRAY ELEMENTS 1 THROUGH N
C    (EARLIER FUNCTION VERSIONS HAVING BEEN DELETED FROM
                                                    STORAGE)
      SUBROUTINE STAT1(X, N, XMEAN, STDEV)
      DIMENSION X(1)
      SUM = SUMD = 0.
     ⎡DO 1 I = 1, N
   1 ⎣SUM = SUM + X(I)
      XMEAN = SUM/N
     ⎡DO 2 I = 1, N
   2 ⎣SUMD = SUMD + (X(I) − XMEAN)**2
      STDEV = SQRT(SUMD/N)
      RETURN
      END
```

The name "STAT1" is not mentioned after the SUBROUTINE statement that begins the subprogram. The idea is that the *dummy argument list* contains not only the names of variables whose values are required *from* the calling program, but also the names of variables whose values are to be *returned* to the calling program. Any *calling statement* must as usual provide a list of arguments matching the dummies in number, order, and mode. Sample program 7-12 calls the STAT1 subprogram to compute mean and standard deviation (stored as "A" and "B" respectively) for 300 examination grades. (It also calls a "SORT" subprogram, discussed below.)

```
C SAMPLE PROGRAM 7-12
C THIS CALLING PROGRAM USES THE STAT1 AND SORT SUBPROGRAMS
      DIMENSION GRADE(300)
      READ, GRADE
      CALL STAT1(GRADE, 300, A, B)
      PRINT, A, B
      CALL SORT(GRADE, 300)
      PRINT, GRADE
      STOP
      END
```

THE CALL STATEMENT

The form of the *calling statement* is quite different from that for function subprograms:

Function subprogram: A = XMEAN(GRADE, 300)
                         ↗   ↖
                      function   arguments (include
                       name   only values
                                       passed *to* the
                                       subprogram)

Subroutine subprogram: CALL STAT1(GRADE, 300, A, B)
                             ↑   ↖
                         subprogram   arguments (including
                           name   values to be passed
                                            in both directions)

The CALL statement transfers control to the subroutine subprogram; when RETURN is executed, control transfers to the next executable statement after CALL.

ALTERATION OF ARGUMENT VALUES

The SORT subprogram referred to in sample program 7-12 (above) appears below (sample program 7-13). It illustrates the *second* advantage of the *subroutine* form over the *function* form: ability to alter the values of arguments within the subprogram. The sorting problem (treated earlier in sample program 6-9) requires such reassignment of values, to accomplish storage interchanges.

```
C SAMPLE PROGRAM 7-13
C THIS SUBROUTINE SUBPROGRAM MAKES SAMPLE PROGRAM 6-9
                                     PERMANENTLY AVAILABLE
      SUBROUTINE SORT(X, N)
      DIMENSION X(1000)
      LIMIT = N − 1
      DO 2 INDEX = 1, LIMIT
      NSMALL = INDEX
      ISTART = INDEX + 1
      DO 1 I = ISTART, N
 1    IF (X(I) .LT. X(NSMALL)) NSMALL = I
      SAVE = X(NSMALL)
      X(NSMALL) = X(INDEX)
 2    X(INDEX) = SAVE
      RETURN
      END
```

The conversion of sample program 6-9 to *subroutine subprogram* form is thus accomplished by inserting the SUBROUTINE statement, extracting the READ and PRINT statements, and substituting RETURN for STOP. Note that the "1000" in the DIMENSION statement does not now actually describe the dimensions of the array to be handled at execution time.

If you look back now at sample program 7-12, you should see that the calling program, after printing the mean and standard deviation, calls the SORT subprogram and then reprints the 300 grades in ascending order.

THE COMMON STATEMENT

The COMMON statement provides a method for making values available to both main program and subprograms *without mentioning them as arguments*. If a subprogram began,

> SUBROUTINE FORM
> COMMON A, B, C, K
> --------------------------

and a main program contained the statements

> COMMON X, Y, Z, J
> --------------------------
> CALL FORM
> --------------------------

the values A and X would share a single storage location, as would B and Y, C and Z, and K and J. This would also have been the case, if these names had appeared in *argument lists:*

SUBROUTINE FORM (A, B, C, K)   (subprogram)

CALL FORM (X, Y, Z, J)   (calling statement in main program)

In both usages, the variables listed need not agree *in name,* but must agree in total *storage length* and in *mode*. However, the following statements match satisfactorily by these criteria:

COMMON A, B, C, D, E   COMMON X(4), TORQUE

Thus the COMMON statement may be used to declare dimensionality (in lieu of a DIMENSION statement); and *only* storage length and mode must be matched, not actual *order* of names. In the example above, A and X(1) share a location, as do B and X(2), etc.

It may be useful to outline the actual method employed by the compiler, in arranging the storage. In reaction to the COMMON statement, it reserves storage for the accompanying list of variables in a special "COMMON" area of storage, in the order in which they are named. Since this reaction is the same whenever the statement is encountered, and the compiler always begins the reservations at the beginning of the COMMON area, variables so listed in main programs and subprograms automatically share storage locations that are simply referenced by different names.

Sample program 7-14 shows the SORT subprogram rewritten to eliminate the entire argument list, by using the COMMON statement:

```
C SAMPLE PROGRAM 7-14
C THIS VERSION OF THE SORT SUBPROGRAM MAKES USE OF THE
C                       COMMON STATEMENT, FOR ALL ARGUMENTS
      SUBROUTINE SORT
      COMMON X(1000), N
      LIMIT = N − 1
      DO 2 INDEX = 1, LIMIT
      NSMALL = INDEX
      ISTART = INDEX + 1
      DO 1 I = ISTART, N
1     IF (X(I) .LT. X(NSMALL)) NSMALL = I
      SAVE = X(NSMALL)
      X(NSMALL) = X(INDEX)
2     X(INDEX) = SAVE
      RETURN
      END
```

When a variable has been mentioned in a COMMON list, it must *not* be mentioned in an argument list. Sample program 7-15 (below) shows a calling program that mentions SORT without any arguments at all; the necessary values have been assigned locations in the COMMON area.

```
C SAMPLE PROGRAM 7-15
C THIS CALLING PROGRAM USES THE 7-14 VERSION OF SORT
      COMMON GRADE(300), WASTE(700), NUMBER
      DATA NUMBER/300/
      READ, GRADE
      CALL SORT
      PRINT, GRADE
      STOP
      END
```

Notice that the variable WASTE has been used simply to fill part of the COMMON storage area, so that NUMBER (main program) and N (subprogram) are properly positioned.

```
      COMMON GRADE(300), NUMBER
```

would have caused an error; and the subprogram COMMON statement must mention a genuine specific storage length; that is,

```
SUBROUTINE SORT
COMMON X(1), N
```

would not work.

For Review

subprogram
statement function
function name
dummy arguments
calling statement
returned value
function subprogram
RETURN statement
calling program
main program
subroutine subprogram
subprogram name
dummy arguments
CALL statement
COMMON statement

Examples

CUBRT(A) = A ** (1./3.)
CUBRT
    A
SUM = SUM + CURBRT (64.0)
    4.0
FUNCTION CUBRT(A)
RETURN

SUBROUTINE STAT1(X, N, XMEAN, STDEV)
    STAT1
    X N XMEAN STDEV
CALL STAT1(A, 50, XM, SX)
COMMON X(1000), N, XMEAN, STDEV
COMMON A(1000), N, XM, SX

Programming Exercises

7-1. Write a *statement function* that will have three integer arguments, representing hours, minutes, and seconds. The function is to return, as an integer, the total number of *seconds* represented by the three arguments. Test this by including it in a program using a calling statement with actual arguments 3 hours, 21 minutes, 14 seconds.

7-2. Rewrite the statement function in Exercise 7-1, as a complete *function subprogram*. Also write a calling program to test the subprogram (use the 7-1 suggested arguments).

7-3. Write a *function subprogram* that will examine a single-dimensioned real array, and return an integer signal value "0" if any zero elements are discovered; otherwise, it will return the signal value as "1". Include the size of the array as an argument. Test with a calling program using the entire 72-item data deck, split into two 36-element arrays for two separate "calls" of the function.

7-4. Write a *function subprogram* that returns (as an integer) the total *number* of *nonzero* elements found in an array of N elements. Test with a calling program that uses the entire data deck (72 elements).

7-5. Write a *function subprogram* that returns the *smallest* value of any *real array*. Test it by writing a calling program that uses the entire data deck (72 elements).

7-6. Write a *function subprogram* that returns the arithmetic mean of the *diagonal* elements (upper left to lower right diagonal) of any *square* real array. Test by also writing a calling program that treats the first 25 data values as a 5 x 5 array.

7-7. Write a *subroutine subprogram* that will reverse the procedure indicated in Exercise 7-1; that is, given any number of seconds, it will return the equivalent time in hours, minutes, and seconds. (Do you see why this must be in *subroutine* form?) Test it with a calling program, using 12,074 seconds as argument. (*Note*: the MOD function described in Chapter 4 may be useful in the subprogram.)

7-8. Adjust the subprogram and calling program in Exercise 7-7 by placing all arguments in COMMON. Test again.

7-9. Write a *subroutine subprogram* that will replace all elements of a single-dimensioned array ("N" elements) by their own logarithms (base 10). (Why is the *subroutine* form required?) Test with a calling program using the first 20 data values.

CHAPTER 8

OTHER VARIABLE TYPES

EXPLICIT TYPE SPECIFICATION

We have been using two major types of variables: *real* and *integer*. Three other modes are usually available: *double precision, complex,* and *logical*.[1] There is no *implicit* specification convention for any of these types (such as the first-character distinction between real and integer names). Therefore, the programmer must declare each of these modes by using *explicit type specification* statements:

> DOUBLE PRECISION X, Y, B(12)
> COMPLEX GAUGE, CROSS (10)
> LOGICAL MAN, BOY, PARENT(2)

Note that when a *subscripted* variable is to be typed by one of these statements, dimension information may appear within the statement, and should not then be repeated in DIMENSION (or COMMON) statements.

DOUBLE PRECISION VARIABLES

Double precision variables are effectively in *real* mode, but are stored in "longer" locations that permit representation of numbers with greater *precision* (usually, approximately twice as many significant digits). Since actual

---

[1] A CHARACTER specification, available only in WATFIV, is discussed in Chapter 10.

125

storage is in *exponential* form (see Chapter 2), the *range* of possible values (determined by the *exponent* storage length) is not affected by the double precision declaration. For example, the results of

$$\text{X} = 1111111. ** 2 \quad \text{and} \quad \begin{array}{l} \text{DOUBLE PRECISION X} \\ \text{X} = 1111111.\text{D}+0 ** 2 \end{array}$$

are stored (assuming 7-digit single precision and 16-digit double precision)[2] as

$$.1234567\text{E}+13 \quad \text{and} \quad .1234567654321000\text{E}+13$$

The usefulness of the double precision arrangement to the programmer arises in several situations. First, some problems require accuracy to a greater number of digits than ordinary ("single") precision provides. The use of the mathematical constant π might be restricted to

$$\text{PI} = 3.141593$$

in single precision. But

$$\begin{array}{l} \text{DOUBLE PRECISION PI, ANSWER} \\ \text{PI} = 3.141592653589793 \end{array}$$

may be useful for a problem in which a highly precise answer is needed.

DOUBLE PRECISION CONSTANTS

The *constant* shown in the last example is written in ordinary decimal form; constants written with more than seven digits are recognized as *double precision* mode by the compiler. However, constants written with less than eight digits· must be specified as *double precision* by using a variant of exponential notation, substituting "D" for "E". For example,

$$\begin{array}{l} \text{DOUBLE PRECISION TWO} \\ \text{TWO} = 1.\text{D}+0/.3\text{D}+1 \end{array}$$

results in storage of 16 "threes" in the TWO location; but

$$\begin{array}{l} \text{DOUBLE PRECISION TWO} \\ \text{TWO} = 1./3. \end{array}$$

would succeed in placing only *seven* digits of the result in storage. That is, we would obtain

---

[2] The "7" and "16" are usual for IBM 360 series, RCA Spectra series, and some other computer systems. These numbers are used as examples, throughout this section.

$$.3333333000000000E + 0$$

instead of

$$.3333333333333333E + 0$$

A second advantage of *double precision* relates to the *binary* storage form for digits, used by the computer. Binary storage results in approximate representation—"rounding error"—of decimals that do not correspond exactly to sums of available negative powers of the base 2. Since *double precision* increases the number of such negative powers that may be used, it results in closer approximations. In effect, rounding error is pushed further to the right of the number. For example,

$$ONE = 1./3.$$

places only seven "threes" in storage, and nonzero "garbage" follows the last "three."

A third advantage of *double precision* mode is discussed in Chapter 10, in connection with storage of *alphameric* (i.e., nonnumeric) characters. For example, the word

NEGATIVE

requires two named storage locations in single precision, but fits into one *double precision* location.

DOUBLE PRECISION FUNCTIONS

Many of the FORTRAN-supplied functions are duplicated for the special case of double precision arguments (and return double precision results). A "D" usually appears in front of the usual function name. These are:

(1 argument)

DLOG	logarithm (base e)
DLOG10	logarithm (base 10)
DEXP	antilogarithm (base e)
DSQRT	square root
DSIN	sine
DCOS	cosine
DATAN	arctangent
DTANH	hyperbolic tangent
DABS	absolute value
DFLOAT	convert from integer to double precision form
IDINT	convert from double precision to integer form

(2 arguments)

    DATAN2   arctangent of a_1/a_2
    DSIGN a_1 gets sign of a_2

(2 or more arguments)

    DMAX1   largest of arguments
    DMIN1   smallest of arguments

In addition, two specialized functions deal with double precision values. They are both concerned with conversion between single and double precision form:

(1)   DOUBLE PRECISION V

        A = X + SNGL(V)

This use of the SNGL function calls for conversion of V to single precision form for the computation. Note that *mixed expressions*, containing double precision and real or integer modes, are usually evaluated (by the compiler) by conversion to *double precision* — just as mixed expressions containing real and integer modes are evaluated by conversion to *real* mode. That is, the *modal hierarchy* is

    double precision (highest)
    real
    integer (lowest)

Thus if the SNGL function were not used in example (1) above, the arithmetic would be done in double precision.

(2)   DOUBLE PRECISION V

        V = DBLE(X) + 7

The DBLE function converts X to double precision form for the computation. Then, because of the hierarchy rule for mixed expressions mentioned above, this also results in conversion of the "7" to double precision prior to addition. However, the compiler-initiated conversion step (which consumes some execution time) could be avoided by writing

    V = DBLE(X) + 7.D+0

The WATFOR and WATFIV compilers impose a requirement on the programmer using double precision functions, which usually is *not* necessary in FORTRAN. This is the inclusion of the *name* of any double precision functions to be used, in an *explicit type specification* (DOUBLE PRECISION)

statement. (Of course, IDINT and SNGL are exempt from this requirement, since they do not return double precision results).

Sample program 8-1 illustrates the use of double precision variables, constants, and functions.

```
C SAMPLE PROGRAM 8-1
C THIS PROGRAM USES DOUBLE PRECISION VARIABLES AND
C   CONSTANTS, AND CALLS A DOUBLE PRECISION FUNCTION
      DOUBLE PRECISION PI, AREA(45), SUM, SUMD, AMEAN,
                                              SDAREA, DSQRT
      DATA PI/3.141592653589793/, SUM, SUMD/2 * 0.D+0/
      ┌DO 1 I = 1, 45
      │READ, RADIUS
      │AREA(I) = PI * RADIUS ** 2
    1 └SUM = SUM + AREA(I)
      AMEAN = SUM/45.D+0
      ┌DO 2 I = 1, 45
    2 └SUMD = SUMD + (AREA(I) − AMEAN) ** 2
      SDAREA = DSQRT(SUMD/45.D+0)
      PRINT, AMEAN, SDAREA
      STOP
      END
```

Sample program 8-1 (above) computes 45 circle areas from

$$\text{area} = \pi r^2$$

and computes and prints the arithmetic mean and standard deviation of these areas. The output is printed to 16 digits, rather than the usual seven. If we had written

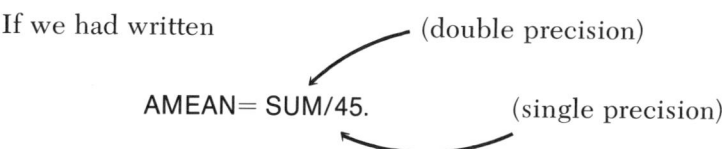

AMEAN= SUM/45.   (single precision)

the result would not be changed, since the rule for *mixed expressions* is conversion to double precision (by the compiler) before execution of the arithmetic operator. The program statement

AREA(I) = PI * RADIUS ** 2
         ↑   ↖
      double   single precision
      precision

does contain a *mixed* expression. We might have written

AREA(I) = PI * DBLE(RADIUS) ** 2

In that case, however, note that DBLE would have to be added to the list in the DOUBLE PRECISION statement, which already contains the name of the DSQRT function.

COMPLEX VARIABLES

The information in this section is of little value to those of us (I include myself) who do not use *complex numbers* in the usual course of events. If the value

$$5.0 + 2.0\ i$$

where $i = \sqrt{-1}$ has no meaning to you, you will not miss anything by skipping to the section on logical variables.

Those who remain will recognize that $i = \sqrt{-1}$ is an *imaginary number*, and that the value above would be obtained as one of the roots of

$$3X^2 - 30X + 87 = 0$$

Complex numbers are always of the general form

$$a + bi$$
$$c + di$$

where a, b, c, and d are real numbers. They may be handled in computation, but the rules are highly specialized. The product of the two values above is obtained from

$$(ac - bd) + (ad + bc)\ i$$

and their quotient is

$$\frac{ac + bd}{c^2 + d^2} + \frac{bc - ad}{c^2 + d^2}\ i$$

FORTRAN provides automatic implementation of such computation procedures, as well as some more complicated ones, when the programmer declares variables to be in *complex* mode. The usual arithmetic operators may be employed. (For the ** operator, the exponent must be in integer mode.)

COMPLEX CONSTANTS

Complex *constants* are written with parentheses enclosing the two components (both in real mode), which are separated by a comma. Thus

COMPLEX X

X = (6.0, 3.25)

If complex values are to be read as data, the same format should be followed on the data card. That is, the effect above would be accomplished by

> COMPLEX X
> ----------------
> READ, X

in conjunction with a data card containing

> (6.0, 3.25)

Complex and simple real values may be mixed in arithmetic expressions, as they may in ordinary mathematical usage. The result is always a complex value. If the above example continued,

> X = X + Y

where Y has not been declared COMPLEX, Y will be used as the complex number

> Y + 0i

COMPLEX FUNCTIONS

Some of the functions already examined for *real* and *double precision* modes are available for *complex* arguments (and return a *complex* result); they are designated by a "C" in front of the usual name. Furthermore, some functions (beginning with "CD") deal with *complex* arguments in *double precision* mode:

CLOG	logarithm (base e)	CDLOG
CEXP	antilogarithm (base e)	CDEXP
CSQRT	square root	CDSQRT
CSIN	sine	CDSIN
CCOS	cosine	CDCOS
CABS	absolute value	CDABS

Additionally, four new functions apply only to manipulation of complex values:

(1)
> COMPLEX X
> ----------------------
> A = REAL(X) + B

The REAL function returns the first (*real*, in the mathematical sense) portion of the complex value.

(2)
> COMPLEX X
> ----------------------
> A = AIMAG(X) + B

The AIMAG function returns the second (*imaginary*) portion of the complex value (using it as a real number, disregarding i).

(3) COMPLEX X, CMPLX

X = CMPLX(A, B)

The CMPLX function combines any two real arguments into a complex number. The arguments may be real variables, constants, or arithmetic expressions. Thus

COMPLEX V, Y, CMPLX

V = CMPLX(A, B + 6.3)
Y = CMPLX(B, 8.0)

both arithmetic statements are valid. Note that the last statement is in correct form, whereas the expression in parentheses would *not* be recognized as a legal complex *constant*. That is,

Y = (B, 8.0)

would not be legal. Also observe that the last two examples indicate that functions returning *complex* results must be declared in *explicit type specification* statements (in WATFOR and WATFIV only).

(4) COMPLEX V, W, CONJG

W = CONJG(V)

The CONJG function returns the complex *conjugate* of the complex argument; the *conjugate* is defined

$$\text{conj}(a + bi) = (a - bi)$$

The last two functions (CMPLX and CONJG) are also usually available for *double precision* arguments (and return *double precision complex* values):

DCMPLX
DCONJG

Sample program 8–2 illustrates the use of complex variables, constants, and functions.

```
C SAMPLE PROGRAM 8-2
C THIS PROGRAM USES COMPLEX VARIABLES AND CONSTANTS,
C                  AND FUNCTIONS PERTAINING TO THEM
      COMPLEX X, Y, PROD, QUOT, XNEW, YNEW, POWER, CMPLX
      READ, X, Y, Z
```

```
    PROD = X * Y
    QUOT = X/Y
    XNEW = X + (6.0, 3.0)
    YNEW = Y + CMPLX(Z, 3.0)
    M = REAL(X) + AIMAG(Y)
    POWER = (XNEW + YNEW) ** M
    PRINT, PROD, QUOT, XNEW, YNEW, POWER
    STOP
    END
```

Two data values are required for each *complex* variable in the input list (therefore, a total of five input values are needed for sample program 8–2). And the output will consist of two real (in the programming sense) numbers for each *complex* variable in the output list. (Therefore, there are 10 output values in sample program 8–2.)

LOGICAL VARIABLES AND CONSTANTS

We have seen that the declaration of variables as DOUBLE PRECISION or COMPLEX does not alter the programmer's usual intention of performing arithmetic computation and numerical input and output. But the declaration of any variable as LOGICAL conveys a rather different purpose. A *logical variable* has only two possible values: *"true"* and *"false."* Logical constants are represented as one of these two words, surrounded by decimal points:

```
    LOGICAL MAN, BOY, CHILD
    MAN = .TRUE.
    BOY = .FALSE.
```

LOGICAL-VALUED EXPRESSIONS

Obviously, variables such as these cannot be combined with other variables in arithmetic. However, their values may be defined (or changed) by *logical-valued expressions*. We have seen such expressions (in Chapter 5) within the parentheses of the *Logical IF statement*. They may appear *without* the "IF" arrangement only when the variable mentioned to the left of the equal sign has been declared LOGICAL. Thus

```
            MAN = AGE1 .GE. 21.0
```

is a valid statement (continuing the example above), and in effect says, "If AGE1 (an arithmetic *real* variable) is equal to or greater than 21.0, assign the value .TRUE. to MAN; otherwise, assign the value .FALSE. to MAN."

A *logical-valued expression* must contain *either*:

(a) *arithmetic variables and arithmetic constants* separated by relational and logical operators, *or*

(b) *logical variables* separated by relational and logical operators, *or*

(c) combinations of *logical variables, arithmetic variables,* and *arithmetic constants,* separated by relational and logical operators, *or*

(d) a single *logical constant.*

Examples of the four possible forms appear below:

(a) Arithmetic variables and constants:

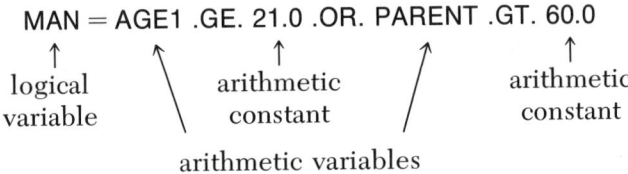

(In the example above, MAN is assigned the .TRUE. value if *either* of the statement parts is true. In the example below, the .TRUE. value is assigned only if *both* parts of the statement are true):

MAN = AGE1 .GE. 21.0 .AND. PARENT .GT. 60.0

(b) Logical variables:

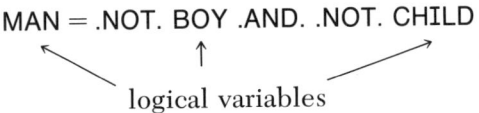

(If BOY and CHILD both have current values of .FALSE., the value .TRUE. will be assigned to MAN; if either BOY or CHILD is .TRUE., MAN will be assigned as .FALSE.)

(c) Combinations of (a) and (b):

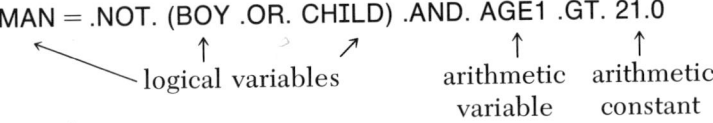

(Note that the first part of this statement represents another method of writing the last example above, in (b).)

(d) There is no possibility of mentioning *logical constants* (.TRUE. or .FALSE.) in the mixtures shown in (a), (b), and (c) above. However, the shortest *logical-valued expressions* contain only a single logical constant:

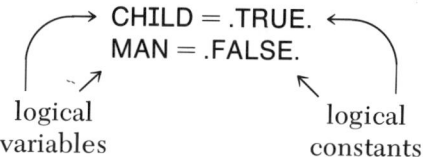

Sample program 8-3 (below) employs a logical variable, which is assigned a .TRUE. value only if a *right triangle* is encountered in a data set. (The Pythagorean theorem is being used: the right-triangle condition is proved by showing that the square of one side is equal to the sum of squares of the other two sides).

```
C SAMPLE PROGRAM 8-3
C THIS PROGRAM USES A LOGICAL VARIABLE
      LOGICAL RIGHT
      DO 1 K = 1, 100
      READ, A, B, C
      AA = A ** 2
      BB = B ** 2
      CC = C ** 2
      RIGHT = AA .EQ. BB + CC .OR. BB .EQ. AA + CC .OR. CC .EQ. AA + BB
    1 PRINT, K, A, B, C, RIGHT
      STOP
      END
```

INPUT/OUTPUT OF LOGICAL VARIABLES

The format-free output representation for .TRUE. is "T", and for .FALSE. it is "F". Therefore, output lines from sample program 8-3 will look like this:

```
1    0.3000000E 01    0.4000000E 01    0.6000000E 01    F
2    0.3000000E 01    0.4000000E 01    0.5000000E 01    T
```

When logical variables appear in *input* lists, the data card is scanned until any "T" or "F" is encountered. Thus, keypunching of the full constant .TRUE. or .FALSE. is not necessary.

THE LOGICAL IF STATEMENT AGAIN

In Chapter 5, we included inside the parentheses of Logical IF statements *only* statements from category (a) above—that is, using only *arithmetic* variables and constants. It is also possible to include statements of types (b) or (c)—that is, those using *logical* variables, and combinations of *arithmetic* and *logical* variables:

IF (MAN .AND. BOY) DIFF = AGE1 − AGE2

logical variables

(The statement at the right is executed only if both MAN and BOY currently are stored as .TRUE.)

IF (MAN .OR. AGE2 .GE. 12.0) FARE = FULL

logical variable   arithmetic variable   arithmetic constant

(The statement at the right is executed if MAN is currently .TRUE., or the value stored in AGE2 is equal to or greater than 12.0.)

Sample program 8–4 (below) uses logical variables and operators within a Logical IF statement, as a convenient (though never absolutely *necessary*) form in a personnel-selection problem. Given a 5000 card deck containing on each man's card his age (years), height (inches), weight (pounds), marital status (0 = single, 1 = married), IQ test score, and number of years of education, the specifications being sought are:

Age:	less than 35 years
Height:	equal to or greater than 67 inches
Weight:	between 150 and 170 pounds, inclusive
Marital status:	single
Intelligence:	*either* IQ score greater than 120, *or* more than 12 years of education.

```
C SAMPLE PROGRAM 8-4
C THIS PROGRAM SELECTS MEN WITH CERTAIN QUALIFICATIONS
      LOGICAL AGE, HEIGHT, WEIGHT, MARITL, INTELL
      DO 1 I = 1, 5000
      READ, NAGE, NH, NW, NSM, IQ, NYEARS
      AGE = NAGE .LT. 35
      HEIGHT = NH .GE. 67
      WEIGHT = NW .GE. 150 .AND. NW .LE. 170
      MARITL = NSM .EQ. 0
      INTELL = IQ .GT. 120 .OR. NYEARS .GT. 12
    1 IF (AGE .AND. HEIGHT .AND. WEIGHT .AND. MARITL .AND. INTELL)
                                                         PRINT, I
      STOP
      END
```

You should see that the program could be shortened, by substituting after the READ statement, for the next six statements,

```
1      IF (NAGE .LT. 35 .AND. NH .GE. 67 .AND. NW .GE. 150 .AND. NW .LE.
       170 .AND. NSM .EQ. 0 .AND. (IQ .GT. 120 .OR. NYEARS .GT. 12)) PRINT, I
```

This style uses *arithmetic* variables, rather than *logical* variables.

For Review	*Examples*
explicit type specification	REAL IN, JOB
	INTEGER ALLEN, BOB
	DOUBLE PRECISION PI, X, Y
	COMPLEX GAUGE, CROSS(10)
	LOGICAL MAN, BOY, PARENT(2)
double precision variable	PI,X,Y
double precision constant	PI = 3.141592653589793
	X = 1.4D+3
double precision function	Y = DSQRT(X)
complex variable	GAUGE,CROSS
complex constant	GAUGE = CROSS(1) + (6.0, 3.25)
complex function	CROSS(2) = CSQRT(GAUGE)
logical variable	MAN,BOY,PARENT
logical constant	MAN = .TRUE.
	BOY = .FALSE.
logical-valued expression	I .GT. 3 .AND. .NOT. (MAN .OR. BOY)

Programming Exercises

8-1. The exact value of 20! is 2,432,902,008,176,640,000. Write a program that obtains the value in single precision and in *double precision*, for comparison.

8-2. Write a *subroutine subprogram* that will return the arithmetic mean and standard deviation (see sample program 7-11), as *double precision* values, for elements 1 through N of any DOUBLE PRECISION one-dimensional array. Test your subprogram with a calling program using the entire data set (72 elements) as the argument array.

8-3. To solve the quadratic equation

$$aX^2 + bX + c$$

we have examined earlier the solution for both roots,

$$\frac{-b \pm \sqrt{b^2 - 4ac}}{2a}$$

If $b^2 - 4ac$ (the *"discriminant"*) is negative, the roots are *complex numbers*. Write a program that reads six sets of coefficients a, b, and c, and produces both roots of each equation. The program should switch to COMPLEX storage locations for computations and output, when the discriminant is found to be negative. Remember that

$$\sqrt{-d} = \sqrt{d}\sqrt{-1} = \sqrt{d}\ i$$

and that complex numbers cannot be "automatically" generated by attempting to obtain square roots of negative arguments.

8-4. For two *complex numbers* (a + bi) and (c + di), the *quotient* is obtained from

$$\frac{a+bi}{c+di} = \frac{ac+bd}{c^2+d^2} + \frac{bc-ad}{c^2+d^2}i$$

Write a subroutine subprogram that returns the result as two real values, operating on four real arguments that have *not* been declared COMPLEX. Test the subprogram with a calling program that (*a*) calls on this subprogram to accomplish the result, for the first four data values (first data card), and (*b*) uses the CMPLX function to form two COMPLEX values from the four real arguments, and prints the result of division using the two COMPLEX values.

8-5. A firm organizes its personnel records with one card for each employee, containing in order:

(1) social security number (written as a continuous 9-digit integer)
(2) age in years (integer)
(3) marital status, keypunched as "TIED" or "FREE"
(4) score (integer) on company's intelligence test
(5) number of years employed (integer)

Write a program that will print the social security number of each employee meeting *all* of the following qualifications:

(a) between 25 and 35 years old (inclusive)
(b) single
(c) score of *at least* 75 on the intelligence test
(d) employed three years or more

Test your program on these three data cards:

```
111111111  24  FREE  78  4
222222222  28  FREE  80  5
333333333  29  TIED  85  3
```

8-6. A *truth table* that frequently appears in logic textbooks shows the logical values (True or False) resulting from various combinations of logical values and logical expressions:

Values		Expressions					
p q	p and q	not (p and q)	not p	not q	not p and not q	not p or not q
T T						
T F						
F T						
F F						

Write a program that "computes" the 24 values for the table, and prints them in the 4 x 6 organization shown. (For a short program, try a two-element *array*, initialize its values with a DATA statement, and do the work with a double DO loop, putting results into a six-element array.)

CHAPTER 9

INPUT/OUTPUT WITH FORMAT; NUMERIC FIELDS

I/O STATEMENT FORM

WATFOR and WATFIV provide convenient *FORMAT-free* input and output statements, which we have used to this point:

        READ, input list   (refers to card reader)
        PRINT, output list   (refers to on-line printer)
        PUNCH, output list (refers to card punch)

When these statements are used, the programmer need not further specify I/O equipment, nor describe the precise *form* and *position* of values on data cards or printer page.

However, these two compilers provide as an option, and most FORTRAN compilers require as mandatory, input/output statements that specify *by number* (a) the input/output equipment unit desired, and (b) a FORMAT statement containing detailed instructions on form and position of values listed (as variable names, usually) in the I/O statements. The general form[1] is

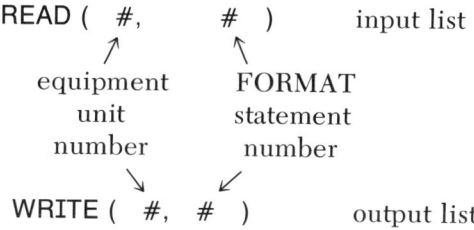

[1] Though the general form shown is the same for WATFOR/WATFIV and standard FORTRAN compilers, one difference persists: WATFOR and WATFIV permit *arithmetic expressions* in output lists following WRITE (#, #), while standard FORTRAN compilers permit variable names only.

EQUIPMENT UNIT NUMBERS

The word READ now becomes a general verb meaning *"input"*; the card reader is but one of many input devices that may be "on-line" to the computer. There usually is a console typewriter, and there may be magnetic tape drives, paper tape drives, magnetic disks, etc. The *equipment unit number* (the first number in parentheses following READ) is used to select among the alternative devices, which are uniquely numbered by the individual installation.

Similarly, the word WRITE is used as a general *output* verb; the *equipment unit number* selects between available on-line devices such as high-speed printers, the console typewriter, a card punch, magnetic tape units, etc.

The *equipment unit number* always appears; it may be written as an integer *constant*, or as an integer *variable*, whose value must have been assigned prior to execution of the I/O statement. The integer *variable* is useful in this position when a program is to be tested on one system and run on another, or there is the possibility that assigned equipment unit numbers may change for other reasons. Thus something like

READ (IN, 150) X, Y, Z

WRITE (IOUT, 175) PROD, ANS, I, J

may appear throughout a program (assume a large number of input and output statements to make the technique worthwhile). The program should then say earlier,

IN = 5
IOUT = 6

or, using the DATA initialization statement,

DATA IN, IOUT/ 5, 6/

The idea is that an equipment unit number change may be inserted by altering one or two cards, rather than dozens of I/O statements. (The numbers used in the example above will appear in sample programs to represent the card reader (5) and the on-line printer (6).)

The *FORMAT statement number* may be omitted, with the meaning that values are to be transmitted in storage form (binary code). Thus

WRITE (2) X, Y, Z, I

calls for reproduction of the binary representations currently occupying the named locations. The same material might then be read back into storage (assume equipment unit number 2 above is a card punch) by

READ (5) X, Y, Z, I

Remember, however, that omission of the parentheses altogether, an option in WATFOR and WATFIV, is interpreted as referring to decimal, exponential, and integer notation, not to binary storage form; and that such omission is illegal for most FORTRAN compilers.

THE FORMAT STATEMENT

The FORMAT statement is nonexecutable. FORMAT statements may be physically placed almost anywhere in the source program, since they are really ignored during execution until mentioned in an input or output statement by number. Thus, each FORMAT statement must be numbered, and may be referenced by more than one input and/or output statement within the program. (I/O statements must contain the FORMAT statement number written as a *constant* only.) For example,

```
10   FORMAT (F10.2, I6)
     READ (5, 10) A, J
     WRITE (6, 10) A, J
     -------------------------------------
     WRITE (6, 10) ANSWER, NUMBER
```

However, any number of FORMAT statements may appear within the program. Thus, three *different* FORMAT statements might have been referenced in the example above.

The word FORMAT (which begins the actual statement; i.e., usually appears beginning in column 7) is followed by parentheses that contain detailed instructions for form of output, including (as we shall see) vertical position, horizontal position, type of notation (e.g., decimal, exponential, integer), number of decimal places, and "labels" to appear with output values.

FIELDS, RECORDS, AND FILES

We begin the study of FORMAT notation by defining some of the terms used in the discussion that follows.

A *field* is any set of characters (columns) to be treated as a unit for transmission, storage, and so on. We shall refer to the *field* as being "w" characters in *width*.

A *record* is a set of *fields* treated as a unit during transfer of information. For punched cards, each card is considered a separate *record*. Thus a card *record* may have 8 10-column fields, or 20 4-column fields, and so on. In connection with printer output, each line of print is considered a separate record. If the print line is 120 characters long (132 is also common), then it may contain 8 15-column fields, or 20 6-column fields, etc. For other media (e.g., magnetic tape), record length may be variable, and is indicated by special "end-of-record" marks, inserted as the initial inscription is performed.

A *file* is a collection of *records* treated as a unit. Suppose a payroll problem involves a punched card for each employee showing his name, wage rate, tax rate, social security number, and hours worked, and that there are 3750 employees. There are then five *fields* per *record*, and 3750 *records* in the *file;* the *file* consists of one or more boxes or drawers of cards.

A *numeric field* contains a number. However, it may include, in addition to numeric characters, certain special characters: decimal point, plus sign or minus sign—and certain alphabetic characters: E for numbers in exponential form, D for numbers in double precision form. The following record contains four numeric fields:

$$124.78 \quad -175 \quad 1.8E13 \quad 1.3D14$$

An *alphameric field* may contain *any* combination of characters that may be keypunched, including alphabetic and special characters as well as digits. The following record contains two alphameric fields and one numeric field:

JOHN JONES	858 ASPEN WAY	145.78
alphameric field	alphameric field	numeric field

As this example implies, the division of the record into fields is at least partially the responsibility of the programmer; for example, the 858 could be treated as a *numeric* field. For that matter, the 145.78 could be treated as *alphameric*; and the "JOHN JONES" could be treated as two alphameric fields, or as many as ten alphameric fields (each one character wide).

FORMAT NOTATION FOR NUMERIC FIELDS

We now list the characters that may appear *within the FORMAT statement,* when the programmer is referring to *numeric* fields:

Notation Character	Meaning
F	Real variable; in decimal form
E	Real variable; in exponential form
D	Real variable; in double precision form
I	Integer variable
G	Stands for *"General";* may be used for any numeric form above, and also for Logical and Complex variables.
P	*"Scale factor";* requests a shift of the decimal point, during transfer of real values

Of these possibilities, the two in most common use for numeric fields are F and I. Sample program 9-1 shows a usage example.

```
C SAMPLE PROGRAM 9-1
C THIS IS PROGRAM 3-1, WRITTEN WITH PROGRAMMER-SUPPLIED
                                             OUTPUT FORMAT
       ┌DO 16 I = 1, 100
       │FAHREN = 1.8 * I + 32.
   16  └WRITE (6, 20) I, FAHREN
   20   FORMAT (I10, F10.1)
        STOP
        END
```

F NOTATION IN OUTPUT

In sample program 9-1, the specification

F10.1

calls for ordinary decimal notation ("F"),[2] in a field *10* characters wide, including *one* postdecimal digit. The general form is

nFw.d

in which "n" may be used to repeat the specification, "w" indicates the total width of the field, and "d" the postdecimal width. The "n" (if it appears), "w", and "d" must all be *integer constants*. If "n" is omitted, a value of "1" is assumed. The statements

WRITE (6, 105) A, B, C
105   FORMAT (2F12.2, F5.0)

arrange that the A and B values will both appear in 12-column fields, each with two postdecimal digits; while C will be printed in a 5-column field, with no postdecimal digits. In the absence of instructions to the contrary, they all appear on the same record—in this case, side by side on a single line of print, which is a total of 29 characters wide. Note that "blanks" are considered as "characters," in this usage.

Commas may be used to separate FORMAT notation expressions, but are not mandatory unless ambiguity would result from omission (usually because a "d" runs into an "n"). For example,

(F10.2,3F5.1)

---

[2] The letter F derives from "Floating Point," a term used to describe the storage/transfer method mentioned earlier: the decimal point is "floated" to the position indicated by the stored exponent value.

would produce error if written

(F10.23F5.1)

However, FORMAT 105 (above) could have been written without the comma:

105   FORMAT (2F12.2F5.0)

RIGHT-JUSTIFICATION

Values output in numeric fields are always *right-justified* by the computer; that is, when the field specified in FORMAT is wider than necessary (which is usually the case), blank characters are filled in to the *left* of the number. This follows the usual handwriting convention:

$$\left.\begin{matrix} 124.65 \\ 1.72 \\ 3826.33 \end{matrix}\right\} \text{rather than} \left\{\begin{matrix} 124.65 \\ 1.72 \\ 3826.33 \end{matrix}\right.$$

Therefore, a change in the size of "w" actually affects the *horizontal position* of the output values. For example, if the three numbers on the left above are specified as F30.2 instead of F20.2, the effect would be displacement of the numbers to the *right* (inserting more blanks at the left). This is shown in sample program 9–2.

```
C   SAMPLE PROGRAM 9-2
C   THIS FORMAT ALTERS PROGRAM 9-1 BY MOVING THE REAL
C                           OUTPUT COLUMN FURTHER TO THE RIGHT
20      FORMAT (I10, F25.1)
        DO 16 I = 1, 100
        FAHREN = 1.8 * I + 32.
16      WRITE (6, 20) I, FAHREN
        STOP
        END
```

Note that the movement of the FORMAT statement to the top has *no* effect during execution.

TRUNCATION OF DIGITS; ROUNDING

The "d" value used by the programmer in nFw.d specifies the number of postdecimal digits to be printed. The WATFOR and WATFIV compiler programs arrange for proper *rounding* of the last (rightmost) printed digit. This is illustrated in sample program 9–3:

```
C   SAMPLE PROGRAM 9-3
C   ROUNDING ARRANGED BY WATFOR AND WATFIV
```

```
        A = 2./3.
        PRINT, A
        WRITE (6, 10) A, A, A
10      FORMAT (F9.4, F9.2, F9.0)
        STOP
        END
```

The output appears as follows:

```
              0.6666666E 00
              0.6667      0.67         1.
```

SIZE OF "w" AND "d"

We have already observed that large "w" specifications merely create extra blanks at the left of the field, shifting digital output to the right. They actually provide a useful "automatic" method for horizontal displacement. For example,

F60.2

arranges for printing of the output number right-justified approximately in the *middle* of a 120-column printer page. Similarly,

F120.2

would end the printed value at the extreme right of the page. Thus the *maximum* "w" size is actually equal to the width of the permissible *record* on the output device being used. For output on punched cards,

F80.2

would be legal, but larger "w" values would produce execution errors. But note that

F70.2, F80.2

would produce an execution error on *either* output device, since this specifies a record 150 characters wide.

The *minimum* "w" size presents a more difficult question. The total field width specified must be large enough to accommodate (1) the number of predecimal digits currently indicated in storage (i.e., size of the stored exponent),[3] (2) the number of postdecimal digits specified by "d," (3) the decimal point,

---

[3] But even if the stored exponent is zero (no predecimal digits), the "w" field must allow for a leading zero printed by the computer. That is, .1234567E 00 is printed as 0.1234567.

which is always printed when F notation is used, (4) a minus sign, if the stored value is negative.

If the "w" specified in FORMAT proves too small, execution error results; in most systems, the printer produces *asterisks* across the requested "w" columns. Two "safety" measures available when the programmer is uncertain as to the probable size of output values are:

1. Use of fairly large "w" specifications, which of course create extra blanks at the left, for unused portions of the field;
2. Use of exponential notation (specifying "E" rather than "F" in FORMAT; to be discussed shortly).

The "d" specification has a *minimum* value of *zero*; note that the zero must be written, so that

$$F10.$$

is an incomplete (illegal) specification. It should be

$$F10.0$$

As to the *maximum* value for "d", first we should observe that it must always be somewhat *smaller than the "w" used;* in most systems, allowance for a leading (predecimal) zero, the decimal point, and a possible minus sign dictate the rule

$$w \geq d + 3$$

For example, F5.2 will just work, for a negative value with one or no predecimal digits:

$$-0.45$$

Second, there is obviously no point in specifying "d" as larger than the *precision* limit provided for real values. In single precision, for instance,

$$F15.7$$

makes sense; though some of the postdecimal digits may still be "garbage":

$$146.3333289$$

↑
seven signif-
icant digits

However, the specification

$$F15.10$$

is *guaranteed* to have *at least* three nonsignificant (imprecise) digits in the postdecimal field.

For the stored value 12.34567 (actually stored in the form .1234567E 02), various specifications and results are shown below:

FORMAT Specification	Output Result	
F5.0	12.	
F5.1	12.3	
F8.1	12.3	
F8.3	12.346	
F4.2	****	(execution error)
F5.3	*****	(execution error)

I NOTATION IN OUTPUT

The general notation form for *integer* variables is

$$nIw$$

As usual, "n" may be omitted, in which case it has an assumed value of "1". The output value is right-justified in the specified field, and will be moved to the right by increasing the value of "w". Thus the value 1234 will appear in I7 as

$$bbb1234$$

(where "b" stands for "blank"), and in I5 as

$$b1234$$

Execution error will result from overly narrow "w" size. Thus the value 1234 cannot be handled in I3. As in the case of F notation, the programmer should also leave room for a minus sign in the field, for negative integer values.

CONSISTENCY BETWEEN LIST AND SPECIFICATION MODES

In both input and output, *real* variables in the (input or output) list must be matched with F, E, or D specifications in FORMAT; and *integer* variables must be matched with I specifications.[4] Execution error results from any mismatch. For example,

---

[4] Except that G notation may be used for either mode. This will be discussed shortly.

```
          WRITE (6,25) KING, ABLE, BAKER
     25   FORMAT (2I7, F10.2)
```

fails in execution, since ABLE cannot be transferred in I format.

Thus if the programmer wants to output a real value in integer form (i.e., printing only predecimal content, without printing the decimal point), he must convert to integer mode prior to the output statement. Whereas the statement

```
     20   FORMAT (2I10)
```

would lead to execution error in sample program 9-1, integer output is successfully arranged in sample program 9-4:

```
C SAMPLE PROGRAM 9-4
C THIS VERSION PRINTS ALL THE OUTPUT IN INTEGER MODE
     ┌DO 16 I = 1, 100
     │ MFAREN = 1.8 * I + 32. + .5
  16 └ WRITE (6,20) I, MFAREN
  20   FORMAT (2I10)
       STOP
       END
```

(A *rounding constant* has been used to produce temperatures correct to the nearest whole degree.)

E NOTATION IN OUTPUT

The general specification form for *exponential notation* is

$$nEw.d$$

The programmer's use of exponential notation for output is normally predicated on his expectation of very large or very small real values. For example, execution error would result from attempting to print the stored value "100 billion" (stored as .1000000E 12) in F14.2. (Figure it out, if you don't see why!). But E14.7 results in

$$0.1000000E\ 12$$

For *small* real values, E notation produces significant digits, when F notation may produce many nonsignificant zeros. For example, for the stored value .0000001234567 (stored as .1234567E-06), F14.7 produces

$$0.0000001$$

whereas E14.7 produces

$$0.1234567E\text{-}06$$

Since the exponential output form is printed in the manner stored—that is, with the decimal at the *left* of the significant digits—the ideal "d" value in E specification is the *precision* limit being used. For "d" actually specifies the total number of significant digits to be printed. Thus we have used "7" in the examples above. The "w" portion of the field should follow the rule

$$w \geq d + 7$$

to allow for (1) the leading zero, (2) the decimal point, (3) the four characters of exponent description, and (4) a possible minus sign for negative values.

The standard FORMAT provided by the WATFOR and WATFIV compilers, when the *FORMAT-less* output statements are used, is

       (for integers)   I12
       (for real values) E16.7

This is illustrated in sample program 9-5.

```
C SAMPLE PROGRAM 9-5
C THIS VERSION DUPLICATES THE STANDARD WATFOR/WATFIV
                                             OUTPUT FORMAT
      DO 16 I = 1, 100
      FAHREN = 1.8 * I + 32.
      PRINT, I, FAHREN
   16 WRITE (6, 20) I, FAHREN
   20 FORMAT (1X, I12, E16.7)
      STOP
      END
```

That is, both output statements in sample program 9-5 have exactly the same effect. (The "1X" in FORMAT 20 is used for printer carriage control, which will be discussed in Chapter 10.)

LENGTH OF LIST VERSUS NUMBER OF SPECIFICATIONS

For both input and output activities, three situations may be distinguished:

1. *List and specifications agree in number.* For example,

        WRITE (6,77) A, B, K, C
   77 FORMAT (2F10.2, I5, F10.2)

There are four variables in the output list, and four specifications (using "n" instead of writing (F10.2, F10.2, I5, F10.2)).

2. *List longer than provided for by specifications (i.e., too few specifications in FORMAT).* For example,

> WRITE (6,78) A, B, K, C
> 78   FORMAT (2F10.2, I5)

In such instances, the specifications are *reused*, starting from the nearest left parenthesis. But an important result of this reuse is a *shift to a new record*. In output, this means that the "C" value will appear on a print line *below* the A, B, and K values:

Result of (2F10.2, I5, F10.2)				Result of (2F10.2, I5)		
6.75	4.76	56	5.55	6.75	4.76	56
				5.55		

Since the word WRITE selects a new record each time an output statement is reached in execution, the right-hand design (above) would also result from

> WRITE (6, 78) A, B, K
> WRITE (6,78) C

regardless of whether FORMAT number 78 said

> (2F10.2, I5)

or

> (2F10.2, I5, F10.2)

(In the latter case, there would be "extra" specifications for both output lists, and in the former there would be "extra" specifications for the second output list. These cause no problem, as explained in (3) below.)

For *input*,

> READ (5, 77) A, B, K, C
> 77   FORMAT (2F10.2, I5, F10.2)

would select the four values from the same record (reading a total of 35 columns of a single card); but the specification "shortage" in

> READ (5,78) A, B, K, C
> 78   FORMAT (2F10.2, I5)

would cause the "C" value to be read from a *second* data card. Note that

> WRITE (6,90) A, I, J
> 90   FORMAT (F10.2, I5)

would produce execution error, because the integer variable "J" will become matched with an F specification.

3. *List shorter than provided for by specifications (i.e., "extra" specifications in FORMAT).* For example,

    WRITE (6, 80) A, B, K, C
  80 FORMAT (2F10.2, I5, 5F10.0)

In this situation, "extra" specifications are simply ignored. That is, data transmission halts when the input or output *list* has been satisfied.

Repetition of a *group* of specifications may be called for by placing the group in parentheses and indicating the number of repetitions with an integer constant ahead of the left parenthesis. For example,

    WRITE (6,12) JNUM, X, L, Y, M, Z, N
  12 FORMAT (I6, 3(F10.2, I5))

In this example, there are seven specifications (matching the seven listed variables). That is, the effect is as though written

  12 FORMAT (I6, F10.2, I5, F10.2, I5, F10.2, I5)

D NOTATION IN OUTPUT

Double precision values may be output using *either* F or D notation in FORMAT; but E notation may not be used. Actually, the D notation acts simply as a substitute for E, when double precision values are listed. Thus

    DOUBLE PRECISION PI

    WRITE (6,100) PI, PI
  100 FORMAT (F18.15, D20.6)

produces

  3.141592653589793 0.314159D 01

G NOTATION IN FORMAT

The *general* specification ("G") may be substituted for F, E, I, D, or L (Logical); thus it is usable for real, integer, double precision, complex, and logical variables. The general form is

    nGw.d

The interpretation of the "w" and "d" portions depends on the mode referred to in the input or output list (and, for real variables, on the size of the stored value):

Mode of Variable In I/O List	Interpretation of Gw.d
Integer	Equivalent to Iw
Real (including double precision and complex)	d is the *total number of significant digits* to be transferred
	If the value is in the range .1 to 10^d, F form is used in output; otherwise, E form is used
Logical	Equivalent to Lw

There are two possible advantages from using G FORMAT notation:

1. Obviously, it offers a safe, lazy method for insuring against mismatching of *I/O list* and *FORMAT* modes. Thus

```
      WRITE (6, 88) A, B, I, MAN, GAUGE, X
   88 FORMAT (6G15.7)
```

will work, regardless of whether the variables listed are real, double precision integer, complex, or logical.

2. It provides a method, for *real* values, of limiting output to only the *significant* digits. If, for example, we say (for a seven-digit precision computer) F14.7, we may get

$$1248.7658723$$

in which the four rightmost digits cannot really be trusted. But with G14.7, we obtain

$$1248.765$$

However, output columns will not be as neat in *decimal alignment* as with F notation:

F14.7	G14.7
1248.7658723	1248.765
3.3165876	3.316587
44.3333333	44.33333
0.0004747	0.4747474E-03

(Note that the last G output is in exponential notation, since the stored value is outside the range .1 to 10^d = .1 to 10000000.)

When G notation is used in *input* FORMAT, the usual rules (discussed below) for F, E, D, I, and L notation apply, depending on the mode of the list variable(s).

P NOTATION: THE SCALE FACTOR

The *scale factor* ("P") is a method of specifying a shift of the decimal point during input or output of *real* values (usable therefore only with F, E, D, or G specifications). For example, if X is in storage as the value 12.34567 (stored .1234567E 02), the use of the scale factor in *output* causes the following conversions:

Specification	Output
F10.2	12.34
0PF10.2	12.34
1PF10.2	123.46
3PF10.2	12345.67
−2PF10.2	0.12
−3PF10.2	0.01

As may be gathered from these examples, the "P" notation used in output FORMAT actually serves to *add* the constant mentioned in front of "P" to the stored exponent. The effect is that "1P" shifts the decimal point one place to the right, and "−1P" shifts it to the left.

For *input*, however, conversion is in the opposite direction. That is, if 12.34 appeared on a data card, the input FORMAT specification 1PF10.2 would result in storing the value

        1.234   (stored as .1234000E 01)

Thus in input the constant in front of "P" is *subtracted* from the exponent that would otherwise have been stored.

The appearance of the *scale factor* in any FORMAT statement is assumed to apply to *all* F, E, D, and G specifications that follow in the same statement, unless another scale factor cancels the effect. Thus

        WRITE (6,10) A, B
  10   FORMAT (2PF14.4, 0PF14.4)

would result in a shift of the decimal for A and avoid the shift for B.

Note that the application to D or E notation does not actually change the *size* of the number, since it changes both the printed position of the decimal *and* the size of the printed exponent:

        C = 1234.567
        WRITE (6, 11) C
        WRITE (6, 12) C
  11   FORMAT (E16.7)
  12   FORMAT (2PE16.7)

produces

0.1234567E 04
12.34567E 02

both of which have the same value.

INPUT FOR NUMERIC FIELDS

Sample program 9-6 (below) uses FORMAT for both input and output, to compute and print the arithmetic mean of "N" data values:

```
C SAMPLE PROGRAM 9-6
C THIS IS PROGRAM 3-11, WITH PROGRAMMER-SUPPLIED INPUT AND
                                                  OUTPUT FORMAT
        SUM = 0.
        READ (5, 15) N
       ┌DO 9 I = 1, N
        READ (5, 16) X
9       └SUM = SUM + X
        XMEAN = SUM/N
        WRITE (6, 16) XMEAN
15      FORMAT (I5)
16      FORMAT (F20.2)
        STOP
        END
```

Equipment unit number 5 is presumed to be the on-line card reader. Since the word READ calls for a new record every time the input statement is executed, data placement for this program must be *one data value per card* (one *field* per *record*). Note carefully that this would still be the case, even if the input FORMAT statement for the data values said

                16   FORMAT (4F20.2)

That is, data cards containing *four* data values each would only be read for the *first* value; the fields to the right of column 20 would be ignored. This is because, as mentioned earlier, input (and output) activity ceases when the input (or output) list has been satisfied. Since the READ statement mentions only one variable name in the list, "extra" data items are ignored, regardless of what the FORMAT statement says (because "extra" FORMAT specifications are ignored).

We have already commented on the reverse effect, when the input list is *longer* than the number of specifications provided in FORMAT: the FORMAT will be reused, but with the effect of a shift to a new record each time reuse occurs. Thus

```
          READ (5,20) A, B, C
     20   FORMAT (F10.4)
```

results in input of the value in columns 1 to 10 of each of *three* different data cards. If, however, the last example had said

```
     20   FORMAT (3F10.4)
```

then A, B, and C would have been read from the first 30 columns of a single card.

DATA CONDENSATION

We have seen that the style of sample program 9-6 (above) permits only one data value per card. "Packing" of data—that is, use of multiple *fields* per *record*—is frequently desirable. This is most conveniently arranged by providing *array* storage for all or part of the data. Sample program 9-7 (below) shows the general method for handling the entire data set in array form.

```
C SAMPLE PROGRAM 9-7
C THIS VERSION WORKS FOR EXACTLY 750 DATA VALUES, "PACKED"
                                              EIGHT PER CARD
        DIMENSION X(750)
        READ (5, 30) X
        SUM = 0.
       ┌DO 1 I = 1, 750
    1  └SUM = SUM + X(I)
        WRITE (6, 30) SUM/750.        (legal only in WATFOR/WATFIV)
        STOP
   30   FORMAT (8F10.2)
        END
```

In this example, there are 750 elements in the input list. Therefore, the specifications in FORMAT statement 30 must be reused many times during execution of the single READ statement. The effect of each reuse is to select a new record (the next card, in this case). Thus the total effect of the arrangement, when the input list is long, is to interpret the FORMAT statement as specifying the number of *fields* to be input from each *record*.

As demonstrated in Chapter 6, the conversion of this program to work for an unspecified number of data values would be accomplished by (1) raising the number in DIMENSION to a larger *maximum*, (2) using a *parameter card*, and (3) using the *indexed list* form in an input statement. The FORMAT arrangement need not change, as shown in sample program 9-8:

```
C SAMPLE PROGRAM 9-8
C THIS VERSION WORKS FOR UP TO 5,000 DATA VALUES, PUNCHED
                                           EIGHT PER DATA CARD
      DIMENSION X(5000)
      READ (5, 10) N
      READ (5, 30) (X(I), I = 1, N)
      SUM = 0.
     ┌DO 1 I = 1, N
1    └ SUM = SUM + X(I)
      WRITE (6,30) SUM/FLOAT(N)
      STOP
10    FORMAT (I5)
30    FORMAT (8F10.2)
      END
```

Suppose the data set is so large that it cannot be stored; a convenient general program for "packed" data uses an array just large enough to store a single record (in our example, eight data values) at a time:

```
C SAMPLE PROGRAM 9-9
C THIS VERSION WORKS FOR ANY NUMBER OF DATA VALUES, PUNCHED
                                              EIGHT PER CARD
       DIMENSION X(8)
       KOUNT = SUM = 0.
       READ (5, 10) N
1    ┌  READ (5, 30) X
     │ ┌DO 2 I = 1, 8
     │ │KOUNT = KOUNT + 1
     │ │IF (KOUNT .GT. N) GO TO 3
2    │ └SUM = SUM + X(I)
     └  GO TO 1
3      WRITE (6, 30) SUM/FLOAT(N)
       STOP
10     FORMAT (I5)
30     FORMAT (8F10.2)
       END
```

F NOTATION IN INPUT

The data values for the last three sample programs must appear eight per card, each in a field *ten* characters wide. However, the "d" portion of

$$nFw.d$$

may be *overruled,* in input usage, by a decimal point keypunched in the data field. Thus the F10.2 specification would interpret each of the following values in the same manner (as 3.5):

>3.5bbbbbbb
>bbb3.5bbbb
>bbbbbbb3.5

If, however, no decimal point appears in the input field, then the FORMAT "d" specification supplies its position, and *right-justification* in keypunching becomes important. When specified as F10.2, the value 3.5 should be keypunched (without decimal point)

>bbbbbbb35b

If it were punched

>35bbbbbbbb

then the F10.2 FORMAT would interpret the number as

>35000000.00

For the last keypunch job shown, a proper FORMAT for interpretation as 3.5 would be F3.1 (or F4.2, etc.).

The examples just used indicate that the unpunched decimal point, whose position is located by "d" in FORMAT, does not actually take up any room on the data card. Thus

>READ (5, 1) A
>WRITE (6, 1) A
>1   FORMAT (F5.2)

used in conjunction with the input data field

>12345

will *not* work, producing an execution error during *output.* The value is successfully read and stored as

>123.45

but a minimum field width of *six* is necessary for output of the value (since decimal points *do* take up output space).

I NOTATION IN INPUT

Right-justification of integers in the specified input fields is important, since blanks to the right of actual digits will be interpreted as zeros. Thus

>123bb

will be interpreted by the specification I5 as 12,300. If 123 is to be stored, I3 should be specified for the data field shown above. On the other hand, if I5 is used, the field should be punched

bb123

From the discussion so far, it should be clear that a continuous string of digits appearing on an input record may be interpreted as separate data values, by the programmer's use of FORMAT. For the data

123456789123

the following statements

```
      READ (5, 16) I, A, J, B, C
 16   FORMAT (I2, F2.0, I3, F2.2, −5PF3.0)
```

produce in storage

$$I = 12$$
$$A = 34.0$$
$$J = 567$$
$$B = .89$$
$$C = 12300000.$$

Note that there is no *consistency* requirement between input data form and FORMAT notation. That is, an input field *without* a punched decimal point does not necessarily contain an *integer*. For the data field 12345,

Mode of Input List Name	FORMAT Specification	Result in Storage
integer	I5	12345
real	F5.2	123.45
real	E5.2	123.45

Similarly, for the data field 12.34,

Mode of Input List Name	FORMAT Specification	Result in Storage
real	F5.d	12.34
real	E5.d	12.34
integer	I2, I3, I4, I5	12

E AND D NOTATION IN INPUT

Input values that are referred to by E specifications in FORMAT may appear in several forms, including ordinary decimal notation. When an exponent does appear, the entire value (including exponent) should be right-justified in the input data field. Each of the following is valid; E6.d could be used to describe the fields.

(1)	1.E+09
(2)	1.E 09
(3)	1.E09
(4)	1.E+9
(5)	1.E9
(6)	1E9
(7)	1.+9
(8)	1.+09

(As the last two examples illustrate, a plus or minus sign *must* appear if "E" is omitted. For *negative* exponents, the minus sign must, of course, always appear.)

As in F input, keypunched decimal points override the "d" part of the FORMAT specification. Therefore, the first five examples above will be stored as "one billion," regardless of the "d" specified in FORMAT. The value stored in the sixth example, however, depends on "d". For the data field bbb1E9,

FORMAT Specification	Decimal Location	Storage Form
E6.0	bbb1E9 ∧	.1000000E 10
E6.4	bbb1E9 ∧	.1000000E 06

If reference to the exponent is omitted from the input data field, the exponent is presumed to be zero. For example,

12.34

will be interpreted as 12.34 by Ew.d, regardless of the value of "d". If the decimal point is not keypunched, the "d" as usual takes control; for the data field

bbbbbb1234

the FORMAT specification E10.2 produces the value 12.34, while E10.1 stores the number as 123.4.

Double precision variables in the input list may be matched (as was the case in *output*) with *either* F or D FORMAT specifications. (The choice does not affect treatment as double precision.) As outlined above for E notation, the "D" need *not* appear in the data field, when a D specification is used.

COMPLEX VARIABLES

Input/output of complex values does not require any special notation. Since each complex value is actually a *pair* of real values, *two* specifications should be used for each COMPLEX name in the list; these may be any combination of F, E, G, and (if names are so declared) D specifications. For example,

```
            COMPLEX CORN
            READ (5, 10) CORN
            WRITE (6, 11) CORN
   10       FORMAT (2F5.2)
   11       FORMAT (E16.7, F10.2)
```

For Review

I/O statement

equipment unit number
FORMAT statement number
FORMAT statement
field, record, file
numeric field
alphameric field
numeric field FORMAT notation
repeated specification
repeated group
scale factor
right-justification
truncation
standard WATFOR/WATFIV FORMAT

Examples

READ (5, 7) N, X, Y
WRITE (6, 7) K
6
7
7 FORMAT (I5,2F10.2)

F10.2, E16.7, D28.16, I6, G15.5
2F10.2
2(F10.2, E16.7)
−2PF10.2
bbb46

I12, E16.7, D28.16

Programming Exercises

Note. The standard data deck contains 6 real data values per card, keypunched in fields of 10, with 2 decimal places. In the following problems, use *formatted* input and output statements. Check with your computer center for appropriate equipment unit numbers for the card reader and printer.

9-1. Write a program that reads all 72 data values (provide array storage), and computes their arithmetic mean. Output the mean in the *center* of the print page, with four decimal places.

9-2. Read in only the *predecimal* portion of the first data value on each card, and compute the arithmetic mean for these 12 values. (*Note.* F10.0 will not work for the input; why?) Output the mean at the extreme *right of the print page, in exponential notation.* (Print 5 significant digits.)

9-3. Read all 72 data values as a 6 x 12 matrix, and then print both (integer) *subscripts* for each *zero* value in the matrix.

9-4. Keypunch a card with a string of 10 consecutive 9's. Write a program that reads the card by interpreting the string as real 99.9, integer 9999, real 0.99, and real 9000. The program should output the values on a single print line in the same form. (But the same FORMAT statement cannot be used for both input and output. Why?)

9-5. Write a program that computes and prints 20! (factorial 20) in double precision, and outputs the result in both decimal and exponential form. (This output does not exactly duplicate that of Exercise 8-1. Why?)

9-6. Write a program that reproduces (on 12 lines) the entire data deck, "spread out" across the entire print page, with all decimal points moved two places to the left.

CHAPTER **10**

ALPHAMERIC AND POSITIONAL FORMAT

FORMAT NOTATION FOR ALPHAMERIC FIELDS

We defined in Chapter 9 that an *alphameric* field may contain any combination of keypunchable characters. We now list the characters that may appear *within the FORMAT statement,* when the programmer is referring to *alphameric* fields:

Notation Character	Meaning
H	Transfer (of following characters) between I/O medium and FORMAT statement
' '	Transfer (of enclosed characters) between I/O medium and FORMAT statement
A	Transfer between I/O medium and named storage locations

HOLLERITH[1] (H) STRINGS AND LITERALS (' '), OUTPUT

In the general form

$$wH$$

"w" is as usual an integer constant describing total field width. (It *must* appear, even for the field width "1".) When used in FORMAT, the meaning is,

---

[1] Named for Herman Hollerith, an inventor of punch-card equipment.

'reproduce verbatim the following w characters." Thus the programmer arranges the transfer of characters *from within the FORMAT statement to the output medium.* For example, the statements

        WRITE (6, 25)
25   FORMAT (20H   HAPPY 1984)

produce the output

    HAPPY 1984

Note that the character count includes blank columns as characters. (There are 10 blanks between the two H's in the FORMAT statement, and, of course, one between HAPPY and 1984.)

An alternative method permits the string of alphameric characters to be enclosed by apostrophes (serving as quotation marks), in which case the wH instruction is not used, and the verbatim reproduction meaning is the same:

        WRITE (6, 25)
25   FORMAT ('   HAPPY 1984')

This is known as *literal transfer.*

We pause to note that the WATFIV compiler permits *literal transfer* in the unformatted PRINT statement:

    PRINT, '   HAPPY 1984'

Sample program 10–1 uses a combination of H and literal notation, to produce column headings.

```
C SAMPLE PROGRAM 10-1
C OUTPUT USE OF H AND LITERAL, FOR COLUMN HEADINGS
      WRITE (6,10)
     ┌DO 1 I = 1, 500
     │READ (5, 11) SALES, PROFIT
     │RATIO = PROFIT/SALES
1    └WRITE (6, 11) SALES, PROFIT, RATIO
10    FORMAT ('   SALES    PROFIT '8H   RATIO)
11    FORMAT (3F10.2)
      STOP
      END
```

The combination of the two forms is used in this program for illustration. Most programmers would write either

10   FORMAT ('   SALES   PROFIT   RATIO')

or

10   FORMAT (28H   SALES   PROFIT   RATIO)

In sample program 10-1, you should also notice the presence of an "extra" specification for the input list, which is ignored when the READ statement is executed.

Thus far, we have not combined *alphameric* and *numeric* notations within the same FORMAT statement; the *output list* has in fact been empty, in the examples shown. Consider, for instance,

```
      WRITE (6, 22) XMEAN
22    FORMAT ('    THE MEAN IS    'F12.4)
```

The output then appears as follows:

```
    THE MEAN IS   123.4567
```

Numeric and alphameric notation may in fact be interspersed in such manner as to "surround" numbers with "labels." Thus

```
         WRITE (6, 40) NPAGE, NCOMMA
40       FORMAT ('ON PAGE' I4 ' THERE ARE' I3 ' COMMAS')
```

The output appears as follows:

```
    ON PAGE 148 THERE ARE 17 COMMAS
```

The arrangement includes provision for three alphameric fields, and two numeric fields, in the output record.

An interesting use of alphameric transfer is the production of "error messages" written by the programmer. Sample program 10-2 (below) shows the technique, examining the parameter entered in sample program 9-8.

```
C SAMPLE PROGRAM 10-2
C RE-WRITE OF PROGRAM 9-8, TO CHECK PARAMETER ENTERED
        DIMENSION X(5000)
        READ (5, 10) N
        IF (N .GT. 5000) GO TO 86
        READ (5, 30) (X(I), I = 1, N)
        SUM = 0.
       ┌DO 1 I = 1, N
1      └SUM = SUM + X(I)
        WRITE (6, 50) SUM/FLOAT(N)
        STOP
86      WRITE (6, 70) N
        STOP
10      FORMAT (I5)
30      FORMAT (8F10.2)
50      FORMAT ('    THE MEAN IS ' F15.4)
70      FORMAT (I10' IS TOO LARGE — MAXIMUM 5000')
        END
```

As soon as the parameter (N) has been read, an IF statement checks its size, and a branch to statement 86 occurs for values over the dimensioned storage. The "error message" is contained in FORMAT number 70. We have also added an alphameric message to be printed with the mean (in FORMAT statement 50).

HOLLERITH STRINGS AND LITERALS IN INPUT

The transfer of alphameric characters from an input medium (e.g., a punched card) *into a FORMAT statement* is also accomplished by wH or literals. The italics emphasize an important difference between this possibility and the "A" notation discussed below. The only purpose of transferring alphameric information into a FORMAT statement is the subsequent reproduction of the *entire unaltered string,* in output. No manipulation of any kind is possible. Thus the following statements read in, and subsequently reproduce, a three-letter abbreviation for common stocks, which appears in columns 3, 4, and 5 of the card deck:

```
          DO 5 I = 1, N
          READ (5, 108) OPEN, CLOSE, VOLUME
          ---------------
          -----------------
          ------------------
     5    WRITE (6, 108) GAIN, RATIO, FUND
     108  FORMAT (5H      3F10.2)
```

In this example, five columns in the FORMAT statement have been left blank, to be filled during execution. Any characters appearing in these FORMAT columns are replaced at each READ execution; therefore, statement 108 could also have been written

```
     108  FORMAT (5H123453F10.2)
```

or

```
     108  FORMAT (5H★★★★★3F10.2)
```

and so on, so long as the correct count is preserved. The *literal* notation may also be used, instead:

```
     108  FORMAT ('     '3F10.2)
```

or

```
     108  FORMAT ('★★★★★'3F10.2)
```

Sample program 10–3 (below) makes use of the literal method, to read and reproduce company names contained in the first 20 columns of each input data card:[2]

```
C SAMPLE PROGRAM 10-3
C THIS PROGRAM USES LITERAL TRANSFER TO REPRODUCE
                                              COMPANY NAMES
         DO 1 I = 1, 500
         READ (5, 10) SALES, PROFIT
         RATIO = PROFIT/SALES
1        WRITE (6, 10) SALES, PROFIT, RATIO
         STOP
10       FORMAT ('*******************'3F10.2)
         END
```

"A" NOTATION FOR ALPHAMERIC FIELDS

The "A" specification transfers alphameric characters between input/output media and *labeled storage*. The word "labeled" signifies that the storage location is referenced by one or more variable names. The general form is

$$nAw$$

in which "w" as usual represents the width of the data field; and "n" is optionally used for repeating specifications.

The instruction is analogous to

$$nIw$$

rather than to

$$wH$$

since the specification describes a field that is *mentioned as a variable in an input or output list*. If, for example, a card contains a four-letter word, followed by a field of six columns containing an integer number:

RICE 21653

the statements

```
         READ (5, 17) VEGTBL, NUMBER
17       FORMAT (A4, I6)
```

place the characters RICE in the VEGTBL storage location, and the integer 21653 in the NUMBER storage location.

---

[2] But, for reasons explained at the end of this chapter (in the "Printer Carriage Control" section), the first column of each card should be left blank.

The use of "A" FORMAT permits some kinds of manipulation of the stored characters, not possible with the "H" and "literal" transfer discussed earlier. First, the stored characters are available whenever referenced by variable name, so that the programmer is not committed to using the same input and output FORMAT, to transfer eventually from input to output medium. Thus our example might continue,

> WRITE (6, 55) NUMBER, VEGTBL
> 55   FORMAT (I10, ' POUNDS OF', A4)

The output is, of course,

> 21653 POUNDS OF RICE

When the READ and WRITE statements are executed for the next data card, the output may be something like

> 446 POUNDS OF PEAS

Second, a string stored in "A" FORMAT may be *altered*, when reproduced in output. The following continuation of the example produces only the first letter of the vegetable:

> WRITE (6, 60) NUMBER, VEGTBL
> 60   FORMAT (I10 ' OF' A1)

The output looks like this:

> 21653 OF R
> 446 OF P

Speaking of alteration, the following statements print the names backwards:

> READ (5, 100) VEG1, VEG2, VEG3, VEG4, NUMBER
> 100   FORMAT (4A1, I6)
> ----------------------
> WRITE (6, 101) NUMBER, VEG4, VEG3, VEG2, VEG1
> 101   FORMAT (I10, 4A1)

The first output is

> 21653ECIR

A third manipulation possibility is *comparison* of two or more storage locations, with alphameric content. (The alphameric strings are actually stored in unique *numerical* representations, so that IF statements operate as usual);

> READ (5, 130) NAME1, NAME2
> 130   FORMAT (2A4)
>   IF (NAME1 − NAME2) 3, 4, 3

This sequence branches to statement 4 only if the two four-character strings are identical.

Since the numeric representation for A1 storage is in ascending numerical order through the alphabet, it is possible to *alphabetize* words in storage, by using a *sorting* program (or subprogram), with reference to characters read in A1 FORMAT.

The examples thus far have been limited to four-character strings because this is a common *maximum* width for a single precision storage location. Declaration of the storage variable as DOUBLE PRECISION may enlarge this (commonly to *eight* characters per location). Thus an eight-character string could be handled by

```
       DOUBLE PRECISION VEGTBL
       READ (5, 65) VEGTBL, NUMBER
   65  FORMAT (A8, I6)
```

Note also, however, that the use of multiple variable names permits storage of long strings. For a 20-character field,

```
       DOUBLE PRECISION TITLE1, TITLE2, TITLE3
       READ (5, 70) TITLE1, TITLE2, TITLE3
   70  FORMAT (2A8, A4)
       WRITE (6, 90) PROFIT, TITLE1, TITLE2, TITLE3
   90  FORMAT (F10.2'COMPANY—',2A8, A4)
```

Output in "A" FORMAT is usually *left*-justified by the computer; therefore the name ROBERTSON, which only occupies one column of the second (TITLE2) field, is correctly printed by these statements.

The use of *array* storage may also be combined with "A" FORMAT, for convenience in handling. Thus the following statements read into storage all 80 columns of a punched card:

```
       DIMENSION COLUMN(80)
       READ (5, 76) COLUMN
   76  FORMAT (80A1)
```

Eighty separate storage locations are used. From what we have said earlier, as few as 10 storage locations might be employed to accomplish the result. In the form above, however, note the interesting possibility of reproducing a single column:

```
       WRITE (6, 800) I, COLUMN(I)
  800  FORMAT ('COLUMN'I3 ' CONTAINS ' A1)
```

The output looks like this:

```
       COLUMN 27 CONTAINS  /
```

The company names treated in sample program 10–3 (above) by a 20-character *literal* in FORMAT are handled in sample program 10–4 (below) by using "A" FORMAT:

```
C SAMPLE PROGRAM 10-4
C THIS PROGRAM USES 'A' FORMAT TO REPRODUCE COMPANY NAMES
      DOUBLE PRECISION CNAME(3)
      DO 1 I = 1, 500
      READ (5,10) CNAME, SALES, PROFIT
      RATIO = PROFIT/SALES
1     WRITE (6, 11) SALES, PROFIT, RATIO, CNAME
      STOP
10    FORMAT (2A8, A4, 2F10.2)
11    FORMAT (3F10.2, 2A8, A4)
      END
```

The DATA statement may be used to initialize *alphameric* storage locations. This technique permits reproduction of messages by using message *names* in an output list, and providing "A" specifications in FORMAT. For example,

```
C SAMPLE PROGRAM 10-5
C TRANSLATION OF CLASS NUMBER CODES TO CLASS NAMES
      DOUBLE PRECISION CLASS(5), STUDT(3)
      DATA CLASS/'FRESHMAN', 'SOPHOMOR','JUNIOR','SENIOR',
                                                   'GRADUATE'/
      DO 1 I = 1, 1000
      READ (5, 10) STUDT, NCLASS
1     WRITE (6, 11) STUDT, CLASS(NCLASS)
10    FORMAT (2A8, A4, I5)
11    FORMAT (2A8, A4, A8)
      STOP
      END
```

In sample program 10–5 (above), the five elements of the CLASS array are initialized with alphameric values by the DATA statement. Each input record contains (1) a student name in columns 2 to 20, read into the three STUDT locations, (2) an integer from 1 to 5 in column 25, indicating class standing (1 = freshman, 2 = sophomore, etc.). Output consists of (1) the student's name, and (2) his class standing name, printed as an alphameric message. Thus if a card contains

        SMITH, JOHN   4

the output will be

        SMITH, JOHN   SENIOR

THE CHARACTER STATEMENT (WATFIV)

The misspelling of **SOPHOMORE** in sample program 10–5 is intentional, to keep within the eight-character limit that usually may be stored in a double precision location. The WATFIV compiler provides a useful *explicit type specification* that (a) provides for longer character strings (up to 120 characters), and (b) also permits reproduction of the strings by *unformatted* output statements. The form is

CHARACTER * #   *name*

where # is the total length (from 1 to 120) of the string to be stored, and *name* is the name assigned by the programmer to the entire string. For example,

```
CHARACTER * 40 OVRDUE
DATA OVRDUE/' THE BALANCE ON THIS ACCOUNT IS OVERDUE'/
  -------------------
  -------------------
  -------------------
PRINT, BAL, OVRDUE
```

In this example BAL is numeric (a dollar balance), and **OVRDUE** is the complete alphameric message initialized in the DATA statement.

We observed earlier that WATFIV would also permit the alternative,

```
PRINT, BAL,' THE BALANCE ON THIS ACCOUNT IS OVERDUE'
```

The CHARACTER specification may be convenient, however, for alternative messages. This is illustrated by sample program 10–6, which prints one of three messages to charge account customers:

```
C SAMPLE PROGRAM 10-6
C USE OF THE CHARACTER SPECIFICATION FOR MESSAGES
      CHARACTER * 35 WORDS(3)
      DATA WORDS(1)/' THIS IS A CREDIT BALANCE'/
      DATA WORDS(2)/' THANK YOU – NO CURRENT BALANCE'/
      DATA WORDS(3)/' PAYMENT DUE WITHIN 30 DAYS'/
      DO 4 I = 1, 7500
      READ, DUE, TRANS, PAID
      BILL = DUE + TRANS - PAID
      IF (BILL) 1, 2, 3
   1  K = 1
      GO TO 4
   2  K = 2
      GO TO 4
   3  K = 3
   4  PRINT, BILL, WORDS(K)
      STOP
      END
```

"Extra" characters provided for (when the message is less than 30 characters in length) are filled in as blanks.

LOGICAL FIELDS

Strictly speaking, the *Logical* field is neither numeric nor alphameric, since only the characters T or F usually appear in the field. The general FORMAT notation is

$$nLw$$

For output, right-justification is observed. Thus

```
      WRITE (6, 100) MAN
100   FORMAT ( 'VALUE OF MAN IS' L5)
```

produces

```
      VALUE OF MAN IS     F
```

For input, however, the data field should contain a T or F in any of the w columns specified; the first such character in the field determines the logical value stored. If no T or F is encountered, the value .FALSE. is assigned. Thus, for FORMAT L5,

Input Data Field	Storage Result
Tbbbb	.TRUE.
bbbbF	.FALSE.
FLIRT	.FALSE.
TAFFY	.TRUE.
WATER	.TRUE.
VAPOR	.FALSE.
12.34	.FALSE.

POSITIONAL NOTATION IN FORMAT

Horizontal and vertical position of input and output fields is determinable to some degree by the notations we have already examined:

1. Execution of a READ or WRITE statement causes a new record to be selected. This effects a downward shift in output, to the next line of the printer page; and a shift to a new data card, in input.

2. Similarly, reuse of FORMAT specifications (resulting from a "shortage" of specifications) has the same record-shifting effect, in both input and output.

3. Horizontal "skipping" may be achieved by use of the "w" in FORMAT. For example, F60.3 "skips" 50 output columns, if the real value (and its decimal point) occupy only 10 characters.

4. Blanks embedded in Hollerith or literal character strings may be used to effect horizontal "skipping":

          10   FORMAT ('   ANSWER IS ' F10.2)

There are, however, several FORMAT notation characters explicitly designed to accomplish horizontal and vertical spacing in output, and to accommodate such spacing on input records:

Notation Character		Meaning
X		Blank column (or "skip" column)
T		Begin in specified column
/		Select new record
Printer Carriage Control { 'b'	or 1Hb or 1X	Single-space printer carriage
'0'	or 1H0	Double-space printer carriage
'1'	or 1H1	Sheet eject (skip to next printer page)
'+'	or 1H+	No vertical movement (printer carriage)

X NOTATION IN FORMAT

The general form for transfer of "blank" characters is

$$wX$$

In this case, as in wH, the preceding integer "w" cannot be omitted, even if the value is "1". The meaning of

$$10X$$

in *output* FORMAT is "output 10 blank columns." In *input*, however, the meaning is actually *skip* 10 columns, which in fact need not be blank on the input record.

It is usually poor practice, in *output* FORMAT, to use the "X" notation in front of F, E, I, D, or G specifications; for the generation of blanks preceding *numeric* output can be accomplished by providing extra room in the "w" portion of the numeric specification. For example,

$$10XF5.2$$

should be written

$$F15.2$$

The second alternative is preferable because output values with large predecimal content, which may lead to execution errors (insufficient "w" size) when the first method is used, may fit within the second FORMAT's larger numeric field. Thus

Output FORMAT	Stored Value	Output Result
10XF5.2 } F15.2	12.34	bbbbbbbbbb12.34 bbbbbbbbbb12.34
10XF5.2 } F15.2	123.45	bbbbbbbbbb***** bbbbbbbbbb123.45

The asterisks at the right of the third output line are, as mentioned earlier, the computer's usual method of signaling a "w" field that is too small to contain the stored value. Yet the value easily "fits" into the F15.2 FORMAT, which produces exactly the *same* result as 10XF5.2, in the case of the smaller value.

In output, however, the X notation is quite useful for inserting blank columns ahead of *alphameric* fields. For example, widespread column headings may be arranged without taking up much FORMAT space:

```
        WRITE (6, 90)
90      FORMAT (20X'SALES'25X'PROFIT'25X'RATIO')
```

In *input*, the wX notation has an important function: the skipping of material, either alphameric or numeric, that appears on input records but is not required as data for the program. Suppose, for example, that the programmer using the data deck described for sample programs 10–3 and 10–4 (above) wants to *ignore* the company name in the first 20 columns of each record, rather than copy it into the FORMAT statement (as in 10–3) or into labeled storage (as in 10–4). Then he may say

```
        READ (5, 10) SALES, PROFIT
10      FORMAT (20X, 2F10.2)
```

Whether the material to be skipped is alphameric or numeric, the use of a wide "w" specification (suggested above for output "skipping") will *not* work. For example, we could not say above

```
10      FORMAT (F30.2, F10.2)
```

The SALES field would be judged as illegally keypunched during execution.

T NOTATION IN FORMAT

A "T" specification in FORMAT provides a direct alternative, in most usages, to the "wX" specification. The general form is

$$Tc$$

where c is an integer constant indicating the *column in which the next data transfer is to begin*. Thus the meaning of

FORMAT (T11, I5)

is the same as

FORMAT (10X, I5)

In each case, an integer is specified as appearing in columns 11 through 15 of the record.

However, the "T" notation also permits READ and WRITE operations to depart from the usual left-to-right order (which wX cannot accomplish). This may be illustrated by reading a data card in reverse field order:

READ (5, 77) C, B, A
77   FORMAT (T71, F10.0, T51, F10.0, T1, F10.0)

The C value comes from columns 71 to 80, the B value from columns 51 to 60, and the A value from the first 10 columns of the card.

/ NOTATION IN FORMAT

The meaning of the *slash* character in FORMAT is "shift to a new record". The general form is simply

/

That is, there are no integer accompaniments.

Production of output on a set of *three* print lines, or three punched cards, or three typed lines, is accomplished by the following statements:

WRITE (IOUT, 18) K, A, B
18   FORMAT (I10/ F10.2 / F10.2)

Output of K is followed by shift to a new record (print line, or card, or type line).[3] This second record contains the A value, and is followed by a third record containing B. Thus the output appearance is

  254
14.21
 1.67

Remember that there are two *other* causes of shift to a new record: execution of the I/O statement, and reuse of the FORMAT specifications. Thus the

---

[3] The effect on *tape* output is placement of "end-of-record" marks following each output value. When the tape is used as input to a printer, the final effect is thus the same as that shown above.

following three arrangements all result in the *same* output design:

    (1)   WRITE (6, 8) A, B
                8   FORMAT (F9.1 / F9.1)

    (2)   WRITE (6, 8) A
                              WRITE (6, 8) B
                8   FORMAT (F9.1)

    (3)   WRITE (6, 8) A, B
                8   FORMAT (F9.1)

    A *slash* in FORMAT referenced by an *input* statement calls for a shift to the next input record. For example, the following statements read information from *four* successive punched cards:

                        READ (5, 19) L, M, A, FOX
             19   FORMAT (2I5 // F10.4 / F5.0)

In this example, L and M are read from the first card, then the "shift, shift" instruction *skips* one card; the A value comes from the third card, and FOX from the fourth. It is evident that a succession of k slashes in mid-FORMAT causes the skipping of k-1 records. However, since the execution of the READ statement itself causes selection of a fresh record, an input FORMAT statement that *begins* with a single slash arranges the *skipping* of one record (card).

    You should see that the arrangement on the left below reads values from the second, fourth, sixth, and eighth cards, while the one on the right reads from the first, third, fifth, and seventh cards:

```
        ⎡DO 1 I = 1, 4                   ⎡DO 1 I = 1, 4
    1   ⎣READ (5, 6) X(I)          1    ⎣READ (5, 6) X(I)
    6    FORMAT (/F10.2)           6     FORMAT (F10.2/)
```

Sample program 10–7 illustrates the use of the X and / notations, in both input and output FORMAT:

```
    C SAMPLE PROGRAM 10-7
    C THIS PROGRAM USES X AND / NOTATION IN BOTH INPUT AND
                                                OUTPUT FORMAT
          DOUBLE PRECISION CNAME(3)
          WRITE (6, 30)
        ⎡ DO 1 I = 1, 500
        | READ (5, 40) CNAME, SALES, PROFIT
        | RATIO = PROFIT/SALES
    1   ⎣ WRITE (6, 50) CNAME, SALES, PROFIT, RATIO
          STOP
```

```
30    FORMAT (30X 'SALES' 20X 'PROFIT' 20X 'RATIO')
40    FORMAT (2A8, A4, 50X, F10.2 / 10XF10.2)
50    FORMAT (' '2A8, A4 / F36.2, 2F25.2)
      END
```

In FORMAT 30 (header output), the X instruction is used to insert blanks before and between the column headings. FORMAT 40 (input) arranges for the company name to be read from the first 20 columns of an initial card, the sales figure to be read from the last 10 columns of the same card, and the profit figure from columns 11 to 20 of a *second* card. (Thus there are two cards per company, a total of 1000 data cards).

The multiline output is arranged by FORMAT 50, which shifts to a new record after the company name, producing the following design:

	SALES	PROFIT	RATIO
ARCO CHEMICAL			
	1248.66	387.45	0.31
BILLINGS STEEL			
	475.00	74.98	0.16

The first notation in FORMAT 50, ' ', is explained in the next section.

PRINTER CARRIAGE CONTROL

High-speed printers are usually equipped with a vertical-paper-movement control system that depends on instructions from the programmer. These instructions are contained in the *first output character* that *would* be produced on an output record, as arranged by a given set of output and FORMAT statements. We say *"would"* because this first character of the output record, having been used for carriage control, is then *discarded, not printed.*

The standard[4] first-character interpretations are:

First Character of Output Record	Preprinting Carriage Movement
blank	single vertical space
0 (zero)	double vertical space
1	space to new paper sheet
+	no vertical spacing
all others	single vertical space

To this point, we have evaded the carriage-control problem by arranging that a *blank* character would be the first character of each output record; this

---

[4] Some systems provide additional characters for such movements as triple spacing, half-page skips, etc.

achieves a single vertical space. The character is really lost, however, so that when we have said

      WRITE (6, 7) K
  7 FORMAT (I10)

the *actual* output record (beginning in physical print column 1) contains only nine total characters (columns):

bbbbbb788

  Thus the simplest way to arrange single spacing (prior to printing the record) is to use numeric specifications with "extra w" room. If, however, a full numeric field of the width specified by "w" is required, a common arrangement is the use of either H or literal alphameric transfer, to provide the (to-be-lost) carriage control character. Thus

  7 FORMAT (1H , I10)

or

  7 FORMAT (' ', I10)

places output (after single spacing) in a genuine field of 10 columns:

bbbbbbb788

Another alternative, for single spacing, uses X notation:

  7 FORMAT (1X, I10)

  One of the last three alternatives shown (1H, or ' ', or 1X) *must* be used for single spacing in some instances, to avoid first-character truncation of *alphameric* fields, which are always left-justified. This is the case in sample program 10–7 (above), in which FORMAT 50 begins with ' ' in order to preserve the first letter of the company name. Although this apparently says, *"print a blank,"* it really means only *"vertical space before printing."*

  Alphameric output accomplished from within FORMAT, by H or literal transfer, may be preceded with a carriage control character (if it appears at the beginning of the record), by the following technique:

  88 FORMAT (' INTEREST RATE')

In this example, the I will actually appear in physical print column 1.

  Since neither the "extra w" nor the "1X" method is available for *double space*, *sheet eject* (new paper sheet), or *suppress space* (no vertical spacing), these carriage control characters are always inserted by H or literal transfer. For example,

     WRITE (6, 15) A, I, J
  15 FORMAT ('1', F10.2 / '0' I10 / '+' I3)

This example also illustrates that each signal for a *new record* (/) within FORMAT will be followed by interpretation of a fresh carriage-control character, which should be provided by the programmer. The arrangement shown above first shifts to a new print page ('1'), prints A in 10 actual columns, then double-spaces ('0') and prints I in 10 actual columns. Finally, the combination of the new-record request (/) and the suppress-space request ('+') accomplish "backward printing" by placing J to the *left* of the I value already printed. The output appears as follows:

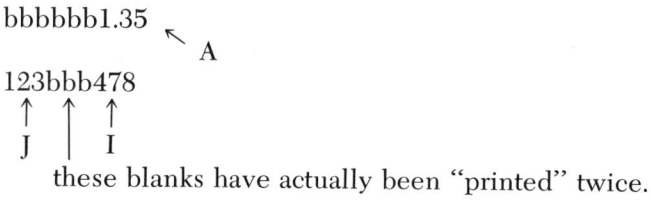

these blanks have actually been "printed" twice.

For Review

	Examples
Hollerith notation	6HMEAN =
literal transfer	'MEAN ='
A notation	3A4
CHARACTER specification	CHARACTER*40 OVRDUE
L notation	3L5
blank (or skip) columns	10X
T notation	T11
new record	/
printer carriage control	' ', '0', '1', '+'

Programming Exercises

10–1. Write a program to read the *third* data value on each card (use wX to skip columns), and print out the (integer) position number (1 to 12) of each *negative* value. Output should shart on a fresh printer page, and read

        ITEM NO.   IS NEGATIVE
        ITEM NO.   IS NEGATIVE
                etc.

10–2. Write a program that will read only the *fifth* data value, from only the *odd-numbered* data cards (1st, 3rd, 5th, ..., 11th), and compute and print their arithmetic mean. (Use / to skip cards, placing the entire data deck behind your program). Using a single output statement, let the output read

MEAN   EXPONENTIAL FORM
XXX.XX   X.XXXXXXXE XX

10–3. Write a program to produce a table of X, $\log_e X$ and $\sqrt{X}$, with suitable *caption labels*, for X = 1.0, 1.1, 1.2, ... 2.0. Print *four* decimal places for the computed values. Double-space the output lines.

10–4. Write a program that will read punched cards and reprint their entire contents verbatim; the contents may be any combination of alphabetic, numeric, and special characters. Let the number of cards to be read and reprinted be determined by an initial *parameter card*. (Hint: the printer *carriage control* problem will prevent you from using "H" or "literal" transfer; try "A" notation).

10–5. If the cards to be copied are guaranteed to have a blank in each column 1, program 10–4 (above) can be written using H or *literal* transfer. Write it, and also provide that the input and output equipment unit numbers may be inserted in a DATA statement, at execution time.

10–6. A card deck contains customer names, keypunched as follows:

columns 1 to 15:   last name (left-justified)
columns 16 to 30:   first name (left-justified)

Write a program that will read the deck and reprint in the order: first *initial* − period − space − last name. For example,

JONES   JOHN

becomes

J. JONES

10–7. Write a program that examines each element of a 40-element array, and prints either "NEGATIVE", "ZERO", or "POSITIVE" for each element, along with the array position number.

10–8. Write a program that will read a set of three punched cards, and print the exact *alphameric* contents of columns 11 to 20, for only those cards containing the letter J in column 80. Test your program on

(11)   (80)
FIRST   I
SECOND   J
THIRD   K

10-9. Write a program which will divide 1.0 by 3.0 (using DOUBLE PRECISION), and produce exactly the following output:

```
                              333
                         0.333333
                    0.333333333
               0.3333D 00
          333.333                  (use a scale factor)
     0.33D 00
     T    F                        (use two logical variables)
```

CHAPTER **11**

SOME ADDITIONAL STATEMENTS

"UNNECESSARY" STATEMENTS?

In this chapter we add some FORTRAN language refinements that might be grouped under the heading, "Statements you can live without." They have been collected here on the author's opinion that their usage, while rarely *necessary*, is sometimes *convenient*. But, of course, this *is* a matter of opinion. We have actually discussed earlier some statements that might be so qualified by other programmers.[1]

Is the DO statement really necessary? Its effect can always be arranged by judicious use of IF statements. Does one really have a need for logical variables? After all, their values may be represented in storage by the programmer as they actually are by the computer, as "1" and "0", rather than ".TRUE." and ".FALSE.". The DATA statement can always be replaced by executable initialization statements. For that matter, is FORMAT really necessary? We seemed to get along without it fairly well for eight chapters — and Chapters 9 and 10 seemed awfully long and complicated.

Any compiler language is inevitably composed of some essential basic statement forms, and many refinements intended to simplify problems in some instances or to provide extra flexibility in others. As a matter of practical experience, I would vote strongly for FORMAT, which is extremely valuable in handling genuine well-designed input records and in preparing

---

[1] In at least two instances, we have already "lowered the bars" by discussing statements *not* recommended for general use by *this* author: the REAL and INTEGER explicit type specifications (Chapter 2), and the COMMON statement (Chapter 7).

good readable output documents; and for the DO statement, which simplifies enormously the *looping* process, in complicated programs.

THE EQUIVALENCE STATEMENT

The specification[2] statement

EQUIVALENCE (ACE, B, CARD)

has the effect of restricting storage reservations to a single location for the variables named. This location will be referenced by *each* of the names given in parentheses in the statement. That is, the mention of ACE, B, or CARD would have the same effect at any point in the program, since the location holds only one value. If more than one set of equivalences is to be mentioned, commas are used between separate parenthesized sets:

EQUIVALENCE (ACE, B, CARD), (XRAY, ROENT)

The EQUIVALENCE statement is reminiscent of the COMMON statement, which also makes a single storage location accessible by two different names. Remember, however, that COMMON arranges this location-sharing between variables appearing in *different* programs or subprograms, while EQUIVALENCE refers to two or more variable names appearing in the *same* program. The effect of EQUIVALENCE could be accomplished by actual identical naming of the variables involved, a device that would *not* have the single-storage effect between programs and subprograms.

EQUIVALENCE is regarded as a convenience in two types of situations. First, it may be used to correct variable name changes that have come about as a result of what the Navy used to call "inadvertence"—to put it more bluntly, programmer error. If a variable referred to as WATCH for part of the program has been referred to as CLOCK for other parts, the insertion at the top of

EQUIVALENCE (WATCH, CLOCK)

may be simpler and less error-prone than rewriting and repunching whole sets of executable statements.

Second, when storage space is tight, further use may be made of storage originally reserved for variables needed only in early parts of the execution,

---

[2] *Specification* statements are those nonexecutable declaratory statements at the beginning of the program, which inform the compiler program of special storage arrangements: REAL, INTEGER, DOUBLE PRECISION, LOGICAL, COMPLEX, DIMENSION, COMMON—and in this chapter, EQUIVALENCE, IMPLICIT, EXTERNAL.

by making it available to variables needed only in later portions. For example, suppose that 500 values of COST are needed early in execution, and 500 values of PRICE in later stages. Although the programmer might save the storage room by calling both variables COST (or PRICE), he can also say

> DIMENSION COST(500), PRICE(500)
> EQUIVALENCE (COST, PRICE)

Note that subscripts are not mentioned in the sample EQUIVALENCE statement. In such cases, COST(1) and PRICE(1) are implied by the statement, leading to "overlay" of the entire arrays. The effect would in fact be the same, if written

> EQUIVALENCE (COST(1), PRICE(1))

THE IMPLICIT STATEMENT

Some compilers (including WATFOR and WATFIV) permit the programmer to design a partial or complete *implicit specification* system for any individual program. That is, he may establish certain alphabetic characters as specifying, when they appear as *initial* characters of variable names, the *type* of the variable as *real, integer, complex, double precision,* or *logical*. This arrangement overrides the usual integer-real predefinitions, and makes unnecessary the use of *explicit* type specification statements (REAL, INTEGER, COMPLEX, DOUBLE PRECISION, LOGICAL). The latter are still permissible, however, and override the IMPLICIT statement for particular variables. Thus

> IMPLICIT REAL(A,B), INTEGER(C —X), LOGICAL (Y,Z)
> REAL TORCH

As shown above, the parentheses may contain either individual letters or an inclusive range indicated by the use of the hyphen (minus sign). In this example, the variables ARROW and TORCH would be recognized as *real*, DOG and WOLF as *integer*, and ZEBRA as *logical*.

The following statement would have no effect, since it duplicates the *implicit* type specification rule built into the FORTRAN compiler program:

> IMPLICIT REAL (A —H, O —Z), INTEGER (I — N)

In WATFIV, the CHARACTER declaration may also be specified in an IMPLICIT statement. For example,

> IMPLICIT CHARACTER*50 (M)

Then all variables beginning with the letter M will be treated as alphameric variables.

STORAGE LENGTH ALTERATION AND INITIALIZATION IN EXPLICIT TYPE STATEMENTS

A common storage length for *integers* provides four "bytes" of memory, sufficient to store numbers up to

$$2^{31} - 1 = 2,147,483,647$$

To save storage space in particular programs, it is possible (depending on the system and compiler used) to declare *half* the usual length, for specific names. In WATFOR and WATFIV, for example,

INTEGER*2 I, J, K, SWIM

This statement declares that I, J, and K (usually integers anyway) and also SWIM (real if not so declared) are to occupy only two "bytes" of memory; they may only reach values of

$$2^{15} - 1 = 32,767$$

Similarly, *real* variables in the same systems are usually allocated *four* "bytes" of memory for single precision, leading to seven-digit precision; and *eight* "bytes" for double precision, leading to 16-digit precision. Instead of the DOUBLE PRECISION declaration, the following statement achieves *double precision* treatment for the variables named:

REAL*8 ARTHUR, JOHN, ROBERT

Logical variables usually occupy *four* "bytes"; but only *one* is really necessary for storing the logical value. Therefore, the following statement saves storage space *without* limiting the possible values stored:

LOGICAL*1 MAN, BOY

It is also possible to allow REAL, INTEGER, LOGICAL, and COMPLEX declaration statements to perform the role of the DATA initialization statement:

```
REAL*8 PI/3.141592653589793/, FRAME/2.7D+5/
INTEGER MARK(20)/20*100/
INTEGER*2 I, J, K/5, 10, 15/
LOGICAL*1 MAN, BOY/.TRUE., .FALSE./
CHARACTER*10 WARN/'IMPOSSIBLE'/
```

In this example, PI and FRAME are declared to be *double precision* as to storage length, and at the same time initial values are stored in each location (during *compilation*). Twenty values of MARK (usual four-byte storage length) are initialized at 100, half-length integers I, J, and K are initialized at 5, 10, and 15 respectively, and MAN and BOY are declared to be logical, with initial values of .TRUE. and .FALSE. provided. The fifth line in the example (CHARACTER) is legal only in WATFIV.

SOME ADDITIONAL STATEMENTS

THE EXTERNAL STATEMENT

In Chapter 7 we indicated that the *arguments* mentioned in *calling statements* may be variables, constants, or more complicated arithmetic expressions. One further possibility is permitted: the use of a *subprogram name* as an argument. When this is done, the *main* program must have an EXTERNAL statement, which specifies that this argument is to be found *outside* both the main program and the subprogram explicitly called by the main program. Sample program 11-1 shows the method:

```
C SAMPLE PROGRAM 11-1
C FUNCTION SUBPROGRAM TO OBTAIN RECIPROCALS OF CERTAIN
                                                 FUNCTIONS OF D
      FUNCTION RECIP(D, FUNCT)
      RECIP = 1./FUNCT(D)
      RETURN
      END

C THIS IS THE CALLING PROGRAM
      EXTERNAL SQRT, ALOG
      RSQRT = RECIP(75.6, SQRT)
      RLOG = RECIP(75.6, ALOG)
      PRINT, RSQRT, RLOG
      STOP
      END
```

The output form this example is, algebraically,

$$\frac{1}{\sqrt{75.6}} \quad \text{and} \quad \frac{1}{\log_e 75.6}$$

ORDER OF SPECIFICATION STATEMENTS

For most compilers, all *specification* statements must precede *executable* statements of the program. Furthermore, many compilers require a particular order of the specification statements used. The following order is generally acceptable:

>Type Statements (REAL, INTEGER, DOUBLE
PRECISION, COMPLEX, LOGICAL, IMPLICIT, CHARACTER)
EXTERNAL
DIMENSION
COMMON
EQUIVALENCE
Statement Function Definitions

THE ENTRY STATEMENT

Occasionally, the programmer wishes to provide different *points of entry* into a subprogram to avoid writing two separate subprograms. In such instances, the ENTRY statement serves to mark the points of entry other than the FUNCTION or SUBROUTINE statement at the top. Its construction is similar to that of these initial subprogram statements:

ENTRY GEOM(N)

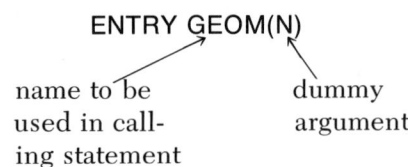

name to be used in calling statement

dummy argument

Sample program 11-2 shows a subprogram with an extra *entry point:*

```
C SAMPLE PROGRAM 11-2
C THIS SUBPROGRAM MAY BE ENTERED AT TWO DIFFERENT POINTS
      SUBROUTINE ABSALL(X, N)
      DIMENSION X(1)
      DO 1 I = 2, N, 2
1     X(I) = ABS(X(I))
      ENTRY ABSODD(X, N)
      DO 2 I = 1, N, 2
2     X(I) = ABS(X(I))
      RETURN
      END
```

If a calling statement says

DIMENSION COST(500)

CALL ABSALL(COST, 500)

the subprogram is entered at the top, and *all* values in the COST array are converted to absolute value. (Since the ENTRY statement is nonexecutable, it is simply ignored (bypassed) during this execution). But if the calling statement says

CALL ABSODD(COST, 500)

only odd-subscripted values in the COST array (first, third, fifth, etc.) are converted to absolute value.

The use of the ENTRY statement can usually be avoided, by adding an extra *argument* to the list. This is illustrated in sample program 11-3:

```
C SAMPLE PROGRAM 11-3
C AN ALTERNATIVE TO PROGRAM 11-2, WITHOUT THE ENTRY STATEMENT
```

```
      SUBROUTINE ABSOL(X, N, INCR)
      DIMENSION X(1)
      DO 1 I = 1, N, INCR
1     X(I) = ABS(X(I))
      RETURN
      END
```

To convert the entire array,

> CALL ABSOL(COST, 500, 1)

To convert only the odd-subscripted values,

> CALL ABSOL(COST, 500, 2)

LABELED COMMON

Many compilers permit the division (as directed by the programmer) of the COMMON storage area into separate "labeled" sections. The insertion of the label that names and identifies as separate such a COMMON area is accomplished by enclosing it between slashes. Thus

> COMMON /FIRST/ A, B, C /LAST/ D, E

establishes two labeled areas. If an unlabeled (*blank* COMMON) area is to be included, it may appear at the first part of the statement without slashes, or be preceded by two consecutive slashes, anywhere in the statement:

> COMMON DELTA, CROSS /FIRST/ A, B, C /LAST/ D, E

is the same as

> COMMON /FIRST/ A, B, C / / DELTA, CROSS /LAST/ D, E

This division into one blank and two labeled areas of COMMON storage would permit the programmer to specify equivalences (i.e., shared storage) in an order other than that originally used. For example, another COMMON statement in the same program could insert variables F and G in the "LAST" area merely by writing

> COMMON /LAST/ F, G

If this statement were written instead as

> COMMON F, G

the new variables would follow DELTA and CROSS in the *blank* COMMON area.

This sort of arrangement may be useful (though not indispensable) when variables in more than two programs are to share COMMON storage. For instance, suppose that two subprograms are in storage, each containing a different COMMON arrangement:

>First subprogram:
>
>COMMON X(100)
>
>Second subprogram:
>
>COMMON W(15, 5)

Now a main program is to be written that calls *both* of the subprograms, passing 100 values to the first and 75 completely different values to the second. A solution *not* using labeled COMMON would require COMMON statements with matching total storage length in the three programs:

>First subprogram:
>
>COMMON X(100), DUMMY(75)
>
>Second subprogram:
>
>COMMON DUMMY(100), W(15,5)
>
>Main program:
>
>COMMON RATE(100), PRICE(15,5)

However, if the subroutine subprogram COMMON statements had originally been written with *labels*, they would not require changing, for:

>First subprogram:
>
>COMMON /S1/ X(100)
>
>Second subprogram:
>
>COMMON /S2/ W(15,5)
>
>Main program:
>
>COMMON /S1/ RATE(100) /S2/ PRICE(15,5)

THE BLOCK DATA SUBPROGRAM

In WATFOR and WATFIV, the DATA statement may be used to initialize variables mentioned in COMMON statements. However, in most FORTRAN compilers, initial values may *not* be entered into areas of *blank* COMMON by use of the DATA statement. This restriction does not apply to *labeled* COMMON; but the use of the DATA statement to store values in labeled COMMON areas requires (in standard FORTRAN) a complete subprogram, which may contain *only specification statements*. The subprogram begins with a BLOCK DATA statement:

```
C SAMPLE PROGRAM 11-4
C THIS IS A BLOCK DATA SUBPROGRAM—ITS SOLE PURPOSE IS
C    INITIALIZATION OF VARIABLES IN LABELED COMMON AREAS
     BLOCK DATA
     DOUBLE PRECISION X(25)
     COMMON /NUM1/ K, L, M /NUM2/ X
     DATA K, L, M/10, 100, 1000/, X/25 * 1.D+12/
     END
```

In this unusual type of subprogram, RETURN is not legal, nor is any other *executable* statement. The subprogram is not *called* by any main program; it is compiled with the main program. We may also observe that this creates one of the rare uses for *labeled* COMMON.

END AND ERR OPTIONS IN THE READ STATEMENT

In sample program 5-12, we introduced the idea of the *sentinel card* used to signal the end of the data deck. The program is reproduced below:

```
C SAMPLE PROGRAM 5-12
C SENTINEL CARD AS ALTERNATIVE TO PARAMETER CARD
C     (SEE PROGRAM 3-11)—ARITHMETIC MEAN OF ANY SET OF
                                              DATA VALUES
      SUM = COUNT = 0.
  15  ⎡READ, X
      ⎢IF (X .EQ. 9999.99) GO TO 86
      ⎢SUM = SUM + X
      ⎢COUNT = COUNT + 1.
      ⎣GO TO 15
  86   XMEAN = SUM/COUNT
       PRINT, XMEAN
       STOP
       END
```

An alternative is shown in sample program 11-5 (below), using an optional form of the READ statement:

```
C SAMPLE PROGRAM 11-5
C THIS PROGRAM USES THE 'END =' OPTION IN THE READ STATEMENT,
C                               TO BRANCH OUT OF THE LOOP
```

```
        SUM = COUNT = 0.
15     ┌READ (5, 30, END = 86) X
       │SUM = SUM + X
       │COUNT = COUNT + 1.
       └GO TO 15
86      XMEAN = SUM/COUNT
        WRITE (6, 30) XMEAN
        STOP
30      FORMAT (F10.2)
        END
```

This usage presupposes that there is a special control character punched on the card following the last actual data card ($ at some installations), which acts as an "end-of-file" mark. When this card is reached during execution of sample program 11–5, a branch to statement 86 results. Thus the "END = #" option in the READ statement substitutes for a programmer-supplied "IF" statement testing a programmer-designed "sentinel card."

The general form of the READ statement with all available options is

```
READ (# #, END = #, ERR = #) input list
      ↑ ↑         ↖         ↖
   equip-  FORMAT  branch   branch to
   ment    state   to # at  # if I/O
   unit    ment    end of   device error
   number  number  file     occurs
```

The sort of "error" specified by ERR is not programmer error, but mechanical or electronic error (e.g., dust interfering with transfer of magnetic tape characters). When END and ERR are both used, their order in the statement is immaterial, and either one may be used alone.

I/O UNIT CONTROL STATEMENTS

Most FORTRAN compilers provide three statements that enable the programmer to manipulate input/output equipment, particularly where *magnetic tape* is the medium being used. In some instances, the statements may be applied to other media as well (e.g., magnetic disk), with comparable results.

In the following examples, # refers to the appropriate *equipment unit number*.

BACKSPACE #

initiates a backspace of one input record.

REWIND #

causes the specified unit to rewind to its starting point. (This is a wise move, prior to beginning any I/O operations referring to a tape unit; that is, the system operator may or may not have started the tape at its rewind point.)

END FILE

is used to place an "end-of-file" mark on the output record. This mark might then be later used by the "END = #" option in a READ statement.

FORMAT STATEMENTS TREATED AS DATA ARRAYS

We have suggested several types of generality that may be written into programs intended for use as part of a permanent program library. These include methods of avoiding predefinition of the size of the data set (e.g., parameter entry, sentinel card), provision of other execution-time options, and designation as function or subroutine subprograms.

When programs are to be applied to various data sets, and with varying requirements for precise form of output, the FORMAT statement is a frequent bottleneck, since it commits the user to particular forms of input and output records. Some compilers provide a flexible alternative, shown in sample program 11–6:

```
      C SAMPLE PROGRAM 11-6
      C FORMAT SPECIFICATIONS TREATED AS DATA
      C THE PROGRAM COMPUTES AND PRINTS AN ARRAY SUM
            DIMENSION IFORM(20), OFORM(20), X(5000)
            READ (5, 40) N, IFORM, OFORM
            READ (5, IFORM) (X(I), I = 1, N)
            SUM = 0.
            DO 1 I = 1, N
    1       SUM = SUM + X(I)
            WRITE (6, OFORM) SUM
            STOP
    40      FORMAT (I5 / 20A4 / 20A4)
            END
```

The only FORMAT statement actually written into this source program is one (statement 40) that serves the first READ statement. That statement reads in the parameter N, and then also reads in two *arrays* in *alphameric* FORMAT. The first of these, IFORM, represents a set of *input* FORMAT specifications, and the second, OFORM, a set of FORMAT specifications for *output*. Each of these arrays contains 20 elements; since each element may be used to store four alphameric characters, 80 characters in all can be stored within each array. In this example, then, an entire 80-column punch card is used to transfer input and output FORMAT specifications into the program *at execution time*.

The two data cards used for these FORMAT specifications should not mention any statement number, or the word FORMAT; they each begin with the left-hand parenthesis. For example, a data deck for sample program 11–6 might begin,

(card 1)	bb750
(card 2)	(10X, 4F10.0)
(card 3)	('1 TOTAL AREA POPULATION IN 1970 WAS' F15.0)
(card 4)	SUFFERN 24335 453865 7761 6654
	etc.

Card 1 contains the parameter N (750), card 2 the input FORMAT specifications, card 3 the output FORMAT specifications, and card 4 begins the actual data set.

In this execution, the actual contents of the IFORM and OFORM arrays are:

Element Number	IFORM	OFORM
1	(10X	('1b
2	,b4F	bbTO
3	10.0	TALb
4	)bbb	AREA
5	bbbb	bPOP
6	bbbb	ULAT
7	bbbb	IONb
8	bbbb	INb1
9	bbbb	970b
10	bbbb	WAS'
11	bbbb	bF15
12	bbbb	.0)b
13	bbbb	bbbb

(13 through 20 all blanks)

The second READ statement, and the WRITE statement, in sample program 11–6, substitute the appropriate *array name* for the usual FORMAT statement number. That is, the general form is

READ (#, name) input list

equipment unit number → name of array containing the alphameric FORMAT specifications

WRITE (#, name) output list

196   SOME ADDITIONAL STATEMENTS

THE ASSIGNED GO TO STATEMENT

For the sake of completeness, we mention the *Assigned GO TO* statement, but with the recommendation that it not be used. The reason is that the *Computed GO TO* statement is more versatile and, in effect, succeeds in four types of situations, for only one of which *Assigned GO TO* offers an alternative. First, the overlapping situation:

Computed GO TO	Assigned GO TO
K = 3	ASSIGN 8 TO K
----------------------------	----------------------------
GO TO (6, 7, 8, 9, 10), K	GO TO K, (6, 7, 8, 9, 10)

In each of the sequences above, the branch is to statement 8.

However, the ASSIGN statement shown at the right is the *only* method for selecting the specific statement number, when the Assigned GO TO form is used. The three types of situation that are *not* amenable to Assigned GO TO treatment are:

1. Determination of the option by reading a *parameter* value (as in sample program 5-15).

2. Use of the DO loop *index* as the condition variable; for example,

    DO 1 I = 1, 5
    GO TO (6, 7, 8, 9, 10), I
    ----

3. *Computation* of the conditioning variable; for example,

    KODE = N/2 − 1
    GO TO (1, 2, 3, 4, 5, 6, 7, 8, 9, 10), KODE

For Review

EQUIVALENCE statement
IMPLICIT statement

storage length alteration

initialization
EXTERNAL statement
ENTRY statement
labeled COMMON
BLOCK DATA statement
END and ERR options

Examples

EQUIVALENCE (WATCH, CLOCK)
IMPLICIT REAL(A), INTEGER(B-H),
                   LOGICAL(I,J)
INTEGER*2 K, L
REAL*8 PI
INTEGER*2 K, L /100, 1000/
EXTERNAL SQRT, ALOG
ENTRY ABSODD(X, N)
COMMON /ONE/ A, B /TWO/ C, D
BLOCK DATA
READ (5, 9, END = 6, ERR = 12)

I/O unit control statements	BACKSPACE 4
	REWIND 4
	END FILE 4
FORMAT statement as data array	DIMENSION IFORM(20)
	READ (5, 40) IFORM
40	FORMAT (20A4)
	READ (5, IFORM) X
Assigned GO TO statement	ASSIGN 8 TO K
	GO TO K, (6, 7, 8, 9, 10)

Programming Exercises

11–1. Write a program to compute the arithmetic mean of a real single-dimensioned array of 30 elements. However, arrange that the usual implicit type specification system is reversed; that is, variable names beginning with I-N are *real*, and all others are treated by the compiler as *integer*. Also arrange that the *sum* and the *mean* share the same storage location, although assigned different names.

11–2. Write a program that will read 10 cards containing four real data values each, and compute and print each four-value arithmetic mean. Make input FORMAT variable—that is, the input FORMAT statement is to be treated as an alphameric data array.

11–3. Arrange *double precision* for all real variable names used in program 11–2 (above), including the FORMAT array name, *without* using the DOUBLE PRECISION specification statement.

11–4. Adjust program 11–3 (above) so that any number of cards may be handled, with reading to halt when an end-of-file mark is encountered. (Use the END option in the READ statement). Test with the end-of-file mark following the *fifth* data card.

APPENDIX **A:**

WATFOR AND WATFIV DIAGNOSTIC MESSAGES

Although many WATFOR and WATFIV error codes and meanings are identical, the number of differences is sufficient to justify separate listing. If you are using the WATFIV compiler, use the table beginning on page 212 (but do read the following instructions, first).

Remember that the listings below actually refer to three levels of "error." Execution of the program is generally not possible when one or more outright language errors are found; these are indicated on your (computer-produced) program listing by

★★★ERROR★★★

On the other hand, an error code accompanied by

★★WARNING★★

indicates that the compiler program has been able to make some "forgiving" assumption about your statement, to allow continued compilation. Finally, a code marked with

★EXTENSION★

serves only as information to the effect that the usage referred to would not be allowed in standard FORTRAN.

The error codes are listed in alphabetical order on the left; section headings indicate the general subject matter diagnosed in each code group. Use the codes, not the section headings, to locate the error meaning.

I. WATFOR DIAGNOSTIC MESSAGES

ASSIGN STATEMENTS AND VARIABLES
- AS-2 ATTEMPT TO REDEFINE AN ASSIGNED VARIABLE IN AN ARITHMETIC EXPRESSION
- AS-3 ASSIGNED VARIABLE USED IN AN ARITHMETIC EXPRESSION
- AS-4 ASSIGNED VARIABLE CANNOT BE HALF WORD INTEGER
- AS-5 ATTEMPT TO REDEFINE AN ASSIGN VARIABLE IN AN INPUT LIST

BLOCK DATA STATEMENTS
- BD-0 EXECUTABLE STATEMENT IN BLOCK DATA SUBPROGRAM
- BD-1 IMPROPER BLOCK DATA STATEMENT

CARD FORMAT AND CONTENTS
- CC-0 COLUMNS 1-5 OF CONTINUATION CARD NOT BLANK (PROBABLE CAUSE—STATEMENT PUNCHED TO LEFT OF COLUMN 7)
- CC-1 TOO MANY CONTINUATION CARDS (MAXIMUM OF 5)
- CC-2 INVALID CHARACTER IN FORTRAN STATEMENT—'$' INSERTED IN SOURCE LISTING
- CC-3 FIRST CARD OF A PROGRAM IS A CONTINUATION CARD (PROBABLE CAUSE—STATEMENT PUNCHED TO LEFT OF COLUMN 7)
- CC-4 STATEMENT TOO LONG TO COMPILE (SCAN-STACK OVERFLOW)
- CC-5 BLANK CARD ENCOUNTERED
- CC-6 KEYPUNCH USED DIFFERS FROM KEYPUNCH SPECIFIED ON JOB CARD
- CC-7 FIRST CHARACTER OF STATEMENT NOT ALPHABETIC
- CC-8 INVALID CHARACTER(S) CONCATENATED WITH FORTRAN KEYWORD
- CC-9 INVALID CHARACTERS IN COLUMNS 1-5. STATEMENT NUMBER IGNORED (PROBABLE CAUSE—STATEMENT PUNCHED TO LEFT OF COLUMN 7)

COMMON
- CM-0 VARIABLE PREVIOUSLY PLACED IN COMMON
- CM-1 NAME IN COMMON LIST PREVIOUSLY USED AS OTHER THAN VARIABLE
- CM-2 SUBPROGRAM PARAMETER APPEARS IN COMMON STATEMENT
- CM-3 INITIALIZING OF COMMON SHOULD BE DONE IN A BLOCK DATA SUBPROGRAM
- CM-4 ILLEGAL USE OF BLOCK NAME

FORTRAN CONSTANTS
  CN-0 MIXED REAL*4, REAL*8 IN COMPLEX CONSTANT
  CN-1 INTEGER CONSTANT GREATER THAN 2, 147, 483, 647 (2**31-1)
  CN-2 EXPONENT OVERFLOW OR UNDERFLOW CONVERTING
                  CONSTANT IN SOURCE STATEMENT
  CN-3 EXPONENT ON REAL CONSTANT GREATER THAN 99
  CN-4 REAL CONSTANT HAS MORE THAN 16 DIGITS, TRUNCATED
                                                  TO 16
  CN-5 INVALID HEXADECIMAL CONSTANT
  CN-6 ILLEGAL USE OF DECIMAL POINT
  CN-8 CONSTANT WITH E-TYPE EXPONENT HAS MORE THAN
                  7 DIGITS, ASSUME D-TYPE
  CN-9 CONSTANT OR STATEMENT NUMBER GREATER THAN 99999
COMPILER ERRORS (Not the programmer's responsibility; notify the
  CP-0 DETECTED IN PHASE RELOC   computer center)
  CP-1 DETECTED IN PHASE LINKR
  CP-2 DUPLICATE PSEUDO STATEMENT NUMBERS
  CP-4 DETECTED IN PHASE ARITH
  CP-5 COMPILER INTERRUPT
DATA STATEMENT
  DA-0 REPLICATION FACTOR GREATER THAN 32767, ASSUME 32767
  DA-1 NON-CONSTANT IN DATA STATEMENT
  DA-2 MORE VARIABLES THAN CONSTANTS IN DATA STATEMENT
  DA-3 ATTEMPT TO INITIALIZE A SUBPROGRAM PARAMETER IN A
                                           DATA STATEMENT
  DA-4 NON-CONSTANT SUBSCRIPTS IN A DATA STATEMENT
                  INVALID IN STANDARD FORTRAN
  DA-5 STANDARD FORTRAN DOES NOT HAVE IMPLIED DO IN DATA
                                                STATEMENT
  DA-6 NON-AGREEMENT BETWEEN TYPE OF VARIABLE AND
                  CONSTANT IN DATA STATEMENT
  DA-7 MORE CONSTANTS THAN VARIABLES IN DATA STATEMENT
  DA-8 VARIABLE PREVIOUSLY INITIALIZED. LATEST VALUE USED
          (CHECK COMMON/EQUIVALENCED VARIABLES)
  DA-9 INITIALIZING BLANK COMMON NOT ALLOWED IN STANDARD
                                                  FORTRAN
  DA-A INVALID DELIMITER IN CONSTANT LIST PORTION OF DATA
                                                STATEMENT
  DA-B TRUNCATION OF LITERAL CONSTANT HAS OCCURRED
DIMENSION STATEMENTS
  DM-0 NO DIMENSIONS SPECIFIED FOR A VARIABLE IN A
                  DIMENSION STATEMENT

DM-1 OPTIONAL LENGTH SPECIFICATION IN DIMENSION STATEMENT IS ILLEGAL
DM-2 INITIALIZATION IN DIMENSION STATEMENT IS ILLEGAL
DM-3 ATTEMPT TO RE-DIMENSION A VARIABLE
DM-4 ATTEMPT TO DIMENSION AN INITIALIZED VARIABLE

DO LOOPS
  DO-0 ILLEGAL STATEMENT USED AS OBJECT OF DO
  DO-1 ILLEGAL TRANSFER INTO THE RANGE OF A DO-LOOP
  DO-2 OBJECT OF A DO STATEMENT HAS ALREADY APPEARED
  DO-3 IMPROPERLY NESTED DO-LOOPS
  DO-4 ATTEMPT TO REDEFINE A DO-LOOP PARAMETER WITHIN RANGE OF LOOP
  DO-5 INVLID DO-LOOP PARAMETER
  DO-6 TOO MANY NESTED DO'S (MAXIMUM OF 20)
  DO-7 DO-PARAMETER IS UNDEFINED OR OUTSIDE RANGE
  DO-8 THIS DO LOOP WILL TERMINATE AFTER FIRST TIME THROUGH
  DO-9 ATTEMPT TO REDEFINE A DO-LOOP PARAMETER IN AN INPUT LIST

EQUIVALENCE AND/OR COMMON
  EC-0 TWO EQUIVALENCED VARIABLES APPEAR IN COMMON
  EC-1 COMMON BLOCK HAS DIFFERENT LENGTH THAN IN A PREVIOUS SUBPROGRAM
  EC-2 COMMON AND/OR EQUIVALENCE CAUSES INVALID ALIGNMENT. EXECUTION SLOWED. (REMEDY—ORDER VARIABLES IN DESCENDING ORDER BY LENGTH)
  EC-3 EQUIVALENCE EXTENDS COMMON DOWNWARDS
  EC-7 COMMON/EQUIVALENCE STATEMENT DOES NOT PRECEDE PREVIOUS USE OF VARIABLE
  EC-8 VARIABLE USED WITH NON-CONSTANT SUBSCRIPT IN COMMON/EQUIVALENCE LIST
  EC-9 A NAME SUBSCRIPTED IN AN EQUIVALENCE STATEMENT WAS NOT DIMENSIONED

END STATEMENTS
  EN-0 NO END STATEMENT IN PROGRAM—END STATEMENT GENERATED
  EN-1 END STATEMENT USED AS STOP STATEMENT AT EXECUTION
  EN-2 IMPROPER END STATEMENT
  EN-3 FIRST STATEMENT OF SUBPROGRAM IS END STATEMENT

EQUAL SIGNS
  EQ-6 ILLEGAL QUANTITY ON LEFT OF EQUALS SIGN

EQ-8 ILLEGAL USE OF EQUAL SIGN
EQ-A MULTIPLE ASSIGNMENT STATEMENTS NOT IN STANDARD FORTRAN

EQUIVALENCE STATEMENTS
  EV-0 ATTEMPT TO EQUIVALENCE A VARIABLE TO ITSELF
  EV-1 ATTEMPT TO EQUIVALENCE A SUBPROGRAM PARAMETER
  EV-2 LESS THAN 2 MEMBERS IN AN EQUIVALENCE LIST
  EV-3 TOO MANY EQUIVALENCE LISTS (MAX = 255)
  EV-4 PREVIOUSLY EQUIVALENCED VARIABLE RE-EQUIVALENCED INCORRECTLY

POWERS AND EXPONENTIATION
  EX-0 ILLEGAL COMPLEX EXPONENTIATION
  EX-2 I**J WHERE I = J = 0
  EX-3 I**J WHERE I = 0, J .LT. 0
  EX-6 0.0**Y WHERE Y .LE. 0.0
  EX-7 0.0**J WHERE J = 0
  EX-8 0.0**J WHERE J .LT. 0
  EX-9 X**Y WHERE X .LT. 0.0, Y .NE. 0.0

ENTRY STATEMENT
  EY-0 SUBPROGRAM NAME IN ENTRY STATEMENT PREVIOUSLY DEFINED
  EY-1 PREVIOUS DEFINITION OF FUNCTION NAME IN AN ENTRY IS INCORRECT
  EY-2 USE OF SUBPROGRAM PARAMETER INCONSISTENT WITH PREVIOUS ENTRY POINT
  EY-3 ARGUMENT NAME HAS APPEARED IN AN EXECUTABLE STATEMENT, BUT WAS NOT A SUBPROGRAM PARAMETER
  EY-4 ENTRY STATEMENT NOT PERMITTED IN MAIN PROGRAM
  EY-5 ENTRY POINT INVALID INSIDE A DO-LOOP
  EY-6 VARIABLE WAS NOT PREVIOUSLY USED AS A PARAMETER – PARAMETER ASSSUMED

FORMAT
(Some FORMAT error messages give characters in which error was detected)
  FM-0 INVALID CHARACTER IN INPUT DATA
  FM-2 NO STATEMENT NUMBER ON A FORMAT STATEMENT
  FM-5 FORMAT SPECIFICATION AND DATA TYPE DO NOT MATCH
  FM-6 INCORRECT SEQUENCE OF CHARACTERS IN INPUT DATA
  FM-7 NON-TERMINATING FORMAT

  FT-0 FIRST CHARACTER OF VARIABLE FORMAT NOT A LEFT PARENTHESIS

FT-1   INVALID CHARACTER ENCOUNTERED IN FORMAT
FT-2   INVALID FORM FOLLOWING A SPECIFICATION
FT-3   INVALID FIELD OR GROUP COUNT
FT-4   A FIELD OR GROUP COUNT GREATER THAN 255
FT-5   NO CLOSING PARENTHESIS ON VARIABLE FORMAT
FT-6   NO CLOSING QUOTE IN A HOLLERITH FIELD
FT-7   INVALID USE OF COMMA
FT-8   INSUFFICIENT SPACE TO COMPILE A FORMAT STATEMENT
           (SCAN-STACK OVERFLOW)
FT-9   INVALID USE OF P SPECIFICATION
FT-A   CHARACTER FOLLOWS CLOSING RIGHT PARENTHESIS
FT-B   INVALID USE OF PERIOD (.)
FT-C   MORE THAN THREE LEVELS OF PARENTHESES
FT-D   INVALID CHARACTER BEFORE A RIGHT PARENTHESIS
FT-E   MISSING OR ZERO LENGTH HOLLERITH ENCOUNTERED
FT-F   NO CLOSING RIGHT PARENTHESIS

FUNCTIONS AND SUBROUTINES
FN-0   NO ARGUMENTS IN A FUNCTION STATEMENT
FN-3   REPEATED ARGUMENT IN SUBPROGRAM OR STATEMENT
           FUNCTION DEFINITION
FN-4   SUBSCRIPTS ON RIGHT HAND SIDE OF STATEMENT
       FUNCTION (PROBABLE CAUSE—VARIABLE TO LEFT OF = NOT
           DIMENSIONED)
FN-5   MULTIPLE RETURNS ARE INVALID IN FUNCTION
           SUBPROGRAMS
FN-6   ILLEGAL LENGTH MODIFIER IN TYPE FUNCTION STATEMENT
FN-7   INVALID ARGUMENT IN ARITHMETIC OR LOGICAL
           STATEMENT FUNCTION
FN-8   ARGUMENT OF SUBPROGRAM IS SAME AS SUBPROGRAM
           NAME

GO TO STATEMENTS
GO-0   STATEMENT TRANSFERS TO ITSELF OR A NON-EXECUTABLE
           STATEMENT
GO-1   INVALID TRANSFER TO THIS STATEMENT
GO-2   INDEX OF COMPUTED GO TO IS NEGATIVE, ZERO OR
           UNDEFINED
GO-3   ERROR IN VARIABLE OF GO TO STATEMENT
GO-4   INDEX OF ASSIGNED GO TO IS UNDEFINED OR NOT IN
           RANGE

HOLLERITH CONSTANTS
HO-0   ZERO LENGTH SPECIFIED FOR H-TYPE HOLLERITH

HO-1 ZERO LENGTH QUOTE-TYPE HOLLERITH
HO-2 NO CLOSING QUOTE OR NEXT CARD NOT CONTINUATION CARD
HO-3 HOLLERITH CONSTANT SHOULD APPEAR ONLY IN CALL STATEMENT
HO-4 UNEXPECTED HOLLERITH OR STATEMENT NUMBER CONSTANT

IF STATEMENTS (ARITHMETIC AND LOGICAL)
  IF-0 STATEMENT INVALID AFTER A LOGICAL IF
  IF-3 ARITHMETIC OR INVALID EXPRESSION IN LOGICAL IF
  IF-4 LOGICAL, COMPLEX, OR INVALID EXPRESSION IN ARITHMETIC IF

IMPLICIT STATEMENT
  IM-0 INVALID MODE SPECIFIED IN AN IMPLICIT STATEMENT
  IM-1 INVALID LENGTH SPECIFIED IN AN IMPLICIT OR TYPE STATEMENT
  IM-2 ILLEGAL APPEARANCE OF $ IN A CHARACTER RANGE
  IM-3 IMPROPER ALPHABETIC SEQUENCE IN CHARACTER RANGE
  IM-4 SPECIFICATION MUST BE SINGLE ALPHABETIC CHARACTER, 1ST CHARACTER USED
  IM-5 IMPLICIT STATEMENT DOES NOT PRECEDE OTHER SPECIFICATION STATEMENTS
  IM-6 ATTEMPT TO ESTABLISH THE TYPE OF A CHARACTER MORE THAN ONCE
  IM-7 STANDARD FORTRAN ALLOWS ONE IMPLICIT STATEMENT PER PROGRAM
  IM-8 INVALID ELEMENT IN IMPLICIT STATEMENT
  IM-9 INVALID DELIMITER IN IMPLICIT STATEMENT

INPUT/OUTPUT
  IO-0 MISSING COMMA IN I/O LIST OF I/O OR DATA STATEMENT
  IO-2 STATEMENT NUMBER IN I/O STATEMENT NOT A FORMAT STATEMENT NUMBER
  IO-3 FORMATTED LINE TOO LONG FOR I/O DEVICE (RECORD LENGTH EXCEEDED)
  IO-6 VARIABLE FORMAT NOT AN ARRAY NAME
  IO-8 INVALID ELEMENT IN INPUT LIST OR DATA LIST
  IO-9 TYPE OF VARIABLE UNIT NOT INTEGER IN I/O STATEMENTS
  IO-A HALF-WORD INTEGER VARIABLE USED AS UNIT IN I/O STATEMENTS
  IO-B ASSIGNED INTEGER VARIABLE USED AS UNIT IN I/O STATEMENTS

IO-C   INVALID ELEMENT IN AN OUTPUT LIST
IO-D   MISSING OR INVALID UNIT IN I/O STATEMENT
IO-E   MISSING OR INVALID FORMAT IN READ/WRITE STATEMENT
IO-F   INVALID DELIMITER IN SPECIFICATION PART OF I/O STATEMENT
IO-G   MISSING STATEMENT NUMBER AFTER END= OR ERR=
IO-H   STANDARD FORTRAN DOES NOT ALLOW END/ERR RETURNS IN WRITE STATEMENTS
IO-J   INVALID DELIMITER IN I/O LIST
IO-K   INVALID DELIMITER IN STOP, PAUSE, DATA, OR TAPE CONTROL STATEMENT

JOB CONTROL CARDS
JB-1   JOB CARD ENCOUNTERED DURING COMPILATION
JB-2   INVALID OPTION(S) SPECIFIED ON JOB CARD
JB-3   UNEXPECTED CONTROL CARD ENCOUNTERED DURING COMPILATION

JOB TERMINATION
KO-0   JOB TERMINATED IN EXECUTION BECAUSE OF COMPILE TIME ERROR
KO-1   FIXED-POINT DIVISION BY ZERO
KO-2   FLOATING-POINT DIVISION BY ZERO
KO-3   TOO MANY EXPONENT OVERFLOWS
KO-4   TOO MANY EXPONENT UNDERFLOWS
KO-5   TOO MANY FIXED-POINT OVERFLOWS
KO-6   JOB TIME EXCEEDED
KO-7   COMPILER ERROR—INTERRUPTION AT EXECUTION TIME, RETURN TO SYSTEM
KO-8   INTEGER IN INPUT DATA IS TOO LARGE (MAXIMUM IS 2147483647)
KO-9   JOB CANCELLED BY OPERATOR

LOGICAL OPERATIONS
LG-2   .NOT. USED AS A BINARY OPERATOR

LIBRARY ROUTINES
LI-0   ARGUMENT OUT OF RANGE DGAMMA OR GAMMA. (1.382E-76 .LT. X .LT. 57.57)
LI-1   ABSOLUTE VALUE OF ARGUMENT .GT. 174.673, SINH, COSH, DSINH, DCOSH
LI-2   SENSE LIGHT OTHER THAN 0, 1, 2, 3, 4 FOR SLITE OR 1,2,3,4 FOR SLITET

LI–3	REAL PORTION OF ARGUMENT .GT. 174.673, CEXP OR CDEXP
LI–4	ABS(AIMAG(Z)) .GT. 174.673 FOR CSIN, CCOS, CDSIN OR CDCOS OF Z
LI–5	ABS(REAL(Z)) .GE. 3.537E15 FOR CSIN, CCOS, CDSIN OR CDCOS OF Z
LI–6	ABS(AIMAG(Z)) .GE. 3.537E15 FOR CEXP OR CDEXP OF Z
LI–7	ARGUMENT .GT. 174.673, EXP OR DEXP
LI–8	ARGUMENT IS ZERO, CLOG, CLOG10, CDLOG OR CDLOG10
LI–9	ARGUMENT IS NEGATIVE OR ZERO, ALOG, ALOG10, DLOG OR DLOG10
LI–A	ABS(X) .GE. 3.537E15 FOR SIN, COS, DSIN OR DCOS OF X
LI–B	ABSOLUTE VALUE OF ARGUMENT .GT. 1, FOR ARSIN, ARCOS, DARSIN OR DARCOS
LI–C	ARGUMENT IS NEGATIVE, SQRT OR DSQRT
LI–D	BOTH ARGUMENTS OF DATAN2 OR ATAN2 ARE ZERO
LI–E	ARGUMENT TOO CLOSE TO A SINGULARITY, TAN, COTAN, DTAN OR DCOTAN
LI–F	ARGUMENT OUT OF RANGE DLGAMA OR ALGAMA. (0.0 .LT. X .LT. 4.29E73)
LI–G	ABSOLUTE VALUE OF ARGUMENT .GE. 3.537E15, TAN, COTAN, DTAN, DCOTAN
LI–H	FEWER THAN TWO ARGUMENTS FOR ONE OF MINO, MIN1, AMINO, ETC.

MIXED MODE

MD–2	RELATIONAL OPERATOR HAS A LOGICAL OPERAND
MD–3	RELATIONAL OPERATOR HAS A COMPLEX OPERAND
MD–4	MIXED MODE – LOGICAL WITH ARITHMETIC
MD–6	WARNING – SUBSCRIPT IS COMPLEX. REAL PART USED.

MEMORY OVERFLOW

MO–0	SYMBOL TABLE OVERFLOWS OBJECT CODE. SOURCE ERROR CHECKING CONTINUES
MO–1	INSUFFICIENT MEMORY TO ASSIGN ARRAY STORAGE. JOB ABANDONED
MO–2	SYMBOL TABLE OVERFLOWS COMPILER, JOB ABANDONED
MO–3	DATA AREA OF SUBPROGRAM TOO LARGE – SEGMENT SUBPROGRAM
MO–4	GETMAIN CANNOT PROVIDE BUFFER FOR WATLIB

PARENTHESES

PC–0	UNMATCHED PARENTHESES
PC–1	INVALID PARENTHESIS COUNT

PAUSE, STOP STATEMENTS
    PS-0   STOP WITH OPERATOR MESSAGE NOT ALLOWED. SIMPLE STOP ASSUMED
    PS-1   PAUSE WITH OPERATOR MESSAGE NOT ALLOWED. TREATED AS CONTINUE

RETURN STATEMENT
    RE-0   FIRST CARD OF SUBPROGRAM IS A RETURN STATEMENT
    RE-1   RETURN I, WHERE I IS ZERO, NEGATIVE OR TOO LARGE
    RE-2   MULTIPLE RETURN NOT VALID IN FUNCTION SUBPROGRAM
    RE-3   VARIABLE IN MULTIPLE RETURN IS NOT A SIMPLE INTEGER VARIABLE
    RE-4   MULTIPLE RETURN NOT VALID IN MAIN PROGRAM

ARITHMETIC AND LOGICAL STATEMENT FUNCTIONS
    (Probable cause of errors: variable on left of = not dimensioned)
    SF-1   PREVIOUSLY REFERENCED STATEMENT NUMBER ON STATEMENT FUNCTION
    SF-2   STATEMENT FUNCTION IS THE OBJECT OF A LOGICAL IF STATEMENT
    SF-3   RECURSIVE STATEMENT FUNCTION, NAME APPEARS ON BOTH SIDES OF =
    SF-5   ILLEGAL USE OF A STATEMENT FUNCTION

SUBPROGRAMS
    SR-0   MISSING SUBPROGRAM
    SR-2   SUBPROGRAM ASSIGNED DIFFERENT MODES IN DIFFERENT PROGRAM SEGMENTS
    SR-4   INVALID TYPE OF ARGUMENT IN SUBPROGRAM REFERENCE
    SR-5   SUBPROGRAM ATTEMPTS TO REDEFINE A CONSTANT, TEMPORARY OR DO PARAMETER
    SR-6   ATTEMPT TO USE SUBPROGRAM RECURSIVELY
    SR-7   WRONG NUMBER OF ARGUMENTS IN SUBPROGRAM REFERENCE
    SR-8   SUBPROGRAM NAME PREVIOUSLY DEFINED — FIRST REFERENCE USED
    SR-9   NO MAIN PROGRAM
    SR-A   ILLEGAL OR BLANK SUBPROGRAM NAME

SUBSCRIPTS
    SS-0   ZERO SUBSCRIPT OR DIMENSION NOT ALLOWED
    SS-1   SUBSCRIPT OUT OF RANGE
    SS-2   INVALID VARIABLE OR NAME USED FOR DIMENSION

STATEMENTS AND STATEMENT NUMBERS
- ST-0   MISSING STATEMENT NUMBER
- ST-1   STATEMENT NUMBER GREATER THAN 99999
- ST-3   MULTIPLY-DEFINED STATEMENT NUMBER
- ST-4   NO STATEMENT NUMBER ON STATEMENT FOLLOWING TRANSFER STATEMENT
- ST-5   UNDECODEABLE STATEMENT
- ST-7   STATEMENT NUMBER SPECIFIED IN A TRANSFER IS A NON-EXECUTABLE STATEMENT
- ST-8   STATEMENT NUMBER CONSTANT MUST BE IN A CALL STATEMENT
- ST-9   STATEMENT SPECIFIED IN A TRANSFER STATEMENT IS A FORMAT STATEMENT
- ST-A   MISSING FORMAT STATEMENT

SUBSCRIPTED VARIABLES
- SV-0   WRONG NUMBER OF SUBSCRIPTS
- SV-1   ARRAY NAME OR SUBPROGRAM NAME USED INCORRECTLY WITHOUT LIST
- SV-2   MORE THAN 7 DIMENSIONS NOT ALLOWED
- SV-3   DIMENSION TOO LARGE
- SV-4   VARIABLE WITH VARIABLE DIMENSIONS IS NOT A SUBPROGRAM PARAMETER
- SV-5   VARIABLE DIMENSION NEITHER SIMPLE INTEGER VARIABLE NOR S/P PARAMETER

SYNTAX ERRORS
- SX-0   MISSING OPERATOR
- SX-1   SYNTAX ERROR–SEARCHING FOR SYMBOL, NONE FOUND
- SX-2   SYNTAX ERROR–SEARCHING FOR CONSTANT, NONE FOUND
- SX-3   SYNTAX ERROR–SEARCHING FOR SYMBOL OR CONSTANT, NONE FOUND
- SX-4   SYNTAX ERROR–SEARCHING FOR STATEMENT NUMBER, NONE FOUND
- SX-5   SYNTAX ERROR–SEARCHING FOR SIMPLE INTEGER VARIABLE, NONE FOUND
- SX-C   ILLEGAL SEQUENCE OF OPERATORS IN EXPRESSION
- SX-D   MISSING OPERAND OR OPERATOR

I/O OPERATIONS
- UN-0   CONTROL CARD ENCOUNTERED ON UNIT 5 DURING EXECUTION (PROBABLE CAUSE–MISSING DATA OR IMPROPER FORMAT STATEMENTS)

UN-1	END OF FILE ENCOUNTERED	
UN-2	I/O ERROR	
UN-3	DATA SET REFERENCED FOR WHICH NO DD CARD SUPPLIED	
UN-4	REWIND, ENDFILE, BACKSPACE REFERENCES UNIT 5, 6, 7	
UN-5	ATTEMPT TO READ ON UNIT 5 AFTER IT HAS HAD END-OF-FILE	
UN-6	UNIT NUMBER IS NEGATIVE, ZERO, GREATER THAN 7 OR UNDEFINED	
UN-7	TOO MANY PAGES	
UN-8	ATTEMPT TO DO SEQUENTIAL I/O ON A DIRECT ACCESS FILE	
UN-9	WRITE REFERENCES 5 OR READ REFERENCES 6, 7	
UN-A	ATTEMPT TO READ MORE DATA THAN CONTAINED IN LOGICAL RECORD	
UN-B	TOO MANY PHYSICAL RECORDS IN A LOGICAL RECORD. INCREASE RECORD LENGTH	
UN-C	I/O ERROR ON WATLIB	
UN-D	RECFM OTHER THAN V IS SPECIFIED FOR I/O WITHOUT FORMAT CONTROL	

UNDEFINED VARIABLES

UV-0	UNDEFINED VARIABLE – SIMPLE VARIABLE
UV-1	UNDEFINED VARIABLE – EQUIVALENCED, COMMONED, OR DUMMY PARAMETER
UV-2	UNDEFINED VARIABLE – ARRAY MEMBER
UV-3	UNDEFINED VARIABLE – ARRAY NAME WHICH WAS USED AS A DUMMY PARAMETER
UV-4	UNDEFINED VARIABLE – SUBPROGRAM NAME USED AS DUMMY PARAMETER
UV-5	UNDEFINED VARIABLE – ARGUMENT OF THE LIBRARY SUBPROGRAM NAMED
UV-6	VARIABLE FORMAT CONTAINS UNDEFINED CHARACTER(S)

VARIABLE NAMES

VA-0	ATTEMPT TO REDEFINE TYPE OF A VARIABLE NAME
VA-1	SUBROUTINE NAME OR COMMON BLOCK NAME USED INCORRECTLY
VA-2	NAME LONGER THAN SIX CHARACTERS. TRUNCATED TO SIX
VA-3	ATTEMPT TO REDEFINE THE MODE OF A VARIABLE NAME
VA-4	ATTEMPT TO REDEFINE THE TYPE OF A VARIABLE NAME
VA-6	ILLEGAL USE OF A SUBROUTINE NAME
VA-8	ATTEMPT TO USE A PREVIOUSLY DEFINED NAME AS FUNCTION OR ARRAY
VA-9	ATTEMPT TO USE A PREVIOUSLY DEFINED NAME AS A STATEMENT FUNCTION

VA–A ATTEMPT TO USE A PREVIOUSLY DEFINED NAME AS A SUBPROGRAM NAME
VA–B NAME USED AS A COMMON BLOCK PREVIOUSLY USED AS A SUBPROGRAM NAME
VA–C NAME USED AS SUBPROGRAM PREVIOUSLY USED AS A COMMON BLOCK NAME
VA–D ILLEGAL DO-PARAMETER, ASSIGNED OR INITIALIZED VARIABLE IN SPECIFICATION
VA–E ATTEMPT TO DIMENSION A CALL-BY-NAME PARAMETER

EXTERNAL STATEMENT
  XT–0 INVALID ELEMENT IN EXTERNAL LIST
  XT–1 INVALID DELIMITER IN EXTERNAL STATEMENT
  XT–2 SUBPROGRAM PREVIOUSLY EXTERNALLED

II. WATFIV DIAGNOSTIC MESSAGES

ASSEMBLER LANGUAGE SUBPROGRAMS
- AL-0 MISSING END CARD ON ASSEMBLY LANGUAGE OBJECT DECK
- AL-1 ENTRY-POINT OR CSECT NAME IN AN OBJECT DECK WAS PREVIOUSLY DEFINED. FIRST DEFINITION USED

BLOCK DATA STATEMENTS
- BD-0 EXECUTABLE STATEMENTS ARE ILLEGAL IN BLOCK DATA SUBPROGRAMS
- BD-1 IMPROPER BLOCK DATA STATEMENT

CARD FORMAT AND CONTENTS
- CC-0 COLUMNS 1-5 OF CONTINUATION CARD NOT BLANK. PROBABLE CAUSE: STATEMENT PUNCHED TO LEFT OF COLUMN 7
- CC-1 LIMIT OF 5 CONTINUATION CARDS EXCEEDED
- CC-2 INVALID CHARACTER IN FORTRAN STATEMENT. A '$' CHAR WAS INSERTED IN THE SOURCE LISTING
- CC-3 FIRST CARD OF A PROGRAM IS A CONTINUATION CARD. PROBABLE CAUSE: STATEMENT PUNCHED TO LEFT OF COLUMN 7
- CC-4 STATEMENT TOO LONG TO COMPILE (SCAN-STACK OVERFLOW)
- CC-5 BLANK CARD ENCOUNTERED
- CC-6 KEYPUNCH USED DIFFERS FROM KEYPUNCH SPECIFIED ON JOB CARD
- CC-7 FIRST CHARACTER OF THE STATEMENT WAS NOT ALPHABETIC
- CC-8 INVALID CHARACTER(S) ARE CONCATENATED WITH THE FORTRAN KEYWORD
- CC-9 INVALID CHARACTERS IN COL 1-5. STATEMENT NUMBER IGNORED. PROBABLE CAUSE: STATEMENT PUNCHED TO LEFT OF COLUMN 7

COMMON
- CM-0 VARIABLE _____ IS ALREADY IN COMMON
- CM-1 OTHER COMPILERS MAY NOT ALLOW COMMONED VARIABLE TO BE INITIALIZED IN OTHER THAN A BLOCK DATA SUBPROGRAM
- CM-2 ILLEGAL USE OF THE COMMON BLOCK OR NAMELIST NAME _____

FORTRAN TYPE CONSTANTS
- CN-0 MIXED REAL*4, REAL*8 IN COMPLEX CONSTANT; REAL*8 ASSUMED FOR BOTH

CN–1   AN INTEGER CONSTANT MAY NOT BE GREATER THAN 2, 147, 483, 647 (2**31–1)
CN–2   EXPONENT _____ ON A REAL CONSTANT IS GREATER THAN 99, THE MAXIMUM
CN–3   REAL CONSTANT HAS MORE THAN 16 DIGITS. TRUNCATED TO 16
CN–4   INVALID HEXADECIMAL CONSTANT
CN–5   ILLEGAL USE OF DECIMAL POINT
CN–6   CONSTANT WITHE E-TYPE EXPONENT HAS MORE THAN 7 DIGITS, D-TYPE ASSUMED
CN–7   CONSTANT OR STATEMENT NUMBER GREATHER THAN 99999
CN–8   EXPONENT OVERFLOW OR UNDERFLOW WHILE CONVERTING A CONSTANT IN SOURCE STATEMENT

COMPILER ERRORS
CP–0   COMPILER ERROR – LANDR/ARITH
CP–1   COMPILER ERROR – LIKELY CAUSE: MORE THAN 255 DO STATEMENTS
CP–4   COMPILER ERROR – INTERRUPT AT COMPILE TIME, RETURN TO SYSTEM

CHARACTER VARIABLE
CV–0   A CHARACTER VARIABLE IS USED WITH A RELATIONAL OPERATOR
CV–1   LENGTH OF CHARACTER VALUE ON RIGHT OF EQUAL SIGN EXCEEDS THAT ON LEFT. TRUNCATION WILL OCCUR
CV–2   UNFORMATTED CORE TO CORE I/O NOT IMPLEMENTED

DATA STATEMENT
DA–0   REPLICATION FACTOR _____ IS ZERO OR GREATER THAN 32767. IT IS ASSUMED TO BE 32767
DA–1   MORE VARIABLES THAN CONSTANTS
DA–2   ATTEMPT TO INITIALIZE THE SUBPROGRAM PARAMETER _____ IN A DATA STATEMENT
DA–3   OTHER COMPILERS MAY NOT ALLOW NON-CONSTANT SUBSCRIPTS IN DATA STATEMENTS
DA–4   NON-AGREEMENT BETWEEN TYPE OF VARIABLE AND CONSTANT _____
DA–5   MORE CONSTANTS THAN VARIABLES
DA–6   A VARIABLE _____ WAS PREVIOUSLY INITIALIZED. THE LATEST VALUE IS USED. CHECK COMMONED AND EQUIVALENCED VARIABLES
DA–7   OTHER COMPILERS MAY NOT ALLOW INITIALIZATION OF BLANK COMMON
DA–8   LITERAL CONSTANT _____ HAS BEEN TRUNCATED

DA-9   OTHER COMPILERS MAY NOT ALLOW IMPLIED DO-LOOPS IN DATA STATEMENTS

DEFINE FILE STATEMENTS
  DF-0   THE UNIT NUMBER IS MISSING
  DF-1   THE FORMAT _____ IS INVALID
  DF-2   ASSOCIATED VARIABLE _____ IS NOT A SIMPLE INTEGER VARIABLE
  DF-3   NUMBER OF RECORDS OR RECORD SIZE _____ IS INVALID

DIMENSION STATEMENTS
  DM-0   NO DIMENSIONS WERE SPECIFIED FOR VARIABLE _____
  DM-1   VARIABLE _____ HAS ALREADY BEEN DIMENSIONED
  DM-2   CALL-BY-LOCATION PARAMETER _____ CANNOT BE DIMENSIONED
  DM-3   DECLARED SIZE OF ARRAY _____ EXCEEDS SPACE PROVIDED BY CALLING ARGUMENT

DO LOOPS
  DO-0   THIS STATEMENT CANNOT BE THE OBJECT OF A DO-LOOP
  DO-1   ILLEGAL TRANSFER INTO THE RANGE OF A DO-LOOP FROM LINE _____
  DO-2   THE OBJECT OF THIS DO STATEMENT _____ HAS ALREADY APPEARED
  DO-3   IMPROPERLY NESTED DO-LOOPS
  DO-4   ATTEMPT TO REDEFINE THE DO-LOOP PARAMETER _____ WITHIN THE RANGE OF THE LOOP
  DO-5   DO-LOOP PARAMETER _____ IS INVALID
  DO-6   ILLEGAL TRANSFER TO STATEMENT NUMBER _____ WHICH IS INSIDE THE RANGE OF THE LOOP
  DO-7   A DO-LOOP PARAMETER IS UNDEFINED OR OUT OF RANGE
  DO-8   BECAUSE OF PARAMETER _____, THIS DO-LOOP WILL TERMINATE AFTER THE FIRST TIME THROUGH
  DO-9   A DO-LOOP PARAMETER MAY NOT BE REDEFINED IN AN INPUT LIST
  DO-A   OTHER COMPILERS MAY NOT ALLOW THIS STATEMENT TO END A DO-LOOP

EQUIVALENCE AND/OR COMMON
  EC-0   _____ HAS BEEN EQUIVALENCED TO A VARIABLE IN COMMON
  EC-1   COMMON BLOCK _____ HAS A DIFFERENT LENGTH THAN WAS SPECIFIED IN A PREVIOUS SUBPROGRAM; GREATER LENGTH USED

EC–2 COMMON AND/OR EQUIVALENCE CAUSES INVALID ALIGNMENT; EXECUTION SLOWED. REMEDY: ORDER VARIABLES BY DECREASING LENGTH
EC–3 EQUIVALENCE EXTENDS COMMON DOWNWARDS
EC–4 SUBPROGRAM PARAMETER _____ APPEARS IN A COMMON OR EQUIVALENCE STATEMENT
EC–5 VARIABLE _____ WAS USED WITH SUBSCRIPTS IN AN EQUIVALENCE STATEMENT BUT HAS NOT BEEN PROPERLY DIMENSIONED

END STATEMENTS
  EN–0 MISSING END STATEMENT; END STATEMENT GENERATED
  EN–1 AN END STATEMENT WAS USED TO TERMINATE EXECUTION
  EN–2 AN END STATEMENT CANNOT HAVE A STATEMENT NUMBER. STATEMENT NUMBER IGNORED

EQUAL SIGNS
  EQ–0 ILLEGAL QUANTITY ON LEFT OF EQUAL SIGN
  EQ–1 ILLEGAL USE OF EQUAL SIGN
  EQ–2 OTHER COMPILERS MAY NOT ALLOW MULTIPLE ASSIGNMENT STATEMENTS
  EQ–3 MULTIPLE ASSIGNMENT IS NOT IMPLEMENTED FOR CHARACTER VARIABLES

EQUIVALENCE STATEMENTS
  EV–0 ATTEMPT TO EQUIVALENCE VARIABLE _____ TO ITSELF
  EV–1 THERE ARE LESS THAN 2 VARIABLES IN AN EQUIVALENCE LIST
  EV–2 MULTI-SUBSCRIPTED EQUIVALENCED VARIABLE _____ HAS BEEN INCORRECTLY RE-EQUIVALENCED. REMEDY: DIMENSION IT FIRST

POWERS AND EXPONENTIATION
  EX–0 ILLEGAL COMPLEX EXPONENTIATION
  EX–1 I**J WHERE I=J=0
  EX–2 I**J WHERE I=0, J .LT. 0
  EX–3 0.0**Y WHERE Y .LE. 0.0
  EX–4 0.0**J WHERE J=0
  EX–5 0.0**J WHERE J .LT. 0
  EX–6 X**Y WHERE X .LT. 0.0, Y .NE. 0.0

ENTRY STATEMENT
  EY–0 ENTRY-POINT NAME _____ WAS PREVIOUSLY DEFINED
  EY–1 PREVIOUS DEFINITION OF FUNCTION NAME IN AN ENTRY IS INCORRECT

EY-2	USAGE OF SUBPROGRAM PARAMETER _____ IS INCONSISTENT WITH A PREVIOUS ENTRY-POINT
EY-3	PARAMETER _____ HAS APPEARED IN AN EXECUTABLE STATEMENT BUT WAS NOT A SUBPROGRAM PARAMETER
EY-4	ENTRY STATEMENTS INVALID IN MAIN PROGRAM
EY-5	ENTRY STATEMENTS INVALID WITHIN RANGE OF DO-LOOP

FORMAT

FM-0	IMPROPER CHARACTER SEQUENCE OR INVALID CHARACTER IN INPUT DATA
FM-1	NO STATEMENT NUMBER ON FORMAT STATEMENT
FM-2	FORMAT CODE AND DATA TYPE DO NOT MATCH
FM-4	FORMAT PROVIDES NO CONVERSION SPECIFICATION FOR A VALUE IN I/O LIST
FM-5	AN INTEGER IN THE INPUT DATA IS TOO LARGE (MAXIMUM = 2,147,483,647 = $2**31-1$)
FM-6	A REAL NUMBER IN INPUT DATA IS OUT OF MACHINE RANGE (1.E-78, 1.E+75)
FT-0	FIRST CHARACTER OF VARIABLE FORMAT NOT A LEFT PARENTHESIS. _____ IS INVALID
FT-1	INVALID CHARACTER ENCOUNTERED IN FORMAT NEAR _____
FT-2	INVALID FORM FOLLOWING A FORMAT CODE
FT-3	INVALID FIELD OR GROUP COUNT NEAR _____
FT-4	A FIELD OR GROUP COUNT GREATER THAN 255.
FT-5	NO CLOSING PARENTHESIS ON VARIABLE FORMAT
FT-6	NO CLOSING QUOTE IN A HOLLERITH FIELD
FT-7	INVALID USE OF COMMA
FT-8	FORMAT STATEMENT TOO LONG TO COMPILE (SCAN STACK OVERFLOW)
FT-9	INVALID USE OF P FORMAT CODE
FT-A	INVALID USE OF PERIOD (.)
FT-B	MORE THAN THREE LEVELS OF PARENTHESES
FT-C	INVALID CHARACTER BEFORE A RIGHT PARENTHESIS
FT-D	MISSING OR ZERO-LENGTH HOLLERITH ENCOUNTERED
FT-E	NO CLOSING RIGHT PARENTHESIS
FT-F	CHARACTERS FOLLOW CLOSING RIGHT PARENTHESIS
FT-G	WRONG QUOTE USED FOR KEY-PUNCH SPECIFIED
FT-H	LENGTH OF HOLLERITH EXCEEDS 255

FUNCTIONS AND SUBROUTINES

FN-1	PARAMETER _____ APPEARS MORE THAN ONCE IN THIS SUBPROGRAM OR STATEMENT FUNCTION DEFINITION

FN-2   SUBSCRIPTS ON RIGHT-HAND SIDE OF STATEMENT FUNCTION. PROBABLE CAUSE: VARIABLE TO LEFT OF = NOT DIMENSIONED
FN-3   MULTIPLE RETURNS ARE INVALID IN FUNCTION SUBPROGRAMS
FN-4   ILLEGAL LENGTH MODIFIER. _____ IS INVALID
FN-5   INVALID PARAMETER
FN-6   PARAMETER _____ HAS THE SAME NAME AS THE SUBPROGRAM

GO TO STATEMENTS
GO-0   THIS STATEMENT COULD TRANSFER TO ITSELF
GO-1   THIS STATEMENT TRANSFERS TO _____, WHICH IS NON-EXECUTABLE
GO-2   ATTEMPT TO DEFINE ASSIGNED GO TO INDEX _____ IN AN ARITHMETIC STATEMENT
GO-3   ASSIGNED GO TO INDEX _____ MAY BE USED ONLY IN ASSIGNED GO TO AND ASSIGN STATEMENTS
GO-4   INDEX OF AN ASSIGNED GO TO IS UNDEFINED OR OUT OF RANGE, OR INDEX OF COMPUTED GO TO IS UNDEFINED
GO-5   ASSIGNED GO TO INDEX _____ MAY NOT BE AN INTEGER*2 VARIABLE

HOLLERITH CONSTANTS
HO-0   ZERO LENGTH SPECIFIED FOR H-TYPE HOLLERITH
HO-1   ZERO LENGTH QUOTE-TYPE HOLLERITH
HO-2   NO CLOSING QUOTE OR NEXT CARD NOT CONTINUATION CARD
HO-3   UNEXPECTED HOLLERITH OR STATEMENT NUMBER CONSTANT

IF STATEMENTS (ARITHMETIC AND LOGICAL)
IF-0   AN INVALID STATEMENT FOLLOWS THE LOGICAL IF
IF-1   ARITHMETIC OR INVALID EXPRESSION IN LOGICAL IF
IF-2   LOGICAL, COMPLEX, OR INVALID EXPRESSION IN ARITHMETIC IF

IMPLICIT STATEMENT
IM-0   THE DATA TYPE _____ IS INVALID
IM-1   THE OPTIONAL LENGTH _____ IS INVALID
IM-3   IMPROPER ALPHABETIC SEQUENCE IN CHARACTER RANGE
IM-4   _____ IS INVALID. FIRST CHARACTER USED
IM-5   IMPLICIT STATEMENT DOES NOT PRECEDE OTHER SPECIFICATION STATEMENTS

IM-6 ATTEMPT TO DECLARE THE TYPE OF A CHARACTER MORE THAN ONCE
IM-7 ONLY ONE IMPLICIT STATEMENT PER PROGRAM SEGMENT ALLOWED; THIS ONE IGNORED

INPUT/OUTPUT
IO-0 I/O STATEMENT REFERENCES STATEMENT NUMBERED _____ WHICH IS NOT A FORMAT STATEMENT
IO-1 VARIABLE FORMAT MUST BE AN ARRAY NAME. _____ IS INVALID
IO-2 INVALID ELEMENT IN INPUT LIST OR DATA LIST
IO-3 OTHER COMPILERS MAY NOT ALLOW EXPRESSIONS IN OUTPUT LISTS
IO-4 ILLEGAL USE OF END= OR ERR= PARAMETERS
IO-5 _____ IS AN INVALID UNIT NUMBER
IO-6 _____ IS NOT A VALID FORMAT
IO-7 ONLY CONSTANTS, SIMPLE INTEGER*4 VARIABLES AND CHARACTER VARIABLES ARE ALLOWED AS UNIT
IO-8 ATTEMPT TO PERFORM I/O IN A FUNCTION WHICH IS CALLED IN AN OUTPUT STATEMENT
IO-9 UNFORMATTED WRITE STATEMENT MUST HAVE A LIST

JOB CONTROL CARDS
JB-0 CONTROL CARD ENCOUNTERED DURING COMPILATION; PROBABLE CAUSE: MISSING CONTROL CARD
JB-1 MIS-PUNCHED JOB OPTION. _____ IS INVALID

JOB TERMINATION
KO-0 SOURCE ERROR ENCOUNTERED WHILE EXECUTING WITH RUN-FREE
KO-1 LIMIT EXCEEDED FOR FIXED-POINT DIVISION BY ZERO
KO-2 LIMIT EXCEEDED FOR FLOATING-POINT DIVISION BY ZERO
KO-3 EXPONENT OVERFLOW LIMIT EXCEEDED
KO-4 EXPONENT UNDERFLOW LIMIT EXCEEDED
KO-5 FIXED-POINT OVERFLOW LIMIT EXCEEDED
KO-6 JOB-TIME EXCEEDED
KO-7 COMPILER ERROR – EXECUTION TIME: RETURN TO SYSTEM
KO-8 TRACEBACK ERROR. TRACEBACK TERMINATED

LOGICAL OPERATIONS
LG-0 .NOT. USED AS A BINARY OPERATOR

LIBRARY ROUTINES
LI-0 ARGUMENT OF DGAMMA OR GAMMA OUT OF THE RANGE 1.382E-76 .LT. X .LT. 57.57

LI-1 ABS(X) .GT. 174.673 FOR SINH, COSH, DSINH OR DCOSH OF X
LI-2 SENSE LIGHT OTHER THAN 0, 1, 2, 3, 4 FOR SLITE OR
       1, 2, 3, 4 FOR SLITET
LI-3 REAL(Z) .GT. 174.673 FOR CEXP OR CDEXP OF Z
LI-4 ABS(AIMAG(Z)) .GT. 174. 673 FOR CSIN, CCOS, CDSIN OR
       CDCOS OF Z
LI-5 ABS(REAL(Z)) .GE. 3.537E15 FOR CSIN, CCOS, CDSIN OR
       CDCOS OF Z
LI-6 ABS(AIMAG(Z)) .GE. 3.537E15 FOR CEXP OR CDEXP OF Z
LI-7 X .GT. 174.673 FOR EXP OR DEXP OF X
LI-8 ARGUMENT OF CLOG, CLOG10, CDLOG OR CDLOG10 IS ZERO
LI-9 ARGUMENT OF ALOG, ALOG10, DLOG OR DLOG10 IS
       NEGATIVE OR ZERO
LI-A ABS(X) .GE. 3.537E15 FOR SIN, COS, DSIN OR DCOS OF X
LI-B ABS(X) .GT. 1 FOR ARSIN, ARCOS, DARSIN OR DARCOS OF X
LI-C X .LT. 0. FOR SQRT OR DSQRT OF X
LI-D BOTH ARGUMENTS OF DATAN2 OR ATAN2 ARE ZERO
LI-E ARGUMENT TOO CLOSE TO A SINGULARITY OF TAN, COTAN,
       DTAN OR DCOTAN
LI-F ARGUMENT OF DLGAMA OR ALGAMA OUT OF THE RANGE
       0.0 .LT. X .LT. 4.29E73
LI-G ABS(X) .GE. 3.537E15 FOR TAN, COTAN, DTAG, DOCTAN OF X
LI-H LESS THAN TWO ARGUMENTS FOR ONE OF MIN0, MIN1,
       AMIN0, ETC.

MIXED MODE
MD-0 RELATIONAL OPERATOR HAS LOGICAL OPERAND
MD-1 RELATIONAL OPERATOR HAS COMPLEX OPERAND
MD-2 MIXED MODE – LOGICAL OR CHARACTER WITH ARITHMETIC
MD-3 OTHER COMPILERS MAY NOT ALLOW SUBSCRIPTS OF TYPE
       COMPLEX, LOGICAL OR CHARACTER

MEMORY OVERFLOW
MO-0 INSUFFICIENT MEMORY TO COMPILE THIS PROGRAM.
       REMAINDER WILL BE ERROR CHECKED ONLY
MO-1 INSUFFICIENT MEMORY TO ASSIGN ARRAY STORAGE. JOB
       ABANDONED
MO-2 SYMBOL TABLE EXCEEDS AVAILABLE SPACE. JOB
       ABANDONED
MO-3 DATA AREA OF SUBPROGRAM EXCEEDS 24K; SEGMENT
       SUBPROGRAM
MO-4 INSUFFICIENT MEMORY TO ALLOCATE COMPILER WORK
       AREA OR WATLIB BUFFER

NAMELIST STATEMENTS
- **NL-0** NAMELIST ENTRY _____ MUST BE A VARIABLE, BUT NOT A SUBPROGRAM PARAMETER
- **NL-1** NAMELIST NAME _____ PREVIOUSLY DEFINED
- **NL-2** VARIABLE NAME _____ TOO LONG
- **NL-3** VARIABLE NAME _____ NOT FOUND IN NAMELIST
- **NL-4** INVALID SYNTAX IN NAMELIST INPUT
- **NL-6** VARIABLE _____ INCORRECTLY SUBSCRIPTED
- **NL-7** SUBSCRIPT OF _____ OUT OF RANGE

PARENTHESES
- **PC-0** UNMATCHED PARENTHESIS
- **PC-1** INVALID PARENTHESIS NESTING IN I/O LIST

PAUSE, STOP STATEMENTS
- **PS-0** OPERATOR MESSAGES NOT ALLOWED; SIMPLE STOP ASSUMED FOR STOP, CONTINUE ASSUMED FOR PAUSE

RETURN STATEMENT
- **RE-1** RETURN I, WHERE I IS OUT OF RANGE OR UNDEFINED; VALUE IS _____
- **RE-2** MULTIPLE RETURN NOT VALID IN FUNCTION SUBPROGRAM
- **RE-3** _____ IS NOT A SIMPLE INTEGER VARIABLE
- **RE-4** MULTIPLE RETURN NOT VALID IN MAIN PROGRAM

ARITHMETIC AND LOGICAL STATEMENT FUNCTIONS
- **SF-1** PREVIOUSLY REFERENCED STATEMENT NUMBER _____ APPEARS ON A STATEMENT FUNCTION DEFINITION
- **SF-2** STATEMENT FUNCTION IS THE OBJECT OF A LOGICAL IF STATEMENT
- **SF-3** RECURSIVE STATEMENT FUNCTION DEFINITION: NAME APPEARS ON BOTH SIDES OF EQUAL SIGN. LIKELY CAUSE: VARIABLE NOT DIMENSIONED
- **SF-4** A STATEMENT FUNCTION DEFINITION APPEARS AFTER THE FIRST EXECUTABLE STATEMENT
- **SF-5** ILLEGAL USE OF FUNCTION NAME _____

SUBPROGRAMS
- **SR-0** SUBPROGRAM _____ IS MISSING
- **SR-1** SUBPROGRAM _____ REDEFINES A CONSTANT, EXPRESSION, DO PARAMETER OR ASSIGNED GO TO INDEX
- **SR-2** SUBPROGRAM _____ WAS ASSIGNED DIFFERENT TYPES IN DIFFERENT PROGRAM SEGMENTS

SR-3 ATTEMPT TO USE SUBPROGRAM _____ RECURSIVELY
SR-4 INVALID TYPE OF ARGUMENT IN RERERENCE TO
             SUBPROGRAM _____
SR-5 WRONG NUMBER OF ARGUMENTS IN REFERENCE TO
             SUBPROGRAM _____
SR-6 SUBPROGRAM _____ WAS PREVIOUSLY DEFINED. FIRST
             DEFINITION IS USED
SR-7 NO MAIN PROGRAM
SR-8 ILLEGAL OR MISSING SUBPROGRAM NAME
SR-9 LIBRARY SUBPROGRAM _____ WAS NOT ASSIGNED THE
             CORRECT TYPE
SR-A METHOD OF ENTERING SUBPROGRAM PRODUCES
      UNDEFINED VALUE FOR CALL-BY-LOCATION PARAMETER

SUBSCRIPTS
  SS-0 ZERO SUBSCRIPT OR DIMENSION NOT ALLOWED
  SS-1 SUBSCRIPT NUMBER _____
  SS-2 INVALID SUBSCRIPT FORM
  SS-3 A SUBSCRIPT OF _____ WHICH IS OUT OF RANGE

STATEMENTS AND STATEMENT NUMBERS
  ST-0 MISSING STATEMENT NUMBER _____
  ST-1 STATEMENT NUMBER GREATER THAN 99999. _____ IS
             INVALID
  ST-2 STATEMENT NUMBER _____ HAS ALREADY BEEN DEFINED
  ST-3 UNDECODEABLE STATEMENT
  ST-4 THIS STATEMENT SHOULD HAVE A STATEMENT NUMBER
  ST-5 STATEMENT NUMBER _____ IN A TRANSFER IS A
             NON-EXECUTABLE STATEMENT
  ST-6 ONLY CALL STATEMENTS MAY CONTAIN STATEMENT
             NUMBER ARGUMENTS
  ST-7 STATEMENT SPECIFIED IN A TRANSFER STATEMENT
             _____ IS A FORMAT STATEMENT
  ST-8 MISSING FORMAT STATEMENT _____
  ST-9 SPECIFICATION STATEMENT DOES NOT PRECEDE
             STATEMENT FUNCTION DEFINITIONS OR EXECUTABLE
             STATEMENTS

SUBSCRIPTED VARIABLES
  SV-0 WRONG NUMBER OF SUBSCRIPTS SPECIFIED FOR
             VARIABLE _____
  SV-1 ARRAY OR SUBPROGRAM NAME _____ IS USED
             INCORRECTLY WITHOUT A LIST

SV-2   MORE THAN 7 DIMENSIONS NOT ALLOWED. _____ IS
                                                                                     INVALID
SV-3   DIMENSION OR SUBSCRIPT IS TOO LARGE (MAXIMUM
                                                                                     $10**8-1$)
SV-4   VARIABLE _____, USED WITH VARIABLE DIMENSIONS, IS
                                                          NOT A SUBPROGRAM PARAMETER
SV-5   VARIABLE DIMENSION _____ IS NOT ONE OF SIMPLE
              INTEGER VARIABLE, SUBPROGRAM PARAMETER, IN
                                                                                     COMMON

SYNTAX ERRORS
  SX-0   MISSING OPERATOR
  SX-1   EXPECTING OPERATOR BUT _____ WAS FOUND
  SX-2   EXPECTING SYMBOL, BUT _____ WAS FOUND
  SX-3   EXPECTING SYMBOL OR OPERATOR, BUT _____ WAS FOUND
  SX-4   EXPECTING CONSTANT, BUT _____ WAS FOUND
  SX-5   EXPECTING SYMBOL OR CONSTANT, BUT _____ WAS
                                                                                     FOUND
  SX-6   EXPECTING STATEMENT NUMBER, BUT _____ WAS FOUND
  SX-7   EXPECTING SIMPLE INTEGER VARIABLE, BUT _____ WAS
                                                                                     FOUND
  SX-8   EXPECTING SIMPLE INTEGER VARIABLE OR CONSTANT,
                                                          BUT _____ WAS FOUND
  SX-9   ILLEGAL SEQUENCE OF OPERATORS IN EXPRESSION
  SX-A   EXPECTING END-OF-STATEMENT, BUT _____ WAS FOUND

TYPE STATEMENTS
  TY-0   VARIABLE _____ HAS ALREADY BEEN EXPLICITLY TYPED
  TY-1   LENGTH OF EQUIVALENCED VARIABLE _____ MAY NOT BE
              CHANGED. REMEDY: INTERCHANGE TYPE AND EQUIVALENCE
                                                                                     STATEMENTS

I/O OPERATIONS
  UN-0   CONTROL CARD ENCOUNTERED ON UNIT _____ AT
              EXECUTION. PROBABLE CAUSE: MISSING DATA OR
                                                                     INCORRECT FORMAT
  UN-1   END OF FILE ENCOUNTERED ON UNIT _____ (IBM CODE
                                                                                     IHC217)
  UN-2   I/O ERROR ON UNIT _____ (IBM CODE IHC218)
  UN-3   NO DD CARD FOR I/O ON UNIT _____ (IBM CODE IHC219)
  UN-4   REWIND, ENDFILE, BACKSPACE REFERENCES READER,
                                                          PRINTER, OR PUNCH
  UN-5   ATTEMPT TO READ ON UNIT _____ AFTER IT HAS HAD
                                                                                     END-OF-FILE

UN–6	_____ IS NOT A VALID UNIT NUMBER (IBM CODE IHC220)
UN–7	PAGE-LIMIT EXCEEDED
UN–8	ATTEMPT TO DO DIRECT ACCESS I/O ON SEQUENTIAL FILE _____, OR VICE VERSA. POSSIBLE MISSING DEFINE FILE STATEMENT (IBM CODE IHC231)
UN–9	FOR I/O ON UNIT _____, WRITE REFERENCES READER, OR READ REFERENCES PRINTER OR PUNCH
UN–A	DEFINE FILE REFERENCES UNIT _____ PREVIOUSLY USED FOR SEQUENTIAL I/O (IBM CODE IHC235)
UN–B	RECORD SIZE FOR UNIT _____ EXCEEDS 32767, OR DIFFERS FROM DD STATEMENT SPECIFICATION (IBM CODES IHC233, IHC237)
UN–C	UNIT NUMBER IS NEGATIVE, ZERO OR TOO LARGE (IBM CODE IHC232)
UN–D	ON UNIT _____, ATTEMPT TO READ MORE INFORMATION THAN LOGICAL RECORD CONTAINS (IBM CODE IHC213)
UN–E	FORMATTED LINE EXCEEDS BUFFER LENGTH (IBM CODE IHC212)
UN–F	I/O ERROR – SEARCHING LIBRARY DIRECTORY
UN–G	I/O ERROR – READING LIBRARY
UN–H	ATTEMPT TO DEFINE THE OBJECT ERROR UNIT _____ AS DIRECT ACCESS (IBM CODE IHC234)
UN–I	RECFM IS NOT V(B) FOR I/O WITHOUT FORMAT CONTROL ON UNIT (IBM CODE IHC214)
UN–J	MISSING DD CARD FOR WATLIB; NO LIBRARY ASSUMED
UN–K	ATTEMPT TO READ OR WRITE PAST END OF CHARACTER VARIABLE BUFFER
UN–L	ATTEMPT TO READ ON UNCREATED DIRECT ACCESS FILE _____ (IBM CODE IHC236)

UNDEFINED VARIABLES
UV–0	VALUE OF _____ IS UNDEFINED
UV–3	SUBSCRIPT NUMBER _____ IS UNDEFINED
UV–4	SUBPROGRAM _____ IS UNDEFINED
UV–5	AN ARGUMENT OF _____ IS UNDEFINED
UV–6	UNDECODEABLE CHARACTERS IN VARIABLE FORMAT

VARIABLE NAMES
VA–0	NAME _____ IS TOO LONG: TRUNCATED TO SIX CHARACTERS
VA–1	ATTEMPT TO USE THE ASSIGNED OR INITIALIZED VARIABLE OR DO-PARAMETER _____ IN A SPECIFICATION STATEMENT
VA–2	ILLEGAL USE OF SUBROUTINE NAME _____

VA-3 ILLEGAL USE OF VARIABLE NAME _____
VA-4 ATTEMPT TO USE PREVIOUSLY DEFINED NAME _____ AS A FUNCTION OR AN ARRAY
VA-5 ATTEMPT TO USE PREVIOUSLY DEFINED NAME _____ AS A SUBROUTINE
VA-6 ATTEMPT TO USE PREVIOUSLY DEFINED NAME _____ AS A SUBPROGRAM
VA-7 ATTEMPT TO USE PREVIOUSLY DEFINED NAME _____ AS A COMMON BLOCK
VA-8 ATTEMPT TO USE FUNCTION NAME _____ AS A VARIABLE
VA-9 ATTEMPT TO USE PREVIOUSLY DEFINED NAME _____ AS A VARIABLE
VA-A ILLEGAL USE OF PREVIOUSLY DEFINED NAME _____

EXTERNAL STATEMENT
XT-0 _____ HAS ALREADY APPEARED IN AN EXTERNAL STATEMENT

APPENDIX B:

TEST OUTPUT FOR EXERCISE PROGRAMS

USE OF THIS APPENDIX

The output values provided below should be referred to when testing each completed exercise program. Check carefully, since the absence of error messages confirms only your use of legitimate WATFOR/WATFIV *language*, but does not guarantee program *logic*.

You may also find the sample output helpful in clarifying the intent of any exercise (prior to writing the program), if the problem statement itself leaves you in any doubt.

TEST DATA

For exercises requiring data, the sample output results from testing on a standard data set, which should be used for each such problem, unless special data are mentioned in the exercise. The set consists of 12 punched cards, coding for which appears in Fig. 11. If your computer center has not "gang-punched" the data cards for you, be sure to follow the indicated column placements when keypunching. Note that the data cards may be kept in proper sequence (of importance, in some exercises) by referring to the last two digits on each card (i.e., postdecimal digits of the sixth data value); for these ascend from 01 to 12.

OUTPUT SHOWN

When any exercise produces more than four lines of output, only the first three lines and the last line are shown below (separated by ------------). Where

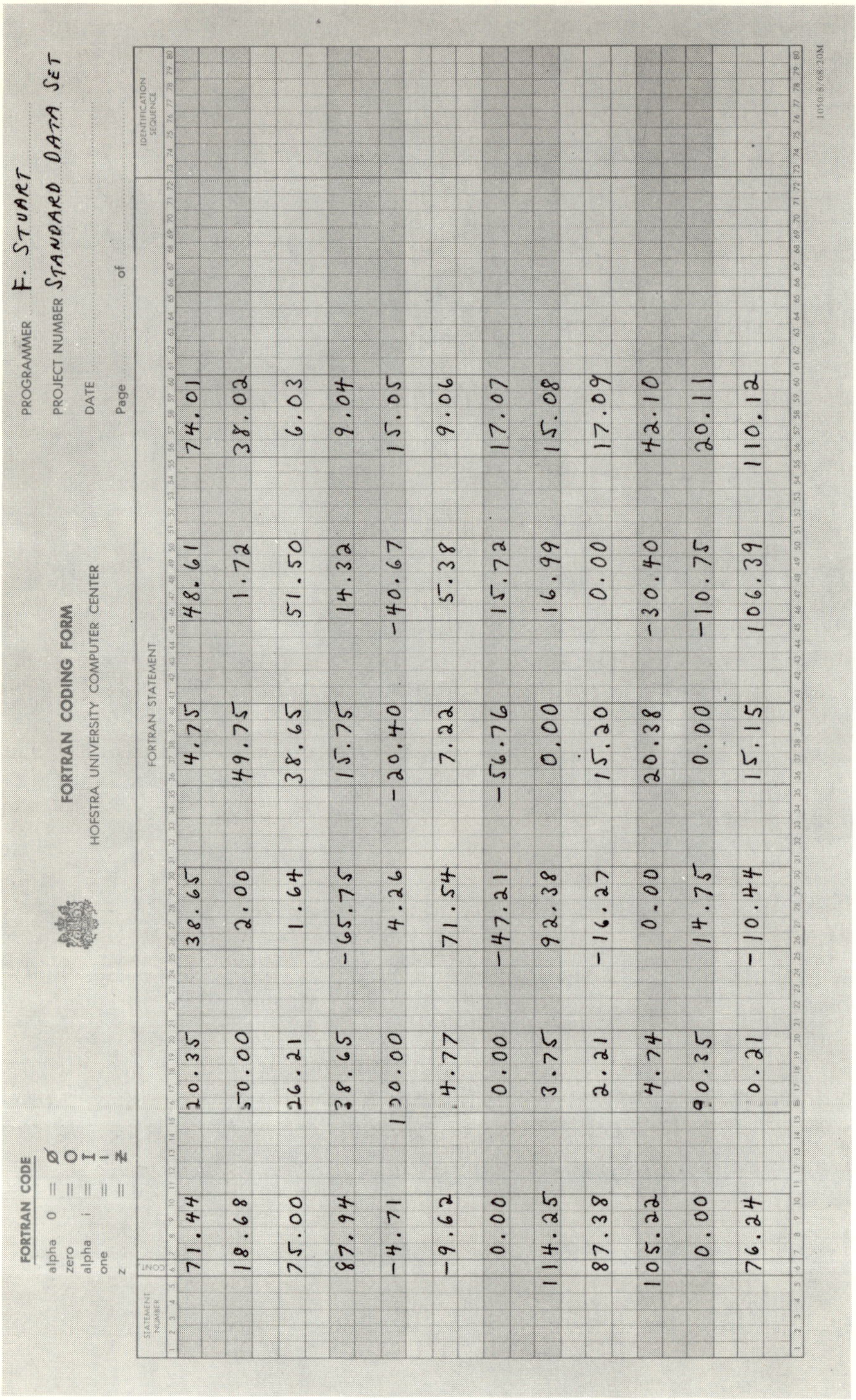

FORTRAN CODE
alpha O = Ø
zero = O
alpha i = I
one = 1
z = Ƶ

FORTRAN CODING FORM
HOFSTRA UNIVERSITY COMPUTER CENTER

PROGRAMMER F. STUART
PROJECT NUMBER STANDARD DATA SET
DATE
Page of

71.44	20.35	38.65	4.75	48.61	74.01
18.68	50.00	2.00	49.75	1.72	38.02
75.00	26.21	1.64	38.65	51.50	6.03
87.94	38.65	-65.75	15.75	14.32	9.04
-4.71	120.00	4.26	-20.40	-40.67	15.05
-9.62	4.77	71.54	7.22	5.38	9.06
0.00	0.00	-47.21	-56.76	15.72	17.07
114.25	3.75	92.38	0.00	16.99	15.08
87.38	2.21	-16.27	15.20	0.00	17.09
105.22	4.74	0.00	20.38	-30.40	42.10
0.00	90.35	14.75	0.00	-10.75	20.11
76.24	0.21	-10.44	15.15	106.39	110.12

1050 8/68 20M

FIG. 11 The standard data set for testing exercise programs.

exponential notation appears, the computer output as actually produced is shown, rather than the precise "correct" answer. That is, where the binary storage method results in a slight understatement of the number, rounding has not been inserted. For example, the first exercise (2–1) has as the last output line

$$350 \quad 0.3687996E\ 03$$

The "correct" answer (from $78.3 + 0.83(350)$) is not

$$368.7996$$

but rather

$$368.80$$

2–1.   100   0.1613000E 03
       110   0.1696000E 03   (twenty-six output lines)
       120   0.1779000E 03
       350   0.3687996E 03

2–2.   1   0.1608000E 02
       3   0.1447200E 03   (thirty output lines)
       5   0.4020000E 03
     59   0.5597448E 05

2–3.   0   0.3414000E 04
     10   0.1707000E 04   (eleven output lines)
     20   0.8535000E 03
   100   0.3333984E 01

2–4.   0.1643495E 01

2–5.   1   0.7787999E 02   0.9575999E 02
      2   0.1557600E 03   0.1915200E 03   (twelve output
      3   0.2336400E 03   0.2872798E 03   lines)
    12   0.9345598E 03   0.1149120E 04

2–6.   1   0.1000000E 01
      2   0.2000000E 01   (twenty output lines)
      3   0.6000000E 01
    20   0.2432896E 19

2–7.   0.2432896E 19   0.2561321E 19

2–8.	2	0.7071063E 05	
	3	0.1709975E 04	
	4	0.2659146E 04	(nine output lines)
	10	0.9330322E 01	

2–9.   0.7287650E 05

2–10.	10	385	
	20	2870	(ten output lines)
	30	9455	
	100	338350	

3–1.   0.1125900E 16   0.1125900E 16

3–2.	1	20	
	2	19	
	3	18	(twenty output lines)
	20	1	

3–3.	1	20	(ten output lines)
	3	18	
	5	16	
	19	2	

3–4.   0.6218198E 03

3–5.	0.7144000E 02	
	0.1867999E 02	
	0.7500000E 02	(seven output lines)
	0.0000000E 00	

3–6.	1	
	2	(fifteen output lines)
	3	
	3	

3–7.	0.4642938E 02
	0.1585358E 02
	0.0000000E 00
	0.0000000E 00

3–8.   0.3529800E 03

3–9.	0.4642938E 02			
	0.1585358E 02			
	0.0000000E 00			
	0.0000000E 00			

4–1.	0.6861600E 02

4–2.	0.4010148E 05

4–3.	0.3000000E 01	0.4000000E 01	0.3999996E 01	0.3999998E 01

4–4.	20	0.3689386E 01	
	21	0.3781522E 01	(twenty-one output lines)
	22	0.3873593E 01	
	40	0.5492929E 01	

4–5.	139	0.4548018E 01	
	141	0.4599727E 01	(fifteen output lines)
	143	0.4651023E 01	
	167	0.5232299E 01	

4–6.	0.2035001E 02	0.2035001E 02	0.1706085E 00	(six output lines)
	0.2000000E 01	0.2000000E 01	0.2923584E 00	
	0.1640000E 01	0.1640000E 01	0.4281616E 01	
	−0.9620000E 01	0.9620000E 01	0.1112213E 01	

4–7.	20	20	
	2	2	
	1	1	(six output lines)
	−9	9	

4–8.	71	
	19	
	75	(twelve output lines)
	88	
	76	

5–1.	3	0.7500000E 02	0.2621001E 02
	4	0.8794000E 02	0.3864999E 02
	8	0.1142500E 03	0.3750000E 01
	10	0.1052200E 03	0.4740000E 01

5-2.	3	0.7500000E 02	0.2621001E 02
	4	0.8794000E 02	0.3864999E 02

5-3.	3	0.7500000E 02	0.2621001E 02
	4	0.8794000E 02	0.3864999E 02

5-4.	1	
	2	(nine output lines)
	3	
	−0.7165000E 01	

5-5.	0.7144000E 02	
	0.1867999E 02	(eight output lines)
	0.7500000E 02	
	0.7624001E 02	

5-6.	15	0.1307673E 13

5-7.	2	0.1867999E 02
	5	−0.4710000E 01
	9	0.8738000E 02
	10	0.1052200E 03

5-8.	7	0.2718252E 01

5-9.	1	71	
	3	75	(six output lines)
	4	87	
	10	105	

5-10.	12

6-1.	0.3166741E 05

6-2.	0.5642544E 03

6-3.	0.1000000E 03	−0.6575000E 02	0.1657500E 03

6-4.	3
	16
	20

6–5.	1	2	0.7144000E 02	0.2035001E 02		0.4589500E 02
	1	3	0.7144000E 02	0.3864999E 02		0.5504500E 02
	1	4	0.7144000E 02	0.4750000E 01		0.3809500E 02
	8	9	0.5000000E 02	0.2000000E 01		0.2600000E 02

(thirty-six output lines)

6–6.	0.1449107E 05				
6–7.	0.6218198E 03	0.3612397E 03	0.8554999E 02		0.8968999E 02
			0.1788100E 03		0.3727798E 03
6–8.	0.7144000E 02	0.2035001E 02	0.3864999E 02		0.4750000E 01
	0.4861000E 02	0.7400999E 02	0.1867999E 02		0.5000000E 02
	0.2000000E 01	0.4975000E 02	0.1720000E 01		0.3802000E 02
	–0.4710000E 01	0.1000000E 03	0.4260000E 01		–0.2039999E 02

(seven output lines)

6–9.	(same as exercise 6–8)

6–10.	0	1	0	1	0	1	0	1
	1	0	1	0	1	0	1	0
	0	1	0	1	0	1	0	1
	0	0	0	0	0	0	0	0
	0	0	0	0	0	0	0	0
	1	0	1	0	1	0	1	0
	0	1	0	1	0	1	0	1
	1	0	1	0	1	0	1	0

7–1.	12074		
7–2.	12074		
7–3.	1	0	
7–4.	65		
7–5.	–0.6575000E 02		
7–6.	0.4967000E 02		
7–7.	3	21	14

OUTPUT SHOWN

7–8.	3	21	14	
7–9.	0.1853941E 01	0.1308564E 01	------------------	0.1698970E 01
	0.3010300E 00	0.1696793E 01	------------------	0.1587149E 01
	0.1711806E 01	0.7803172E 00	0.1944186E 01	0.1587149E 01
	(three output lines; first two contain eight numbers each)			
8–1.	0.2432896E 19		0.2432902008176640D 19	
8–2.	0.2374847222222221D 02		0.3959797573599078D 02	
8–3.	−0.1424272E 00	−0.7216145E 00	−0.1424272E 00	0.7216145E 00
	−0.2636044E 01	−0.4061633E 01		
	−0.2678197E 00	−0.8164692E 01		
	0.3600675E 01	−0.2065331E 01		
	(six output lines)			
8–4.	0.1884625E 01	0.2949039E 00		
	0.1884624E 01	0.2049038E 00		
8–5.	2	222222222		
8–6.	T F F F F F			
	F T F T F T			
	F T T F F T			
	F T T T T T			
9–1.			23.7484	
9–2.				0.51667E 02
9–3.	1		7	
	1		11	
	2		7	(seven output lines)
	5		9	
9–4.	99.9	9999	0.99	9000.
9–5.	2432902008176639000.		0.2432902008176640D 19	

9-6.   (Is your output spread across the entire print page?)

0.7144	0.2035	0.3865	0.0475	0.4861	0.7401
0.1868	0.5000	0.0200	0.4975	0.0172	0.3802
0.7500	0.2621	0.0164	0.3865	0.5150	0.0603
0.7624	0.1021	−0.1044	0.1515	1.0639	1.1012

(twelve output lines)

10-1.   (Does your output start on a new print page?)
ITEM NO.   4 IS NEGATIVE
ITEM NO.   7 IS NEGATIVE
ITEM NO.   9 IS NEGATIVE
ITEM NO. 12 IS NEGATIVE

10-2.   MEAN   EXPONENTIAL FORM
               10.73   0.1073500E 02

10-3.   X   LOG   SQRT
               1.0   0.0000   1.0000
               1.1   0.0953   1.0488   (eleven output lines)
               1.2   0.1823   1.0954
               2.0   0.6931   1.4142

10-4.

71.44	20.35	38.65	4.75	48.61	74.01
18.68	50.00	2.00	49.75	1.72	38.02
75.00	26.21	1.64	38.65	51.50	6.03
76.24	10.21	−10.44	15.15	106.39	110.12

(twelve output lines)

10-5.   (Same as exercise 10-4).

10-6.   J. JONES

10-7.   1   POSITIVE
         2   POSITIVE
         3   POSITIVE   forty output lines; lines 37 and 38
        40   NEGATIVE   should say ZERO)

10-8.   SECOND

10-9.   (See output sketch accompanying exercise)

OUTPUT SHOWN   233

11-1.   MEAN = 25.68

11-2.   1   0.3379750E 02
        2   0.3010750E 02
        3   0.3537500E 02   (ten output lines)
        10   0.3258499E 02

11-3.   1   0.3379750000000000D 02
        2   0.3010750000000000D 02
        3   0.3537500000000000D 02   (ten output lines)
        10   0.3258500000000001D 02

11-4.   0.3379750000000000D 02
             0.3010750000000000D 02
             0.3537500000000000D 02   (five output lines)
             0.1078750000000000D 02

INDEX

A FORMAT notation, 165, 168-172, 181, 182
ABS function, 61, 62, 67, 92
Absolute value, 61, 62, 67, 69, 92, 127
Addition, 12, 22
Address, 21, 115
Adjustable dimensions, 116
AIMAG function, 132
AINT function, 66, 67
ALGOL, 7
Algorithm, 42, 52, 69
ALOG function, 58-61, 67
ALOG10 function, 59-61, 67
Alphabet, 7, 8
Alphabetization, 171
Alphameric, 127, 144, 165-183, 195, 196
AMAX functions, 64, 67, 68
AMIN functions, 64, 67, 68
AMOD function, 66-68
Analog computer, 1
Antilogarithm, 32, 59-61, 67, 127
Apostrophe, 166
Arc cosine, 62
ARCOS function, 62, 67
Arc sine, 62
Arctangent, 62, 127, 128
Argument, 57-59, 62-68, 109, 111, 119, 121, 189, 190
  dummy, 110-112, 115-118, 122

Arithmetic expression, 19, 20-23, 33, 35, 57, 71, 72, 94, 111, 113, 131, 141
Arithmetic IF statement, 71-79, 85, 88, 111
Arithmetic mean, 48, 49, 82-84, 107, 116-118, 123, 130, 137, 162, 163, 198
Arithmetic operator, 12, 20, 22, 31, 33, 35, 52, 57, 77, 130
Arithmetic statement, 19, 20, 35, 57, 65, 93, 112, 117
Array, 91, 93, 94, 96-100, 103, 107, 108, 115, 116, 120, 122, 123, 137, 139, 157, 158, 162, 171, 182, 187, 190, 195, 196, 198
ARSIN function, 62, 67
Assembler language, 6
Assigned GO TO statement, 197, 198
Asterisk, 7, 19, 22, 103, 148, 176
ATAN function, 62, 67
ATAN2 function, 62, 63, 67
Average deviation, 61, 62, 92

BACKSPACE statement, 194, 198
BASIC, 7
Batch processing, 11
Binary number system, 5, 6, 127, 142
Bits, 5
Blank columns, 15, 45, 145, 146, 159, 166, 174, 175, 179, 181, 182
Blank COMMON, 120-123, 185, 186, 189, 192

235

BLOCK DATA statement, 192, 193, 197
Branch statement, 29, 30, 35, 39, 40, 43, 52, 53, 71-89, 113

Calling program, 112-118, 122, 123, 137
Calling statement, 109-111, 113, 115-118, 122, 189
CALL statement, 119, 119, 122
Card punch, 23
Card reader, 3, 11, 142, 156
Carriage control, 151, 169, 175, 179-182
Centigrade temperature, 17, 21, 26, 27, 29, 30, 36, 39, 41, 42
Central processing unit, 2, 3
CHARACTER statement, 173, 181, 188
Chemical reaction, 36
COBOL, 7
Coding form, 10, 11, 14, 15, 30
Combinations, 51-53, 99, 100, 114
Comma, 23, 45, 63, 71, 130, 145
Comment statement, 18, 35
COMMON area, 120, 121
COMMON statement, 120-123, 185, 186, 189, 192
  labelled, 191-193, 197
Compilation, 11-13, 20, 21, 46, 92, 94, 103, 115
Compiler language, 7
Compiler program, 7, 11, 12, 15, 18, 22, 25, 40, 60, 93, 113, 115, 199
Complex constants, 130-132, 137
Complex functions, 131-133, 137
Complex variables, 125, 130, 132, 137, 138, 162, 187
Computed GO TO statement, 85-89, 197
Computers, advantages, 1
  analog, 1
  digital, 1
  systems, 3, 4
Conditional branch, 29, 30, 35, 39, 40, 71-89
Conjugate, 132
Constants, complex, 130-132, 137
  double precision, 126, 127, 129, 137
  integer, 23, 25-28, 35, 40, 46, 94, 115, 145, 153
  logical, 133, 134, 137
  real, 18-20, 22, 23, 25, 35
Consumption function, 36
Continuation of statements, 15
CONTINUE statement, 43, 44, 53, 73, 74
Control cards, 11, 46
Control statements, 113

COS function, 62, 67
COSH function, 62, 67
Cosine, 62, 68, 127
COTAN function, 62, 67
Cotangent, 62
Cube root, 37, 110, 112

D FORMAT notation, 144, 149, 153, 155, 160, 161, 175
Data, 11, 45-48, 53, 156, 157
  condensation, 156-158
  for testing exercise programs, 13, 54, 162, 226, 227
DATA statement, 103, 104, 107, 108, 142, 172, 173, 182, 185, 188, 192
Debugging, 12, 13
Debug mode, 14, 20
Decimal point, 22, 23, 25, 27, 32, 46, 104, 144, 145, 147, 150, 151, 155, 159-161, 163
Degree-days, 63
Diagnostic messages, 12-14, 18, 20, 21, 36, 46, 199-225
Diagonal array elements, 123
Digital computer, 1
DIMENSION statement, 92-94, 97, 101, 103, 104, 107, 115, 116, 120, 157, 189
  double dimension, 101, 102, 107
  triple dimension, 106, 107
DIM function, 63, 67, 68, 73
Discriminant, 138
Disk, 4, 5, 113, 142
Division, 22, 25, 32, 48, 66, 68
Documentation, 81
DO statement, 39-45, 49-54, 80, 94, 102, 185, 186
Double dimension, 101, 102, 107
Double precision, 125-130, 137, 153, 161, 163, 171, 183, 187, 188, 198
Double precision functions, 127-132, 137
DOUBLE PRECISION statement, 125-130, 153, 171, 183, 188, 198
Dummy argument, 110-112, 115-118, 122

E FORMAT notation, 144, 149-151, 153, 155, 160, 161, 175
ENDFILE statement, 195, 198
End-OF-File mark, 194, 195, 198
END option in READ statement, 193-195, 197, 198
END statement, 22, 35, 113

ENTRY card, 11, 46, 54
ENTRY statement, 190, 197
Equal sign, 19, 20, 41
Equipment unit number, 142, 162, 182, 194
Equivalence, 191
EQUIVALENCE statement, 186, 187, 188, 197
ERR option in READ statement, 193, 194, 197
Error messages, 12-14, 18, 20, 36, 46, 167, 199-225
Execution, 11, 13, 14, 20, 46, 94, 195
EXP function, 59-61, 67
Explicit type specification, 27, 28, 35, 92, 110, 125, 128, 132, 137, 173, 185, 187, 188
Exponential notation, 23-26, 35, 45, 89, 126, 144, 148, 150, 151, 154, 163, 229
Exponentiation, 22, 31-35, 54, 59, 130
Expression, logical, 71, 75, 79, 88, 133-139
  mixed, 26, 27, 44, 58, 128, 129
  real, 41
Extended assignment statement, 64, 65, 84
Extension messages, 12, 13, 21, 23, 199
EXTERNAL statement, 189, 197

F FORMAT notation, 144-150, 153, 158, 159, 175
Factorial numbers, 37, 59, 89, 113-115, 163
Farenheit temperature, 17, 21, 26, 27, 29, 30, 39, 41, 42
Field, 141, 143-145, 156, 157, 159, 165
File, 143, 144
Fixed format, 23
FLOAT function, 66, 67
Floating point, 145
Flowcharting, 80-85
FORMAT statement, 24, 45, 141-183, 185, 195, 196, 198
FORTRAN, 7
Free run mode, 14
Function name, 20, 57-59, 67, 110-113, 122
Functions, FORTRAN-supplied, 57-69, 73, 75, 109, 111
  complex, 131-133, 137
  double precision, 127-132, 137
Function subprogram, 112-117, 119, 122, 123, 190, 195

G FORMAT notation, 144, 149, 153, 154, 175
Geometric mean, 54, 55
GO TO statement, 29, 30, 35, 39, 40, 53
  assigned, 197, 198
  computed, 85-89, 197

  unconditional, 29, 76
Gravitational constant, 36
Grouping, 33-35

H FORMAT notation, 165-170, 180-182
Hexadecimal number system, 6
Hierarchy, 33, 35
Hollerith, 165-169, 175, 181
Hyperbolic cosine, 62
Hyperbolic sine, 62
Hyperbolic tangent, 62, 127
Hyphen, 187

I FORMAT notation, 144, 149, 159, 160, 175
IABS function, 61, 67
IDIM function, 63, 67, 68
IFIX function, 66, 67
IF statement, 30, 43, 71, 168
  arithmetic, 71-79, 85, 88, 111
  logical, 52, 71, 75-79, 85, 88, 111, 133, 135, 136
Imaginary number, 130
IMPLICIT statement, 187, 197
Implicit type specification, 26-28, 187, 198
Implied DO loop, 97
Incrementation, 20, 29, 31, 35, 40-44, 53, 96
Index, DO loop, 40-44, 52, 53, 69, 80, 94-96, 197
Indexed list, 34, 97, 98, 104-107, 157, 158
Initialization, 30, 31, 35, 40, 48, 103, 104, 188, 192, 197
IN-letters, 19
Input, data, 11, 45-48, 53, 54
  equipment, 4, 142, 194
  list, 45-47, 53, 93, 112, 133, 135, 141, 149, 151-154, 156, 157, 160, 161, 167, 169
  statement, 44-47, 53, 93, 141-183, 193, 194-196
Input/output of arrays, 93, 97, 98, 103-107
Integer arithmetic, 25-27, 32, 48, 66
Integers, 19, 25-30, 32, 35, 40, 41, 46, 86, 94, 95, 142, 149, 187, 188
Interchange in storage, 99-101, 107, 119
INT function, 66, 67
ISIGN function, 65, 67, 68

JOB card, 11, 12, 46
Justification, left, 171, 182
  right, 146, 147, 149, 159, 161, 162, 174

Keypunch machine, 8, 9

L FORMAT notation, 174, 181
Labeled COMMON, 191-193, 197
Left justification, 171, 182
Literal transfer, 165-170, 172, 175, 180-182
Logarithms, 32, 58-61, 67-69, 87, 89, 123, 127
Logical expression, 71, 75, 79, 88, 133-139
Logical IF statement, 52, 71, 75-79, 85, 88, 111, 133, 135, 136
Logical operators, 77, 78, 88, 134, 136
Logical variables, 125, 133-139, 174, 185, 187, 188
Loop, 28-30, 35, 36, 39, 41, 43, 44, 48-53, 91, 102, 105, 106, 186

Machine language, 6, 7, 11, 12, 21, 43, 57
Magnetic tape, 4, 6, 8, 11, 142, 143, 194
Main program, 113-116, 120-122, 189, 192
Matrix, 102, 104, 105, 108, 163
MAX functions, 64, 67, 68, 128
Mean, arithmetic, 48, 49, 82-84, 107, 116-118, 123, 130, 137, 162, 163, 198
 geometric, 54, 55
 quadratic, 68
Memory, 3
Messages, error, 12-14, 18, 20, 36, 46, 167, 199-225
 extension, 12, 13, 21, 23, 199
 warning, 12, 13, 18, 65, 199
Microseconds, 1
MIN functions, 64, 67, 68, 75, 128
Mixed expression, 26, 27, 44, 58, 128, 129
MOD function, 66-68, 123
Multiplication, 12, 22, 32

Nanoseconds, 1
Nested DO loops, 49-53, 102, 105, 106

Object program, 7, 11, 12, 14, 21, 22, 103, 113
On-line, 4, 11, 23, 142
Operator, arithmetic, 12, 20, 22, 31, 33, 35, 52, 57, 77, 130
 logical, 77, 78, 88, 134, 136
 relational, 30, 35, 52, 75-77, 88, 134
Output, equipment, 4, 142, 194
 list, 21, 23, 34, 35, 141, 149, 151-154, 156, 167, 169
 statement, 17, 23, 35, 41, 46, 48, 93, 97, 141-183, 196
 for testing exercise programs, 36, 226-234

P FORMAT notation, 144, 155, 156, 162
Paper tape, 6, 8, 142

Parameter, 47, 48, 53, 55, 66, 79, 80, 82, 84, 85, 87, 97, 98, 101, 107, 108, 157, 182, 195-197
Parentheses, 22, 30, 32-34, 41, 57, 63, 71, 72, 77, 86, 94, 104, 105, 111, 130, 132, 135, 142, 153, 186, 187, 196
Payroll, 2
PL-I, 7
Plotter, 3
Precision, 25, 35, 125, 126, 148, 151, 154, 188
Primary storage, 3, 4, 5, 11
Printer, 4, 23, 142, 143, 179
 carriage control, 151, 169, 175, 179-182
PRINT statement, 17, 23, 46, 48, 97
Probability, 114
Program, calling, 112-118, 122, 123, 137
 compiler, 7, 11, 12, 15, 18, 22, 25, 40, 60, 93, 113, 115, 199
 definition, 2, 4, 6
 main, 113-116, 120-122, 189, 192
 object, 7, 11, 12, 14, 21, 22, 103, 113
 source, 7, 11, 12, 18, 22, 44, 46, 54, 143
Punched cards, 4, 6, 8, 11, 14, 22, 45, 144, 165, 168
PUNCH statement, 23, 46
Pythagorean theorem, 135

Quadratic equations, 34, 74, 137
Quadratic mean, 68

Radians, 62, 63, 68
Range, 25, 35, 59, 60, 108, 126
READ statement, 44-47, 53, 93, 141-183, 193, 194-196, 198
REAL function, 131
Record, 143-145, 147, 152, 156-158, 174, 177, 178, 181, 195
Relational operators, 30, 35, 52, 75-77, 88, 134
Remainder, 27, 66, 68, 69
Replacement, 20
RETURN statement, 113, 114, 119, 122, 193
REWIND statement, 194, 198
Right justification, 146, 147, 149, 159, 161, 162, 174
Right triangles, 135
Rounding, 65, 69, 127, 146, 147, 150, 229

Samples, 108
 systematic, 96
Scale factor, 144, 155, 156, 162
Secondary storage, 4, 5, 11, 113

Semicolon, 15, 22
Sentinel card, 79, 80, 82, 84, 88, 89, 193-195
Sheet eject, 180
SIGN function, 65, 67, 68
Significant digits, 125, 149-151, 154, 163
Sine, 62, 63, 127
SIN function, 62, 63, 67
SINH function, 62, 67
Slash, 22, 104, 175, 177, 178, 181, 191
SNGL function, 128
Sorting, 100, 101, 119-122, 171
Source program, 7, 11, 12, 18, 22, 44, 46, 54, 143
Special characters, 6-8, 18, 144
Specification statements, 186, 189, 193
SQRT function, 57, 58, 61, 67, 109
Square root, 37, 57, 58, 61, 67, 68, 109, 117, 127
Standard data set, 13, 54, 162, 226, 227
Standard deviation, 117, 118, 130, 137
Statement continuation, 15
Statement function, 109-112, 122, 189
Statement numbers, 15, 29, 40, 50, 71, 72, 86, 197
STOP statement, 22, 29, 35
Storage location, 18, 20, 21, 24, 27, 91, 94, 115, 120, 121, 169
  primary, 3, 4, 5, 11
  secondary, 4, 5, 11, 113
Subprogram, 109-123, 186, 189, 190, 192, 193
  function, 112-117, 119, 122, 123, 190, 195
  subroutine, 117-123, 137, 138, 190, 192, 195
Subroutine subprogram, 117-123, 137, 138, 190, 192, 195
Subscript omission, 93, 97, 103, 106, 107
Subscripts, 91-108, 115-117, 125, 187
Subtraction, 22, 65, 68
Summation, 30, 31, 35, 48

T FORMAT notation, 175-177, 181

TAN function, 62, 67
Tangent, 62
TANH function, 62, 67
Tape, 177
  magnetic, 4, 6, 8, 11, 142, 143, 194
  paper, 6, 8, 142
Temperature, 17, 21, 26, 27, 29, 30, 36, 39, 41, 42, 64
Testing of programs, 13, 54, 162, 226-234
Trigonometric functions, *see* individual functions
Triple dimension, 106, 107
Truncation, 25-27, 32, 35, 48, 65-67, 89, 146
Truth table, 139
Type declaration statements, 27, 28, 92, 110, 125, 128, 132, 137, 173, 185, 187, 188

Unconditional branch, 29, 30, 35, 39, 40, 53, 76
Undefined variable, 14, 20, 31

Variable names, 13, 18-21, 45, 46, 169, 170, 186, 198
Variables, 18, 19, 22, 23, 25
  complex, 125, 130, 132, 137, 138, 162, 187
  double precision, 125-130, 137, 153, 161, 163, 171, 183, 187, 188, 198
  integer, 19, 25-28, 29, 35, 40, 41, 46, 86, 94, 95, 142, 149, 187, 188
  logical, 125, 133-139, 174, 185, 187, 188
  real, 25, 35, 45, 149, 187, 188
  subscripted, 91-108, 115-117, 125
  undefined, 14, 20, 31
Video display, 3

Warning messages, 12, 13, 18, 65, 199
Waterloo, University of, 7
WRITE statement, 23, 141-183, 196

X notation, 175, 176, 178-181

3880

WATFOR
WATFIV
FORTRAN PROGRAMMING

By Fredric Stuart, Hofstra University

This is an introduction to FORTRAN which takes full advantage of the WATFOR/WATFIV compilers. It contains the full FORTRAN IV language along with Format-free input/output options and extensive compilation and execution error diagnostics. The core-resident compiler executes and compiles hundreds of programs per minute.

Includes 107 sample programs, 81 program exercises, standard data set and trial output for all exercises.

JOHN WILEY & SONS, Inc.
605 Third Avenue, New York, N.Y. 10016
New York • London • Sydney • Toronto

ISBN 0-471-83471-8